Discovering NewcastleGateshead

A walking guide to NewcastleGateshead
plus parkland strolls and
visits to coastal attractions

Peter Donaghy and John Laidler

SIGMA Leisure

Published by Sigma Leisure - an imprint of
Sigma Press, Stobart House, Pontyclerc, Penybanc Road
Ammanford, Carmarthenshire SA18 3HP

British Library Cataloguing in Publication Data

A CIP record for this book is available from the British Library

ISBN: 978-1-85058-913-6

Typesetting and Design by: Sigma Press, Ammanford, Carms

Printed by: Berforts Group Ltd

Disclaimer: The information in this book is given in good faith and is believed to be correct at the time of publication. Where appropriate, attention has been drawn to matters of safety. The authors and publisher cannot take responsibility for any accidents or injury incurred whilst following these walks. Only you can judge your own fitness, competence and experience.

Foreword

I'm a Geordie and I love Newcastle. The River Tyne is in my blood. The Northumbrian coast enchants me. I also love walking, possibly the best way of taking exercise gently and of pausing to smell the roses. So it's not surprising that I should be a fan of a book on walks around Tyneside.

It's an easy book to follow. On reading the list of walks my mind harked back to some of my favourite childhood haunts – Leazes Park, through which I walked with my family on our way to the Leazes synagogue every Saturday, and at other times fished for tiddlers in the lake. It was from here that one could suss the St. James Park roar and compute by how many goals the Magpies had trounced the visitors.

As children we holidayed in Tynemouth and Whitley Bay. My sister and I learned to swim and dive in what we called the Egg Pool, so named because its smooth rocky outline was the shape of a perfect egg. I wonder if it's still there offering safe swimming to youngsters.

I can't see or hear the word Jesmond without my mind flooding with images of my schooldays at Central High, once known as the 'Brown' school, a reference to the colour of our school uniform which distinguished us from the 'Green' school (Church High) and the 'Blue' school (La Sagesse). Here I learned lessons in more than latin and chemistry, lessons in life that still stand me in good stead.

As I lighted on the heading 'Crossing the bridges' I almost had to gulp down my emotions. From the time I went to study medicine in London I returned home each vacation by train over a bridge across the Tyne. Despite myself I wept each time. From the impersonal southern metropolis the return to the familiar embrace of Newcastle's sooty outlines was almost more than I could bear.

Nowadays contemplating Anthony Gormley's Angel of the North moves me in exactly the same way. We can't escape our origins nor should we want to but glory in them. I'm sure this book will illuminate and glorify the origins of each and every reader, and walker who follows

Miriam Stoppard

There are not many destinations that you can fully explore on foot but NewcastleGateshead is such a compact place, walking is one of the best ways to discover its delights. From Hadrian's Wall to NewcastleGateshead's seven famous bridges, visitors and residents can really make the most of what we have to offer by putting on their walking shoes. *Discovering NewcastleGateshead* has gathered together some of best walks available, including exploring the city centre, the surrounding parkland and further afield to the coast.

Walking is one of my favourite past times so be it a day out along the River Tyne or walking the dogs across Newcastle's Town Moor, it's the perfect way to unwind. This book really helps you explore the area and learn more about the history and heritage of NewcastleGateshead and the wider region.

There are already lots of trails out there but I've lived here 30 years and I'm still finding new ones. *Discovering NewcastleGateshead* is a great book for visitors new to the area or for residents looking to know more about the fantastic place where we live.

Sarah Stewart
Chief Executive of NewcastleGateshead Initiative

Preface

This book aims to help people explore and discover many fascinating parts of Newcastle and Gateshead and their immediate surrounds. We have chosen the relatively recent designation NewcastleGateshead for our title as this reflects the enhanced cultural identity shared by these two administratively different centres of population, particularly as a result of regeneration on both sides of the River Tyne. NewcastleGateshead Initiative, a public-private partnership, supported by Newcastle and Gateshead Councils, aims to promote NewcastleGateshead as a world-class place to live, work, invest, learn and visit.

Twenty-six carefully crafted walks lead readers to all the major places of interest as well as to many nooks and crannies that may well be new to long-standing residents. Indeed as two people who have each lived here for over seventy years, we have been surprised to learn so much about our own heritage. For many users this book may be a trip down memory lane while, for newcomers and visitors, we hope to provide a useful introduction to the delights of this area.

The walks can be done in any order but newcomers at least may find it helpful to get their bearings by starting with the introductory Walks 1 and 2. The walks are relatively short but you will need to allow time to visit the interiors of some of the buildings as well as to admire their external features. We suggest you read through the walk in advance so that you can plan where you may wish to stop and perhaps where you may be able to enjoy some refreshments.

You can expect some inclines, given the nature of the topography on both sides of the River Tyne, and we have endeavoured to give some indication of any particular steep sections and provide alternative routes for easier access where appropriate. At the same time, even though these walks are intended to be undertaken during daylight hours, users need to be aware of town traffic and other conditions.

NewcastleGateshead offers a good public transport system and we have designed our walks to start and finish within easy reach of Metro Stations and bus stops. To obtain up-to-date transport information and timetable you are advised to contact Nexus: Tel 01912020747 or via the website www.nexus.org.uk

For the sixteen Town and Urban walks we have included outline maps which may prove useful to those who want to take short cuts or to combine parts of more than one walk.

The Green and Parkland Places section provides opportunities to enjoy some rural walks within the boundaries of Newcastle and Gateshead. While in the Beyond NewcastleGateshead section we have included some walks in order to explore the delights of the coastal areas: Whitley Bay, Cullercoats, Tynemouth and North Shields. In addition, in this section, we have suggested using the ferry to cross the River Tyne from North to South Shields and how to experience a walk under the Tyne to the historic town of Jarrow.

Brief information is given about certain people, streets and buildings alongside the directions for the walks. However, on some occasions more detailed insights are provided. In such cases the name of the person or place is highlighted in bold and the details then appear in boxed vignettes. This is intended to help users follow the walks more easily and at the same time enable readers to acquaint themselves at their leisure with the background information.

We have tried to ensure that the descriptions are correct at the time of writing. However, a lot is happening in both Newcastle and Gateshead as both regeneration and economic factors continue to make their mark. Users may find that buildings have been demolished, restoration is taking place and new structures have arisen, likewise that establishments have gone out of business or have changed hands and names have been altered (even of banks!). Similarly opening hours may vary and may need to be checked via the websites provided. On a positive note, however, more information panels and heritage plaques are appearing thus providing more assistance in the discovery adventure.

Some suggestions for quiz questions have been included in order to make the walks more family-friendly. The location of the material needed to answer the questions is indicated in the text by the letters Qu followed by the number of the question. Adults, of course, will be able to pose or amend the questions according to the ages of the children concerned and/or make up their own questions. Although the questions shouldn't stretch the adults too much, the answers have been supplied at the end of the book just in case!

In preparing these walks we have thoroughly enjoyed discovering more about NewcastleGateshead and we just hope that you too will derive pleasure in finding plenty of things to interest you. Good luck and gan canny!

Peter Donaghy and John Laidler
March 2012

Contents

Acknowledgements

We are grateful for all the assistance we have received from the great number of people who have enlightened us about many aspects of NewcastleGateshead. Sometimes it was the result of brief and informal conversations, at others, it was by appointment, telephone call or email. Regardless of the time involved or the method used, everyone has been very helpful. It would be impossible to name all those involved and perhaps invidious to single some out more than others, be they library staff, caretakers, clergy, council employees, city guides, business owners or well-informed private individuals.

In checking the walks we must thank our families and friends and, in particular, Professor Neville Harris and the Revd and Mrs Pullen for their constructive criticism. Our respective wives Jeanne and Gillian have given us invaluable support as well as the time and space to immerse ourselves in this project.

A great number of sources of information were used in researching the walks and we have listed a selection of these at the end of the book. However, of invaluable use have been the two standard histories: *Newcastle upon Tyne: Its Growth and Achievement* by S. Middlebrook (Newcastle Journal, 1950) and *A History of Gateshead* by F.W.D. Manders (Gateshead Corporation, 1980) and the splendid Pevsner Architectural Guide, *Newcastle and Gateshead*, by Grace McCombie (Yale University Press, 2009).

We are indebted to Nexus for permission to reproduce the Metro Map and particularly to John Stephenson and Alice Kevans for providing the maps for the sixteen town and urban walks.

Finally we would like to acknowledge our gratitude to Sigma Leisure for their guidance and their patience in bringing this book to fruition. While any errors or omissions are solely our responsibility, any corrections can be forwarded to us through Sigma.

A little history

The concept of 'NewcastleGateshead' is fairly recent, and arises from the need to present a joint case for culture, business and tourism. Nevertheless, the geographical proximity of Gateshead and Newcastle resulted in there being some degree of relationship, although not always friendly, between them for several centuries. During the 19th and 20th centuries the two local authorities cooperated to build six bridges across the River Tyne. But the 21st century has seen a much greater gelling together of their common interests. However, their story begins some 1900 years ago.

The Swing Bridge is sited on the narrowest part of the River Tyne between Gateshead and Newcastle. It was very near this line that a Roman bridge was constructed in the second century during the reign of Emperor Hadrian (117-138) and named Pons Aelius to honour his family name. The east end of the defensive system, which we know as Hadrian's Wall, was originally to finish at the Roman bridge and there is a possibility that a small fort was built to guard the bridge. Some years later, around the end of the 2nd century, a fort, named Pons Aelius after the bridge, was built on the site of the present castle in Newcastle. This could be said to be the beginning of Newcastle's recorded history.

Gateshead's history also began around that time. Roman coins and artefacts have been found in the area and there would have been a settlement of some sort on the south end of the bridge. It is possible that it was on the south side of the river that the inevitable small settlement to supply the needs of Roman soldiers was established.

Following the Romans' withdrawal in the early 5th century and subsequent invasions by Jutes, Saxons and Angles, there emerged, in the 6th century, a number of independent Anglo-Saxon kingdoms. The northern-most of these was Northumbria. The spread of Christianity here resulted in the development of monastic settlements. Bede refers to Utta as Abbot of Gateshead in 653. The name of the settlement on the north bank, Monkchester, indicates the presence of a monastery there. An Anglo-Saxon cemetery, presumed to be Christian, was built on the site of the Pons Aelius fort.

Newcastle gained its name from the 'new castle' built in 1080 by Robert Curthose, son of William 1, to strengthen the defence of the important Tyne crossing. This was replaced almost 100 years later, in Henry II's reign, by a sturdy stone castle. The small settlement that grew around the castles was gradually transformed into a fully-fledged town with a market and charter. A town wall was constructed in the 13th and 14th centuries to give protection, mainly from the Scots, to the townsfolk, merchants and craftsmen as they carried on their daily lives. Commercial trade included the exporting of wool, skins and lead and, later, coal. There were four parish churches inside the wall. The castle's strong stone keep, sections of the town wall and three of the old churches can still be seen today.

At the same time Gateshead was developing, within the domain of the Bishops of Durham to whom William had delegated sufficient authority for them to rule, effectively, as a kingdom within a kingdom from the mid-12th century. By the end of the 12th century Gateshead had grown into a substantial borough. Notable activities included fisheries on the Tyne and milling. The 13th century St Edmund's Chapel, although somewhat altered, still serves as a place of worship. Gateshead continued to grow during the 13th and 14th centuries.

During this time the Bishops of Durham and the burgesses of Newcastle disagreed about many issues including the control of the bridge and the navigational rights on the river as well as the transport of coal from Gateshead mines. Newcastle was set upon limiting Gateshead's development. Indeed for a few months in 1553 circumstances enabled a take-over of Gateshead by Newcastle. The matter did not rest there and by the end of the 16th century, the Gateshead mines had been ceded to Newcastle.

The question as to who could ship the coal to its various destinations was settled in 1530. From then Newcastle had a monopoly in the export of coal and this provided the main impetus to Newcastle's growth into a major town. However, even though coal had to be shipped from Newcastle, Gateshead's mines also thrived as production increased to meet the growing demand for Tyneside's coal.

Although the coal trade was predominant, from the 18th century there was an increase in other industrial development in Gateshead and Newcastle. This included iron works, lead manufacture, potteries, glass making, tanning and glue works. The existence of coal and iron industries was an important driver in the development of shipbuilding and ship repairing along both banks of the Tyne particularly at Wallsend and Jarrow. The growth of the railways brought further opportunities, including the establishment of the Greenesfield works in Gateshead and the Stephenson works in Newcastle. Both towns experienced increases in population. Like other industrial towns there was a great deal of poor housing and inadequate working conditions. However, local industrial grandees built impressive properties in suburban locations such as Low Fell and Jesmond.

Civic pride had long been a feature of both towns and this was, perhaps, evidenced further after local government reorganisation under the Municipal Corporations Act of 1835. It should also be noted that both towns have benefitted from the generosity of local benefactors in the provision of recreation land and other facilities.

Gateshead elected a Mayor and Town Clerk and in 1844 a new Town Hall was built. This was replaced by the Town Hall in West Street in 1870 and the adjacent Free Library in 1885. Windmill Hills became Gateshead's first public park in 1861 to be followed by Saltwell Park from 1876. Plans were discussed for an art gallery although it was not until 1917 that the Shipley Art Gallery was opened. Gateshead became a Municipal Borough in 1975.

Newcastle had been governed by a Mayor and bailiffs from around 1300. From 1400 it was recognised as a county in its own right. In the 1650s a new Guildhall and Exchange was constructed and in 1691 a Mansion House was built as the Mayor's official residence. In the 1830s and 1840s, Richard Grainger, assisted by architects such as John Dobson, redeveloped the centre of the town. In 1858 the corporation built a Town Hall and Corn Exchange in the Groat Market, although both Grainger and Dobson strongly opposed its location -which spoilt a splendid view towards the historic St Nicholas' Church, Black Gate and Castle. Leazes Park became Newcastle's first public park in 1873. A public library was built in 1884 and the nearby Laing Art Gallery in 1904. In 1882 Newcastle became a city and St Nicholas' Church was made into a cathedral.

By the end of the 20th century the area's traditional heavy industries had all but disappeared. Government action and local initiatives have resulted in a shift to modern light and high-tech industries as well as recognition of the importance of commerce, retailing, leisure and tourism. Regeneration schemes have completely changed the character of the town centres and both sides of the river.

Regeneration in NewcastleGateshead is continuing in the 21st century, as you may discover on these walks.

1. An introduction to Newcastle

Start: Haymarket Metro Station
Finish: Monument Metro Station
Distance: 2.75 miles
Route: Haymarket, Northumberland Street, Grey's Monument, Grey Street, Dean Street, Guildhall, Quayside, St Nicholas' Cathedral, Bigg Market, Grainger Street, Monument Metro Station
Accessibility: On pavements throughout with one steep climb
Refreshments: Cafés and pubs throughout the route

For those new to Newcastle it might be useful to get your bearings before embarking on any of the other walks. This walk will provide some contemporary and historical insights, indicate where many of the places of interest lie and show, where appropriate, the starting points for some other walks. We will explore the Haymarket and Barras Bridge areas on other occasions (starting point for Walks 3, 4 and 5) but today we are going in the opposite

Theatre Royal

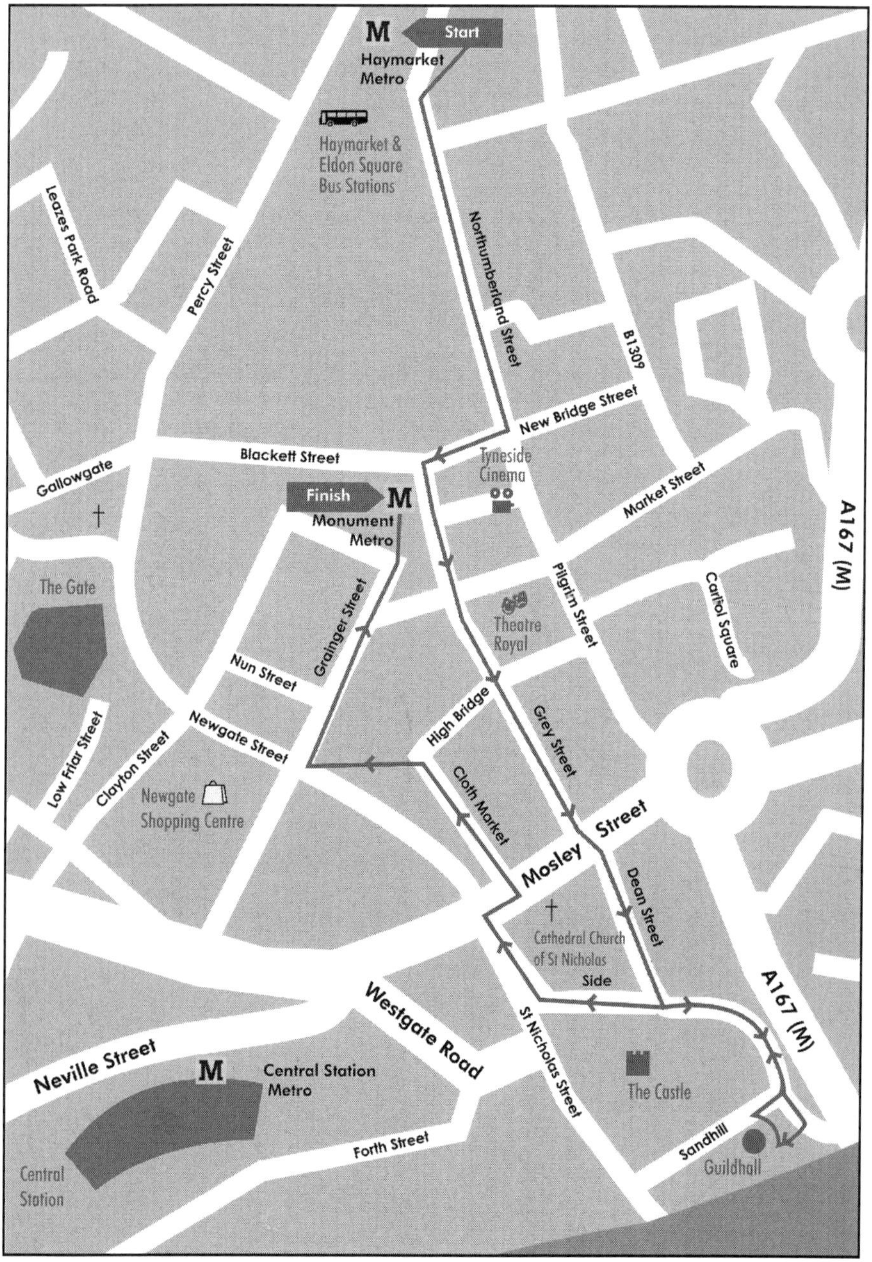
Start
M
Haymarket Metro
Haymarket & Eldon Square Bus Stations
Leazes Park Road
Percy Street
Northumberland Street
B1309
New Bridge Street
Blackett Street
Gallowgate
Tyneside Cinema
Finish
M
Monument Metro
Market Street
A167 (M)
The Gate
Grainger Street
Pilgrim Street
Carliol Square
Theatre Royal
Nun Street
High Bridge
Grey Street
Newgate Street
Low Friar Street
Clayton Street
Newgate Shopping Centre
Cloth Market
Mosley Street
Dean Street
Cathedral Church of St Nicholas
Side
A167 (M)
Westgate Road
St Nicholas Street
Neville Street
M
Central Station Metro
The Castle
Sandhill
Forth Street
Guildhall
Central Station

direction, from the Haymarket Metro Station down pedestrianized **Northumberland Street** on route to the River Tyne.

Northumberland Street

It is hard to imagine that in the 18th century, this street was once the site of pleasant urban dwellings behind which were private gardens. Gradually, retail outlets came to occupy the lower floors of the buildings as Newcastle grew into an important commercial city. Now lined by familiar high street shops, Northumberland Street has become the city's main shopping street. Unfortunately many of the establishments are behind rather plain brick and rendered facades with only the occasional trace of what was once a more uniformly pleasant thoroughfare. However, if you can avoid being distracted by the buskers, street traders, market researchers, petition-gatherers, *Big Issue* vendors and fellow pedestrians and look above the rather garish frontages of many of the commercial outlets, you will find some elegant facades and interesting details.

The second street on the left is Ridley Place, like many streets it is named after a noted local family, in this case the **Ridley Family** with their ancestral home at Blagdon Hall. Once a pleasant 19th-century residential street it now contains a miscellany of commercial premises. On the corner of Ridley Place with Northumberland Street there is a branch office of Virgin Money. The fine clock is a reminder of the former occupant.

Ridley Family

The Ridleys are a landowning family who have played a prominent role in north-eastern economic, political and social affairs for several hundred years. As well as being generous local benefactors, they have occupied a wide range of important positions. They have been mayors, members of parliament and held posts in the legal, military and business worlds. Their country estate is at Blagdon in Northumberland and in its grounds is the Cale Cross which once stood in the market place near the Quayside (see below). They are remembered in a number of memorials in St Nicholas' Cathedral.

The third road on your left is Northumberland Road leading to the City Hall, City Pool and Northumbria University. If you walk 50 metres down this road, on the right-hand side, on the side wall of the shop building, you will see two interesting relief panels reflecting aspects of local heritage in *Newcastle through the Ages* (Henry & Joyce Collins, 1974). Beside two mythical creatures you find local creative geniuses such as Armstrong, Stephenson, Grainger and Dobson whose significance we shall discover on these walks.

A few metres further down Northumberland Street, between Marks and Spencer and the **Eldon Square Shopping Centre,** is the narrow passageway of **Prudhoe Chare**. Here you will find the

A history in mosaic

Prudhoe Chare

You will come across several such narrow alleyways or 'chares' on these walks. On the wall just beyond the Northumberland Arms pub is a collection of sculptures rescued from diverse buildings demolished in the 1970s. They include representations of the heads of prominent local citizens and figures from mythology. There is a section of the city's coat of arms with the seahorse and the beginning of the city's motto *Fortiter De...* (see below: Sir John Marley). These are said to have come from the old City Library and the old Town Hall. There is also reference to the YMCA.

Eldon Square Shopping Centre

This is now the name of a shopping centre, the construction of which began in 1969. This has not been without controversy, particularly when it involved the demolition of two sides of the original elegant city square in Blackett Street, now called Old Eldon Square. Since it opened in 1976, this huge indoor mall has continued to spread its tentacles across a wide area and is accessible from a number of other city streets. With the completion of St Andrew's Way in February 2010, Eldon Square now occupies 1.4 million square feet, making it one of the biggest in-town shopping centres in the UK. It contains a vast array of major high street stores, specialist outlets, cafés and restaurants as well as leisure facilities. A Shopper's Directory and map is available at the information desk, some 100 metres from the main entrance. A short way further on there is an open area that is often used for displays and for carol singing at Christmas by local school and other choirs. Here there is a clock to commemorate the visit of the Queen in her silver jubilee year (1977) and a statue *Man with Pigeons* presented by the property developers to the Mayor to commemorate the opening of the Centre.

Northumberland Arms pub, a small entrance into the shopping centre and some interesting stonework **(Qu 1**).

Return to Northumberland Street. Next to Eldon Square, above Phones4u, you will see three attractively decorated windows advertising some of the wares of one of the previous occupiers who is indicated by the letters DS (the jewellers, David Summerfield).

Some 40 metres further on, a plaque high on the wall above the store Bank, refers to this being the site of the 18th-century Orphan House founded by John Wesley in 1743 and used as the headquarters of Methodism in the north of England. On the next building, in niches above the shop front of The Carphone Warehouse, there are statues of four historical local people: **Roger Thornton, Harry Hotspur, Sir John Marley and Thomas Bewick**.

A few metres further along Northumberland Street you are at the department store Fenwick founded by **John James Fenwick** in 1882. It is well worth crossing to the opposite side of the street to appreciate the magnificent frontage.

Glancing down to the end of the next street on your right (Brunswick Place) you can see Brunswick Methodist Church (1820). It has been referred to as the 'cathedral of northern Methodism'. Following modifications in the 1980s, in addition to its continuing ministry, it offers a variety of other facilities, including a coffee shop and a base for several caring associations.

On the opposite side of Northumberland Street there is an example of one of the 19th-century houses which were converted into shops (previously Amos Atkinson, currently Moss). However, the fancy plasterwork is more modern and is said to date from the

Roger Thornton (died 1429)

Roger Thornton is claimed to be Newcastle's 'Dick Whittington'. He came from very humble origins to become a rich merchant, Member of Parliament and several times Mayor of Newcastle in the early 15th century. His generosity as a benefactor, especially of local churches, earned him the title 'Patron of Newcastle' (Charleton, 1890). He was buried in All Saints' Church and his magnificent monumental brass is now in St Nicholas' Cathedral. He was said to be responsible for creating Newcastle's status as a town and county outside the jurisdiction of the geographical county of Northumberland in which it stands.

Harry Hotspur (1364-1403)

Henry Percy, first son of the 1st Earl of Northumberland, is believed to have earned the nickname 'Harry Hotspur' because of his fiery and impulsive character and his bravery. He was killed at the battle of Shrewsbury in rebellion against the King and subsequently immortalised in Shakespeare's play, *Henry IV, Part I.* Strictly speaking his connection is with Northumberland. The Percys have been associated with Alnwick since they first occupied the castle in 1301. However, the significance of his family to the region as a whole is also recalled in the name of nearby Percy Street.

Sir John Marley (1590-1673)

John Marley was mayor and skilful defender of Newcastle, in support of the King, for some ten weeks in 1644 against a vastly superior force of Scots on the side of the Parliamentarians in the Civil War of 1642-46. His actions earned the town its motto, *Fortiter Defendit Triumphans* (Triumphing by Brave Defence) which was bestowed by a grateful King Charles I. Some of the town was destroyed. Sir John was imprisoned in the castle and then committed to the Tower of London from where he succeeded in escaping abroad.

Thomas Bewick (1753-1828)

Thomas Bewick, the noted wood engraver, illustrator, writer, artist and naturalist has been described as "the most celebrated artist ever produced by Northumbria" (Marshall Hall, 2005). He was apprenticed at the age of fourteen to the Newcastle engraver Ralph Beilby, whose brother William's glass enamelling is now so highly regarded. Examples of the works of both Bewick and the Beilby family can be found in the Northern Spirit Gallery of the Laing Art Gallery.

Bewick lived most of his working life in Newcastle with a workshop adjacent to St Nicholas' Cathedral. He spent the latter part of his life in Gateshead where he died. His illustrations of animals and birds have brought him worldwide fame, in particularly through his *A History of British Birds* (1804). He was an acute observer of rural life and produced many humorous scenes such as his depiction of the 'town and country tooth drawers'. The Bewick Collection on the 6th floor of Newcastle City Library contains an extensive number of his books, tools and other materials, while there is a permanent exhibition of his life and work at his birthplace in Cherryburn, Northumberland (owned by the National Trust and open to visitors. Tel 01661-843276). He also has a street, a square and a block of flats in Newcastle, together with a street in Gateshead, named after him.

John James Fenwick (1846-1905)

A grocer's son from Richmond, Yorkshire, J.J. Fenwick started out in 1860 as an apprentice draper in Stockton. He came to Newcastle eight years later and found work in a firm of mercers. In 1882 he opened his own ladies tailoring business in Northumberland Street, no doubt helped by the compensation for 'unfair dismissal' that he had received from his previous employers! In no time he had acquired two houses further up the street where he was able to base the present store. His business acumen enabled him to lay the foundations of a very successful business that has continued to flourish under the private ownership of the Fenwick family.

The exiting frontage was built in1915 and restored in 1996. Fenwick's, as it is commonly called, has gradually expanded to its present considerable size with additional entrances in Blackett Street (see below) and Eldon Square. It offers a wide range of fashion clothing, household goods and foodstuffs together with restaurants and cafés. The window displays are particularly noted for their animated Christmas scenes that have delighted generations of children (and adults!) for some forty years. Although Newcastle continues to have the company's flagship store, there are eight other stores under the Fenwick name, for example, in London, Canterbury and York, together with two Bentalls and one William & Griffin within the business.

coronation of Queen Elizabeth II. The adjacent access lane leads to Princess Square and the City Library.

You now arrive at the crossroads at the south end of Northumberland Street. To the left is New Bridge Street West leading to the City Library and the Laing Art Gallery. On the right is Blackett Street leading to Grey's Monument and the Monument Metro Station as well as to Old Eldon Square, Gallowgate and St James' Park, Chinatown and the Town Walls. Straight ahead is **Pilgrim Street**.

At the crossroads turn right into Blackett Street, named after John Blackett an 18th -century mayor and member of the prominent local family whose family seat is Matfen Hall, now an hotel and golf club. On your left is a well-known local landmark in the shape of the golden-lady clock above the attractive early 1890s premises of the Northern Goldsmiths. On the Pilgrim Street side of the building a sign states that they are 'Manufacturers of Watches and Chronometers to the Admiralty', while on the Blackett Street

Golden lady

side the claim is to be 'The Ring Shop for the World'.

A few metres further on from the Northern Goldsmiths is another elegant establishment, the jewellers, Reid and Sons (1906). Here too the clock is of note as it bears the inscription 'Greenwich Time'. This is said to be because, at one time, it had the distinction of a link to Greenwich to secure actual Mean Time.

Continuing ahead, on the right, just beyond an entrance to the Metro Station and near the entrance to the Monument Mall (1990) look out for two stone benches with glass backs, two of nine such seats that offer thoughts on 'things to do' **(Qu 2)**.

You now arrive at the area of the city known as 'The Monument' with its towering memorial to Earl Grey, the Metro Station, an entrance to Eldon Square Shopping Centre and the junction of three key streets: Blackett Street, Grey Street and Grainger Street.

Turn left and cross with care to Grey's Monument (starting point for Walk 7). The gentle curves of the Eldon Buildings enable this part of Blackett Street to merge neatly into Grey Street. While Blackett Street itself continues ahead with two contrasting buildings to admire, Emerson Chambers and Fenwick's.

Now standing near Grey's Monument you are at the apex of Grey Street and Grainger Street. Grey Street has been described as 'one of the best streets in England' (Pevsner and Richmond, 2002) and is often acknowledged as one of England's finest streets in popular polls. Since 1991, like its neighbouring streets, it is now labelled as being part of Grainger Town, a reference to the early 19th century redevelopment of Newcastle by the developer Richard Grainger.

On your left, within Eldon Buildings, is The Charles Grey, formerly the Eldon Grill, one of the 1960s in-places. If you can manage to climb several flights of stairs you can still enjoy food and drink there and

Pilgrim Street

This street was so named because it was the route travelled by pilgrims, possibly making their way to the nearby Friary of the Franciscans or Grey Friars, said to possess relics of St Francis, or, as is more generally thought to be the case, travelling further afield beyond the city walls to Jesmond and the Shrine of Our Lady. There is evidence of pilgrims making their way here in the13th century where the Pilgrim Gate provided an important point of passage through the town wall. Such was the popularity of the route, at least until the dissolution of the friaries and monasteries in the 1530s, that inns and resting places for pilgrims sprang up in the immediate area. The Pilgrim Gate itself was eventually demolished in 1802, long after the pilgrimages had ceased. The only trace now of the Friary lies in the name of nearby High Friars Lane where you will find the entrance to the Tyneside Cinema.

Contrasting styles

appreciate some splendid views of Grey's Monument and its surroundings **(Qu 3)**.

It is worth spending a few moments to look ahead and admire the classical gracefulness of Grey Street before continuing down the street. Once you proceed on your way you will need in general to glance upwards to appreciate the dramatic columns, decorative carvings, plinths, windows and balconies of so many of the buildings.

The initial section is conveniently pedestrianized and it may contain 'Grey Street Gardens'. This is one of several projects by **Newcastle NE1** whose helpful street rangers you may also encounter on your walks. Here you will find one of the ScratchBikes stations for bicycle hire.

Newcastle NE1

This is an independent limited company, formed in 2009 for an initial five-year term. Its activities are overseen by a Board of Directors which has local business, Council, academic and leisure representation.

Broadly speaking, its aim is to champion Newcastle City Centre. It manages the Newcastle Business Improvement District (BID). There are around 90 BIDS in the UK and Newcastle's is the biggest. It fulfils its aim through various business initiatives and a number of physical projects.

Examples of the former include extended opening hours the 'alive after five' initiative, a bike hire scheme and the appointment of street rangers. Physical projects have included Monument Movies - a projection of films on a large screen near Grey's Monument - and the installation of 'pocket parks'. In a city centre context, pocket parks provide small, sometimes themed, spaces for rest and relaxation. Pocket parks may be permanent structures, for example, the Sir Bobby Robson Memorial Garden at St James' Park and St Nicholas' Square outside St Nicholas' Cathedral. Other pocket parks may be temporary but some could be put into storage and used on future occasions, an example is the Grey Street Gardens installation.

Continue ahead and admire, on your right, the Central Exchange Buildings containing the Central Arcade, and, on your left, the H&M store, formerly Waterstone's. Earlier, this was the premises of Mawson, Swan and Morgan, also booksellers. The wrought iron street lamps which are still outside were due to Joseph Swan being the inventor of the incandescent lamp **(Qu 4)**.

You pass Hood Street on your left and then Lloyds Bank. This is the area where the Franciscans once had their friary (see Pilgrim Gate above). It also became the site of a property (Anderson Place) that Richard Grainger purchased and then demolished as part of his development plan. Before you use the traffic lights to go across Market Street, walk a few paces to your left to read the bronze plaque on the side of the current property **(Qu 5)**.

Beyond Market Street stands the **Theatre Royal** designed by the brothers **John and Benjamin Green**.

You will see that the street adjacent to the theatre, which contains the stage door entrance, is appropriately called Shakespeare Street. Continue down the left-hand side of Grey Street where you can admire the many fine buildings. On both sides you will pass entrances to a street called High Bridge. This refers to the former existence of a bridge over the Lort Burn that flowed down here (see below).

Proceed ahead towards the traffic lights. On the left, a plaque on the General Buildings, Nos 24-18, commemorates the bicentenary of the distinguished architect **John Dobson** and

Theatre Royal

The current theatre dates from 1837 but it is not the first of this name. The original Theatre Royal that opened in Mosley Street in 1788 was demolished in 1836 as part of Richard Grainger's plan to redevelop the town centre with the construction of Grey Street. Sadly the only evidence remaining of that theatre is in the shape of a back alley on the former site named Drury Lane (see below). Grainger sited the replacement in a prime position towards the top of his new Grey Street and he engaged John and Benjamin Green to produce this classical building.

Unfortunately the interior was largely destroyed by fire in 1899. However, it was remodelled by the London theatre architect Frank Matcham and re-opened in 1901. Several alterations have been made since then including a major restoration in 2011 to recreate Matcham's original design in time for 175th anniversary of the theatre in 2012.

It boosts a reputation as one of the UK's leading theatres. It is the regional home of the Royal Shakespeare Company (RSC), the National Theatre, Opera North and Rambert Dance Company. Its annual Christmas pantomine is an important part of the Tyneside festive season and attracts packed houses. Pasqualino's bar-restaurant, accessible from Market Street, is available to both theatre-goers and the general public.
For further information see: www.theatreroyal.co.uk

John Green (1787-1852) and Benjamin Green (1811-1858)

John Green was born in Northumberland and after working with his father in a building business in Corbridge, in around 1820, he set up in Newcastle as an architect and civil engineer. One of his early designs, in the fairly plain style which he favoured, was the Literary and Philosophical building in Westgate Road (1825).

His son Benjamin trained in London with the draftsmen A.C. Pugin (famous for architectural drawings of Gothic churches and father of A.W.N. Pugin who designed St Mary's Cathedral) and then, in the 1830s, joined his father in the Newcastle practice. In his designs, Benjamin tended towards a more elaborate style than his father.

The partnership produced a wide variety of work in Northumberland and Durham, ranging from farms, churches, monuments and mansions to roads and bridges. Their most famous work in Durham is probably Penshaw Monument (1844), erected in memory of John George Lambton, first Earl of Durham. Although they were credited jointly with many of their projects it is possible that Benjamin concentrated on the architectural aspects while John undertook any subsequent engineering work.

Their important contributions to Grainger's 19th-century redevelopment of Newcastle included the Theatre Royal in Grey Street (1837) and Benjamin' Green's column for Grey's Monument (1838). Happily, both of these iconic buildings remain for the enjoyment of Newcastle folk and visitors

John Dobson (1787-1865)

"Dobson is a figure of great importance, of whom all of us who live and work in the North East can justifiably feel proud" (Faulkner and Greg, 2001). The son of a market gardener, he was born in North Shields in 1787. He soon showed a talent for drawing and at an early age he became apprenticed to David Stephenson the leading local architect-builder of

the time. He lived all his life on Tyneside, apart from an influential year or so he spent in his early twenties broadening his horizons in London. It was there that he became personally acquainted with several important artists and it seemed he might have chosen to be a watercolourist. However, his skill and love of drawing led him to pursue architecture as his career. While the vast majority of his work was to be in the North East, his services were often sought further afield including designs for buildings in Edinburgh, Leeds, Norfolk, Lincolnshire and even for a Gothic castle in Germany.

The 19th-century boom in church building placed great demands on his services but that did not prevent him from designing a vast number of other diverse constructions in a variety of architectural styles. He could claim responsibility for countless stately homes, city dwellings, schools, gaols, bridges, railway stations and indeed the Jesmond cemetery in which he would eventually be buried. It is just sad to think that the city-centre street named in his honour is such a soulless carriageway.

his contribution to the building of Grey Street. You will find that he was also responsible for a number of significant buildings that you will encounter on these walks but it has to be recognised that several other architects also made important contributions to the renaissance of Newcastle.

At the junction with Mosley Street (named after Alderman Mosley, 1717-1798, an influential figure in the development of the town) cross at the traffic lights to proceed down Dean Street. This was once a deep-sided valley or dene through which ran the Lort Burn, before the valley was filled in and the burn culvetted to its outflow into the River Tyne (see below). It is curious to find that 'dene' became 'Dean' in the street name. About halfway down, on the left-hand side, you pass the site of another of the bridges that once crossed the Lort Burn, the Low Bridge, marked now only by the name on the wall, by the steps, next to the entrance to the multi-storey car park.

There are some very fine facades on the right-hand side of the street. Note in particular the brightly-coloured Cathedral Buildings (1901) next to Cathedral Stairs. As the name suggests, the narrow passageway leads to the rear of St Nicholas' Cathedral, as well as to the site of the workshop of the engraver Thomas Bewick (see above).

Some 20 metres further down is Milburn House built 1905 by Alderman J.D. Milburn, a member of another prominent

Ship-like Milburn House

land and shipowning family. The maritime connection is reflected in its liner-like shape and the deck-style (A-G) labelling of the floors. The interior was restored in the early 1990s to its original Arts and Crafts style as befits such prestigious office accommodation. Some public restaurants, that you pass later, nestle in the lower decks on the other side of the building.

Opposite Milburn House before Dean Street reaches the mid-19th century railway viaduct by Robert Stephenson, look for a narrow opening called Painter Heugh. It's amazing now to think that, before the dene was covered over, boats (called painters) which used to ferry goods from larger vessels on the Tyne were able to be moored here.

Follow the road as it curves left and becomes the Side. In 2005 John Maine created the public art project *Tributary* with diagonal lines of cobblestones placed at intervals across the block-paved roadway. This was to reflect the movement of the Lort Burn as it flows down to the River Tyne. Unfortunately heavy traffic and road works have taken their toll and the artwork currently appears in a sad condition.

You are entering the Quayside area with its variety of bars and restaurants. On each side of the doorway of the Akenside Traders pub, there are duplicate information panels where you can read some rather unflattering comments about an 18th-century character, Mark Akenside A few steps further on, a plaque marks the previous site of a market cross, the Cale Cross (see above, Ridley Family). Continue along the Side as it bears right to arrive at the base of the Tyne Bridge where you will find a commemorative plaque **(Qu 6)**.

Cross the road at the traffic lights to arrive at the River Tyne. From here you have fine views; to the left, of The Sage, the Millennium Bridge and the Baltic, and to the right, of the Swing Bridge and the High Level Bridge with the Queen Elizabeth Metro Bridge just visible behind.

At the riverside turn right along the riverside path and walk a short distance to find two plaques commemorating visits by the Cutty Sark at the time of the Tall Ships races. The building to your right is the Guildhall (starting point for Walk 10). Cross over to this building and look for a plaque, with an interesting explanation of the derivation of the name of the Lort Burn, tucked into a corner to the right of a wall lamp **(Qu 7)**.

Continue to the front of the building where you will find a further plaque with some details of the historic Guildhall's former importance as a centre of local government. This area, known as Sandhill, marks the early entrances into Newcastle near the sites of the Roman and the medieval bridges over the Tyne. It was to become an area inhabited by wealthy merchants.

Cross the road at the traffic lights. Immediately in front of you is the Bob Trollop pub, presumably named after Robert Trollop the 17th-century architect who designed the original Guildhall. Walk some 40 metres to the left to two splendid timber-framed merchants' houses built in the16th and 17th centuries, now collectively known as the Bessie Surtees' House. It was from here that in 1772 young Bessie eloped with John Scott, later to become Lord Eldon, Lord Chancellor of England. A plaque marks the window out of which she climbed! The house is now the North East Regional Office of English Heritage and three rooms are open to visitors free of charge, Monday-Friday (Tel 0191-2691200).

Walk back to Bob Trollop's and follow the road as it bears left to return up the Side to pass the Side Photographic Gallery and Cinema. The entrance to the cinema is at No 26 next to Buee at the Side (formerly Side Café) and the Gallery is a few metres ahead on the narrow passage to Battery Steps. Proceeding up the Side you pass the **Crown Posada**.

On your left, just before the railway viaduct, you will see the tall Vermont Hotel, formerly the offices of Northumberland County Council. Bear left to climb steeply up the Side with the intriguingly named Dog Leap Stairs on your left and Milburn House on your right. As you reach the top of the street, look out for a bust above a doorway and a plaque marking the site of the birthplace of John Collingwood **(Qu 8)**.

On your left is the Black Gate entrance to the Castle, while to your right is St Nicholas' Cathedral (starting point for Walks 9 and 14). Ahead are the elegant St Nicholas Buildings and the former General Post Office (1876) now offices and apartments. Bear right towards the Cathedral. At the traffic lights, to the left, is Collingwood Street leading to the Central Station.

However, you need to cross straight ahead to the Cathedral Square building, the site of the Town Hall of 1863, the city's administrative headquarters before the construction of the Civic Centre in Barras Bridge in the 1960s. For a short while, between the demolition of the Town Hall and the erection of the Cathedral Square complex, this really was a delightful open space overlooking St Nicholas' Cathedral and beyond to the Black Gate. What a pity it did not remain that way!

Crown Posada

This a traditional pub, believed to be among the oldest in Newcastle dating back to the 18th century. It was earlier known just as the Crown and it is said to owe its present name to a nineteenth owner, a sea captain who had a wife in Spain and a mistress installed in the Crown. He changed the name to Crown Posada, adding the Spanish word for inn or resting place which could have been rather hurtful to his seemingly unsuspecting wife. The interior is very atmospheric with a partitioned snug and delightful Pre-Raphaelite windows. A good place to enjoy fine ale.

Once over the busy road you are going to turn right but before you do so, look ahead up the Groat Market, named after a form of oats that were once sold here. On the left is the Blackie Boy, another of the older pubs, built on the site of a former blacksmiths. Here a gentlemen's debating club attended by the engraver Thomas Bewick used to meet in the late-18th century. It has been subject to rebuilds, alterations to its facade and to changes of name. A short distance further on is the more modern Thomson House, the head offices and printing works of the local newspaper group, NCJ Media, responsible for The Journal, Evening Chronicle and Sunday Sun.

Now turn right (the Cathedral and the statue of Queen Victoria are on your right) and walk a few metres before turning left up the Cloth Market. This area, once a thriving site for butchers (it was once known as the Flesh Market), and afterwards for the numerous drapers to whom it owns its present name, is now a rather run-down backwater of pubs, takeaways and offices.

Immediately on your right is a rather sad alleyway (Drury Lane) along which were once entrances to the old Theatre Royal on Mosley Street (1788-1836). A few paces further is **Balmbras** pub, frequently recalled in the song Blaydon Races. Almost opposite the pub, behind the solitary tree in the square, there is an information board about the song with a map of 1879 on which is marked the New Town Hall of 1863 (see above). A plaque in the pavement names the square as Morrison's Court in memory of Robert Morrison, an early Christian missionary to China and obviously a skilful linguist **(Qu 9)**.

Continuing up the Cloth Market you will soon find the Old George Yard on your right. If you walk through the archway, beneath the Cloth Market Building of 1870, you come to The Old George, reputed to be the oldest pub in Newcastle and certainly one of the most atmospheric. The yard houses the former stables of the coaching inn as well as an interesting boutique, a guitar shop and a music shop.

A few metres further you arrive at the ornately tiled Beehive Hotel at the corner with

High Bridge. On the opposite corner on the walls of the Sunlight Chambers you will see a freize depicting the benefits of industry and agriculture. This building of 1902 was originally the offices of Lever Brothers, soap manufacturers and competitors to Newcastle's own Thomas Hedley (later Proctor and Gamble). It now houses student accommodation.

The area now opens up to form the Bigg Market which refers to its once being the site of the sale of barley. The name now resonates with the rather frenetic nightlife of its neighbouring pubs and discos. However, there are fine buildings on both sides, one of which, on the right, is the imaginatively decorated Half Moon Chambers, built 1903-5 on the site of a coaching inn. This is by Benjamin Simpson, designer of the likewise charming Emerson Chambers on Blackett Street

Near the top of the Bigg Market you will find a fountain that has been on the move. In 1901, it was moved from outside St Nicholas' Cathedral, to the lower part of the Bigg Market, to make way for Queen Victoria's statue. Then it was moved again in 1998 to its present position in order to free up more space in the Bigg Market. However, it does seem rather an

Balmbras

Balmbras, was once called The Wheatsheaf and run for some twenty-five years by landlord John Balmbra who was immortalised in the song *Blaydon Races*. The song begins,

Ah went to Blaydon Races, twas on the ninth o' June,
Eiteen hundred an sixty two, on a summer's afternoon,
We tuik the bus frae Balmbra's, and she was heavy laden,
Away we went alang Collingwood Street, that's on the road to Blaydon.

It was first performed in John Balmbra's concert room in 1862 by its writer the music hall artist, George (Geordie) Ridley (1835-1864). At the age of eighteen, George Ridley had been crushed by a rail wagon at the Gateshead Iron Works where he worked. This obliged him to look elsewhere for gainful employment and so he put his musical talents to good use as a professional singer and song writer. He delighted in using his songs to portray local characters. In addition to the *Blaydon Races*, one of his best known songs, *Cushie Butterfield*, tells of the love of a keelman (boatman) for 'big lass and a bonnie lass an' she likes hor beer an 'they caal hor Cushie Butterfield'. Sadly his injuries attributed to his early death but his songs live on and *Blaydon Races* has become the 'Geordie anthem', reverberating in particular wherever Newcastle United play.

The music hall tradition continued albeit with several changes of names until the building had to be demolished after a fire and then rebuilt in 1901. However, the pub was renamed Balmbra's in 1962 and the music hall was reinstated as part of the centenary celebrations of the Blaydon Races. This operated as a very popular venue until the 1980s where among the many talented performers, the comedian Dickie Irwin is said to have stood out as the 'reincarnation of Geordie Ridley'.

While the original races were horse races, the song has been recalled every 9th of June since 1981 in the form of a road race between here and Blaydon. Some 4000 competitors take part in what is now a 5.9 mile race. The event is preceded by the singing of the song and the Can-Can performed by a local dance troupe before the Lord Mayor starts the race by ringing Jackie Bell's handbell that features in the song.

anomaly in this popular party area to find a memorial in honour of the Revd. Dr. J.H.Rutherford, an advocate of temperance, with the inscription 'Water is best'!

Just before you arrive at the junction with Grainger Street and Newgate Street, look out for a more deliberate note of humour in the form of one of the 'alternative' plaques that you may encounter on the city's pavements **(Qu 10)**.

Rutherford Fountain

Turn right into Grainger Street and proceed straight ahead towards the Monument. On your left you pass Nun Street and then one of the entrances to the Grainger Market before reaching the traffic lights as the road bears right into Market Street. Cross over the road and turn immediately down Market Street. On the right is the building once occupied by two former household names in Newcastle, the stores Bainbridge's and then Binns.

On the left you will see an entrance to the Central Exchange Buildings and a Visitor Information Office.

Continue ahead and turn left at Grey Street to return to the Monument Metro Station and the end of this walk. You will now have become acquainted with some of the key areas of the city centre and the starting points for some of the other walks.

Quiz questions

1. **Which three dates can you find on the sculptures?**
2. **What are the single words that represent the 'to do' suggestions on these two benches?**
3. **What is the date on Eldon Buildings?**
4. **How many street lamps are there outside H&M?**
5. **Who was once kept prisoner on this site?**
6. **Who officially opened the Tyne Bridge?**
7. **What was the original meaning of 'Lort Burn'?**
8. **Why is John Collingwood famous?**
9. **Why do you think Robert Morrison was a skilful linguist?**
10. **Who was the person who waited here in 1952?**

2. Introduction to Gateshead

Start/Finish:	**Gateshead Metro Station (Gateshead Interchange)**
Distance:	**2 miles**
Route:	**Gateshead Metro Station, West Street, Gateshead Heritage @ St Mary's, The Sage, Baltic, St Edmund's Chapel, Jackson Street, Gateshead Metro Station**
Accessibility:	**On pavements and surfaced paths. Several ascents and descents by steps for which alternative routes are given**
Refreshments:	**Gateshead Old Town Hall, The Sage, the Baltic**

This walk passes several of Gateshead's iconic buildings and should help you to get your bearings before embarking on other Gateshead walks.

Leave Gateshead Metro Station by the West Street North exit and follow the ramp to the main road (West Street). Ahead, at the time of writing, is the site of the major redevelopment project of Trinity Square This follows the demolition in 2010-11 of the towering multi-storey car park, that featured in *Get Carter*, the 1971 film starring Michael Caine, which dominated the Gateshead skyline for so many years.

Turn left and proceed downhill passing a large sculpture, *Sports Day* (Mike Winstone, 1986).

Farewell to famous car park

Cross over to the other side of the street and continue downhill.

A little further on you pass the former Post Office (1897); a plaque informs us that this is the site of the house where the famous engraver and naturalist Thomas Bewick lived and died. To the right of the plaque you can see the hand and toe holds provided so that a policeman could raise himself up to look through the window to check that the Post Office safe was still secure.

Adjacent is the Lloyds Bank building (George Reavell, 1914) which is reckoned to be the only surviving pre-1960s commercial property in Gateshead (Pesvner, 1983). Cross Nelson Street and turn right to look at a plaque which indicates that the Gateshead Dispensary (1832-1946) operated in these premises from 1855 until 1946 **(Qu 1)**.

Return to the main road. A short distance further on you come to a small, ornate clock tower (Gillett and Johnson, 1892) presented by Walter de Lancey

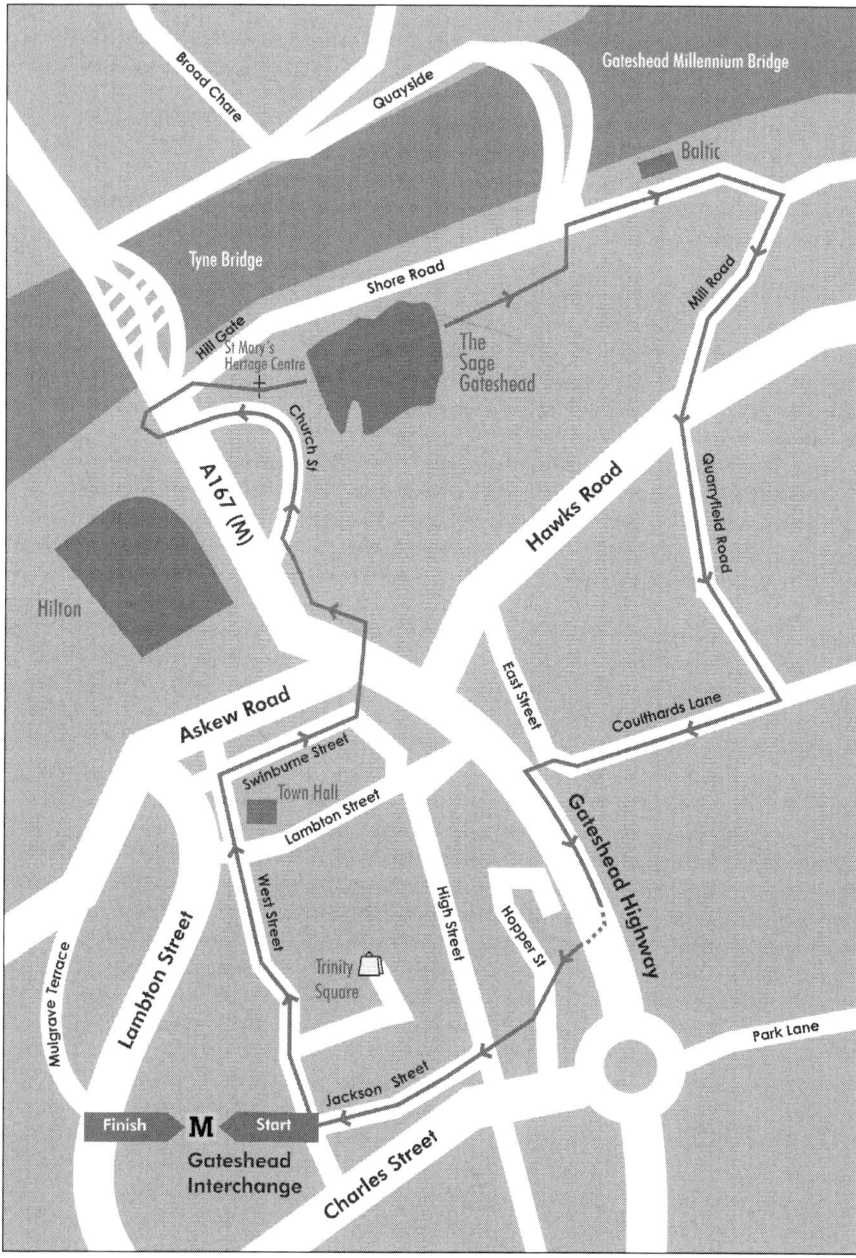
Gateshead Millennium Bridge
Broad Chare
Quayside
Baltic
Tyne Bridge
Shore Road
Mill Road
Hill Gate
St Mary's Heritage Centre
The Sage Gateshead
Church St
A167 (M)
Hawks Road
Quarryfield Road
Hilton
East Street
Askew Road
Coulthards Lane
Swinburne Street
Town Hall
Lambton Street
Gateshead Highway
West Street
High Street
Hopper St
Trinity Square
Mulgrave Terrace
Lambton Street
Park Lane
Jackson Street
Finish
M
Start
Gateshead Interchange
Charles Street

Willson ,who served as Mayor of Gateshead for the third time in 1892. In 1875, with Stephen Aitcheson, he founded Walter Willson's, a major chain of retail grocery shops in the North East and Cumbria; it was taken over by Alldays in the 1990s **(Qu 2)**.

The clock tower stands in front of the old **Town Hall**.

Town Hall

The old Town Hall was completed in 1870. The architect was John Johnstone who designed the now demolished Newcastle Town Hall (1863). The elaborate frontage is surmounted by a statue of Queen Victoria. During earlier refurbishment it was discovered that the statue was unsecure and it is now supported by two stays.

Apart from the expected council chambers and administrative offices, the building also housed the magistrates' court as well as Gateshead's main police station. The latter had appropriate accommodation, including cells and an outside exercise yard. For some years Gateshead's policemen also served as volunteer firemen.

Today the building is partly used by council departments but some of the former chambers can be hired for private functions.

A carefully maintained clock

One of the ground floor rooms has been converted into a café, called Bewicks (open 11.30am-2.00pm, Mon-Fri). An information panel near the café's entrance door gives details of Thomas Bewick's house in Gateshead. The rest of the building is not normally open to the public except for Heritage Days, which are usually held in early September.

Opposite the Town Hall, the brown metal sculpture *Acceleration* (John Creed, 2005) is a pointer to the future as well as a reminder of the busy railway activities which took place nearby.

Go past the Town Hall and turn right into Swinburne Street. Take the next turning on the right, Swinburne Place. A short distance up on your right you can see some of the barred windows of the former police cells. The red-brick building at the end is a former police house.

Walk back to Swinburne Street, turn right and proceed past a terrace of four buildings, dating from the 1870s and 1880s, which are now used for municipal or commercial purposes. First is the former General Post Office, then the former Library, next the

Gateshead Institute Permanent Building Society, and finally The National Provincial Bank of England. You can see the name and the founding date of the last-named near the top of the building. The bank eventually changed its name to the National Provincial Bank and was later absorbed into the Royal Bank of Scotland.

At the end of street use the steps or ramp on the left to descend to the busy crossroads.

You now have to cross two busy roads via pedestrian lights and you might have to exercise patience as you wait for the lights to change. Turn right and cross to the other side of the dual carriageway. Now turn left and cross the road, walking towards the railway arch ahead. The repeated 'No' on the filled-in arches is a temporary art work *No No No No No* (Cath Campbell and Mike Thurlow, 2007) which is said to be deliberately ambiguous and encourages passers-by to question the world around them.

Go down the ramp on the left and through the arch then walk for a few metres along the main road to the first street on your right (Church Street) **(Qu 3)**, **(Qu 4)**.

The small, octagonal concrete building on the corner opposite is a good example of a change of use – in this case from a public toilet to office accommodation (Waste not, want not?). Walk down the left-hand side of Church Street and follow the road as it bears left under the Tyne Bridge to the pedestrian lights ahead.

Turn right and cross the road, then turn left and follow the pavement as it takes a sharp turn to the right. Proceed ahead to come to a plaque in the wall on your right **(Qu 5)**.

Go up the sloping path on the right and continue on this path ahead to arrive at the entrance to the car park and grounds of **Gateshead Heritage @ St Mary's**. In the graveyard the largest memorial is known as the Trollope Mausoleum **(Qu 6)**.

From church to visitor centre

After visiting the heritage centre, leave the grounds and proceed ahead to **The Sage**. You can enter at the west entrance and walk through the building to explore its attractions and then exit at the east entrance. Occasionally, the west entrance is closed; in which case you can turn right and walk round the outside to the east entrance.

After your visit to The Sage we will be making our way to the Baltic. This involves going down several steep flights of steps. To avoid these, follow the bracketed instructions below.

(To take this quite long detour, leave by the east entrance, turn right and walk alongside the building. Carry on in the same direction along a footpath to exit onto a road. Turn left and proceed to the crossroads ahead. To reach the Baltic, go down the road on your left.)

A useful link

Gateshead Heritage @ St Mary's

St Mary's is the oldest building on the quayside having stood there in one form or another for over 800 years. A typical medieval church, built in the late 13th century, it was Gateshead's only church until 1825 and its principal burial ground until 1854. It also served as the focus for local government until local elections were introduced in the 1830s. In 1854 a devastating explosion and fire destroyed huge amounts of property on both sides of the Tyne and St Mary's was badly affected not for the last time. Stones that fell onto the church are preserved just beyond the church grounds. Population began to move away from the industrial quayside and this culminated with a slum clearance programme in the 1930s.

A dwindling congregation eventually led to the closure of the church in 1979. This was followed shortly afterwards by the second fire which destroyed much of the internal furniture and fittings and all of the stained glass windows, including a William Wailes window dedicated ironically to the victims of the 1854 fire. Further devastation was caused by a third fire in 1983.

However, following basic repairs by the Civic Trust, the church was acquired by a leading national company, Phillips Auctioneers, who tastefully adapted the building to their needs and reopened it in 1990 as an auction house. Phillips left ten years later, initially leasing the building to Gateshead Council and then selling it to the Council in 2004. In the early stages of the regeneration of the quayside it was used as a visitor centre and then as a tourist information centre. In 2008, following a major restoration project to bring it back to more of its original appearance, it opened as a heritage centre, Gateshead Heritage @ St Mary's.

Display panels relate the history of Gateshead from Roman times to the present day and comfortable seating areas encourage visitors to spend their time browsing the splendid array of historical records, documents, maps and photographs. A special section is devoted to family history where it is possible to access the Church of England parish records for Gateshead. Several plaques of interest adorn the walls: one in memory of Charles Bertram, churchwarden of St Mary's who lost his life in the warehouse, of which he was co-owner, that was at the heart of the 1854 fire; another, poignantly showing broken oars, recalls the death of the champion rower James Renforth supposedly with his final words, 'What will they say in England?'. The Centre also hosts exhibitions, lectures and concerts. The graveyard contains some interestingly decorated gravestones and a useful trail is available. Admission is free and the Centre is open daily, except on Mondays, and helpful staff are on hand to answer questions. It is certainly a place to visit in order to satisfy one's curiosity about much of Gateshead.

For further information see: www.gatesheadheritage@stmary's; Tel 0191 4334699

Leave The Sage from the east entrance and walk ahead **(Qu 7)**.

Now make your way down to the riverside via a series of steps. At the bottom you arrive near the building known as **HMS Calliope**.

Go down further steps, or use the ramp, on your right into the open area called Baltic Square with Gateshead Millennium Bridge (see Walk 14) ahead and, to your right, the **Baltic Centre for Contemporary Art**, often referred to as the Baltic.

The Sage

This was another bold initiative undertaken by Gateshead Council to breathe new life into a derelict quayside area with the creation of a world-class concert and music centre. This striking building designed by the internationally acclaimed architect Norman (Lord) Foster opened in December 2004 thanks to huge lottery funding and sponsorship by the Newcastle based software company Sage Plc. Its intricate shell-like roof initially received a mixed reception and some not too flattering names. However, it has since become another emblematic image for Gateshead matching that of the Angel of the North. It contains three performance spaces: Hall One with seating for 1700; Hall Two which can accommodate up to 400 and the Northern Rock Foundation Hall which acts a smaller rehearsal and performance room. In addition to function and hospitality rooms, several bars, a café and brasserie, there are some twenty-five rooms in the Music Education Centre. In other words, The Sage is much more than a concert venue.

It sees its purpose as 'a home for music and musical discovery'. It hosts performances of all kind of music including indie, country, folk, jazz, electronic and dance as well as classical. The acoustics in Hall One, which can be altered by raising or lowering the ceiling panels, have been particularly praised. Managed by the North Music Trust it has two tenants: the Northern Sinfonia Orchestra and Folkworks. The former feature regularly and their subscription concerts with guest soloists and other orchestras are extremely popular. Folkworks under the artistic directorship of the world-renowned Northumbrian piper, Katherine Tickell, provides a varied programme of folk music together with support and encouragement to the youth ensemble Folkestra. All age groups and abilities are catered for through weekly classes and summer schools. Nor are its activities confined to the building itself as it offers an outreach programme of concerts and classes in the north-east and Cumbria. The Silver Singers for the over-50s is an example of The Sage's ability to organise and motivate community-based choirs.

The building is open daily for visitors to appreciate its interior, enjoy refreshments and take in the splendid views across the Tyne.

For details of concerts and activities see: www.thesagegateshead.org; or the Welcome desk Tel 0191 4434666

There are a number of information panels in the entrance hall **(Qu 8)**.

On leaving the Baltic walk to the road, turn left and proceed ahead with the Baltic on your left. There are lots of new developments around here. At the junction cross the road to the stainless steel sculpture *Swirl* (Colin Rose, 2009) outside Baltic Place. Turn right and walk up the hill, passing the Baltic Quay apartment blocks on your right. At the crossroads, cross at the pedestrian lights and carry straight on along the road ahead (Quarryfield Road). On your left is the former Saltmeadows, a 1960s industrial estate now being redeveloped.

You pass the Baltic Campus of Gateshead College on your right. On your left you come to Abbots Hill. Baltimore House, an office block, is located here and the adjacent building houses the northern headquarters of the Open University. Turn right and use the pedestrian lights to cross to the other side of the road. Turn left and, via another set of pedestrian lights, proceed ahead.

Carry on and until you come to a blue cycleway sign. Turn right as indicated for the

Gateshead Millennium Bridge

town centre. Walk under the railway bridge and turn left just beyond the entrance to the Union Electric Steel engineering works. Continue parallel to the busy road and at the end of the wall below the flyover, turn right to descend to a subway signed 'To Shopping Centre'. Follow the sign to the town centre passing Park Court on your left and turn left at a minor road. Walk a few metres behind the church and then turn right along Hopper Place to meet a road. On your right is **St Edmund's Chapel** and the adjoining Trinity Community Centre.

Inside St Edmund's you will find a quiet place for worship with interesting stained glass windows, as well as a display of art work. In front of the church, there is a mosaic of a St Cuthbert's cross (St Cuthbert was Bishop of Lindisfarne, otherwise known as Holy Island), incorporating the work of children from a former school, by Mark Todman, mosaic artist with glass by Sue Woolhouse **(Qu 9)**.

On leaving the chapel, go across the road and walk up the left-hand side of Jackson Street. The Metropole Hotel (William Hope, 1896) is on the left-hand corner. The Metropole

HMS Calliope

Her Majesty's Ship (HMS) Calliope is one of the Royal Navy's shore-based establishments, known affectionately as 'stone frigates'. A division of the Royal Naval Reserve, based on the Tyne was set up in 1905. Until the 1960s the reserve unit used two former naval vessels, both renamed Calliope, but moved to its present shore base in 1968, retaining the name HMS Calliope. It serves as a base for around 200 reservists of the Tyne division.

Baltic Centre for Contemporary Art

In the early 1990s Gateshead Council decided to embark on an ambitious project to create a centre for contemporary art in the former Rank Hovis Flour Mills. The grain mills and warehouse had been designed in the 1930s but with the intervention of World War II, construction was postponed and the building did not open until 1950. It was named the Baltic Flour Mills in line with the company policy of calling their mills after seas or rivers. Hundreds of people were employed but its life span was short and following a disastrous fire and with sales falling it closed in 1981. The silos, however, remained open until 1984 to contain an EEC 'grain mountain', a fact that led to some public hostility.

In 1994 an international architectural competition organised by Gateshead Council was won by Dominic Williams of Ellis Williams Architects. Subsequently it took some four years to complete the massive transformation of the building into its present state before it was able to be opened in 2002. There are six floors on which there is flexible space to house both small and substantial exhibitions, studios, lecture rooms, a ground floor café and shop as well as a restaurant on the top floor. Its location on the Gateshead Quays provides the opportunity to obtain stunning views of the Tyne and its bridges.

Baltic aims to 'present a dynamic, diverse and international programme of contemporary visual art' and to this end there are no permanent exhibitions but instead there are regular changes in installations and activities. Emphasis is placed on innovative work and artists are encouraged to work with local people to create new projects. The results at times have been provocative and not always universally popular.

From flour to art

However, two of what the Centre calls its 'blockbuster' exhibitions certainly succeeded in drawing large numbers of participants and viewers. In 2003 Antony Gormley, creator of the landmark *Angel of the North*, enlisted the help of volunteers, aged from two to eighty-five, to have their naked bodies moulded in plaster. He then used the moulds to construct series of sculptures in steel to create *Domain Fields*.

Bodies, albeit rather portly ones, were also in evidence again in 2007 when the Centre staged an exhibition of the work of Beryl Cook. The public loved it, judging by the gales of laughter, but art critics dismissed it as being contrary to the ethos of the Baltic.

In 2011 the staging here of the Turner Prize, for the first time outside of a Tate venue, drew record attendances.

Baltic is open daily and admission is free.

For further information see: www.balticmill.com; Tel 0191 4404949

St Edmund's Chapel

St Edmund's Chapel was founded in 1249 by Nicholas de Farnham, Bishop of Durham, as a chapel and hospital, dedicated to St Edmund and St Cuthbert, on the site of the earlier Holy Trinity Hospital. After the Dissolution of the Monasteries, around 1540, it became part of a private house. By the mid-18th century it was in ruins. However, in 1836 the then owner, Cuthbert Ellison, gave the chapel to the Rector of Gateshead. The chapel was restored in 1836/7 by John Dobson as Holy Trinity Chapel. In 1894/6 the chapel was converted into a new Holy Trinity Church by Stephen Piper. To achieve this, the chapel became the south aisle of the extended building by taking down the original north wall.

Holy Trinity Church became redundant in 1969 but the chapel was partitioned off and was used for weekday services and private prayer. In the meanwhile, following slum clearance programmes, St Mary's, Gateshead's Parish Church, had a dwindling congregation and became redundant in 1979. Hence, there was no Gateshead Parish Church.

In 1980 the two parts of the redundant Holy Trinity building were divided. The 1890s extension was converted into the Trinity Community Centre by Hayton, Lee and Bradock; the original chapel was restored and reverted to the name of St Edmund's Chapel. In 1981 Sunday services were begun and in 1982 it joined with the church of St James and St Bede as the new Parish Church of Gateshead Team Ministry.

Theatre, built at the same time, was situated behind the hotel. The theatre was the largest in Gateshead and one of the first buildings to have electric light. It was converted into the Scala Cinema in 1919 and demolished in 1960.

Walk ahead. After 100 metres, on the right-hand side, you pass the original headquarters building of the Gateshead Industrial Cooperative Society Ltd; the name and date, 1881, are inscribed at the top. The extension to the building is next door **(Qu 10)**.

At the end of the street, over the road on the left is St Joseph's Catholic Church (1859). Cross to the Gateshead Interchange and the end of the walk. The Metro Station is also the starting point for Walks 12 and 13. Buses for Walks 19, 20 and 21 leave from the adjacent Bus Concourse.

Quiz questions

1. Why was the Gateshead Dispensary founded in 1832?
2. Which firm partially funded the restoration of the clock in 2001?
3. What is the name of the bridge ahead of you?
4. What annual running event, usually held in September, crosses the bridge?
5. When did Daniel Defoe live in Gateshead?
6. Which family is now commemorated on the Trollope Mausoleum?
7. Where is there an outdoor performance space near the Sage?
8. On which floor is the viewing box?
9. Which school is remembered in the mosaic outside St Edmund's Chapel?
10. When was the Cooperative Society building extended?

3. West of the Haymarket: Town Moor and Newcastle University

Start/finish: Haymarket Metro Station
Distance: 2 miles
Route: Haymarket, Great North Museum, Exhibition Park, Town Moor, Newcastle University, Haymarket
Accessibility: On pavements and tarmac tracks
Refreshments: Cafés and pubs in Haymarket area, Great North Museum, Forum Café in the University grounds, McKennas at Northern Stage

Palace of Arts: Exhibition survivor

We begin our walk at the top of pedestrianized Northumberland Street at the **Haymarket**. Just beyond one of the stations of the **Tyne and Wear Metro** you will find the striking monument: the **South African War Memorial** (Macklin, 1907). Ahead is **Barras Bridge** although there is no sign of a bridge! The Goddess Victory figure on top of the monument looks out over a busy junction of roads, with university buildings on the left and ecclesiastical and civic buildings on the right **(Qu 1)**.

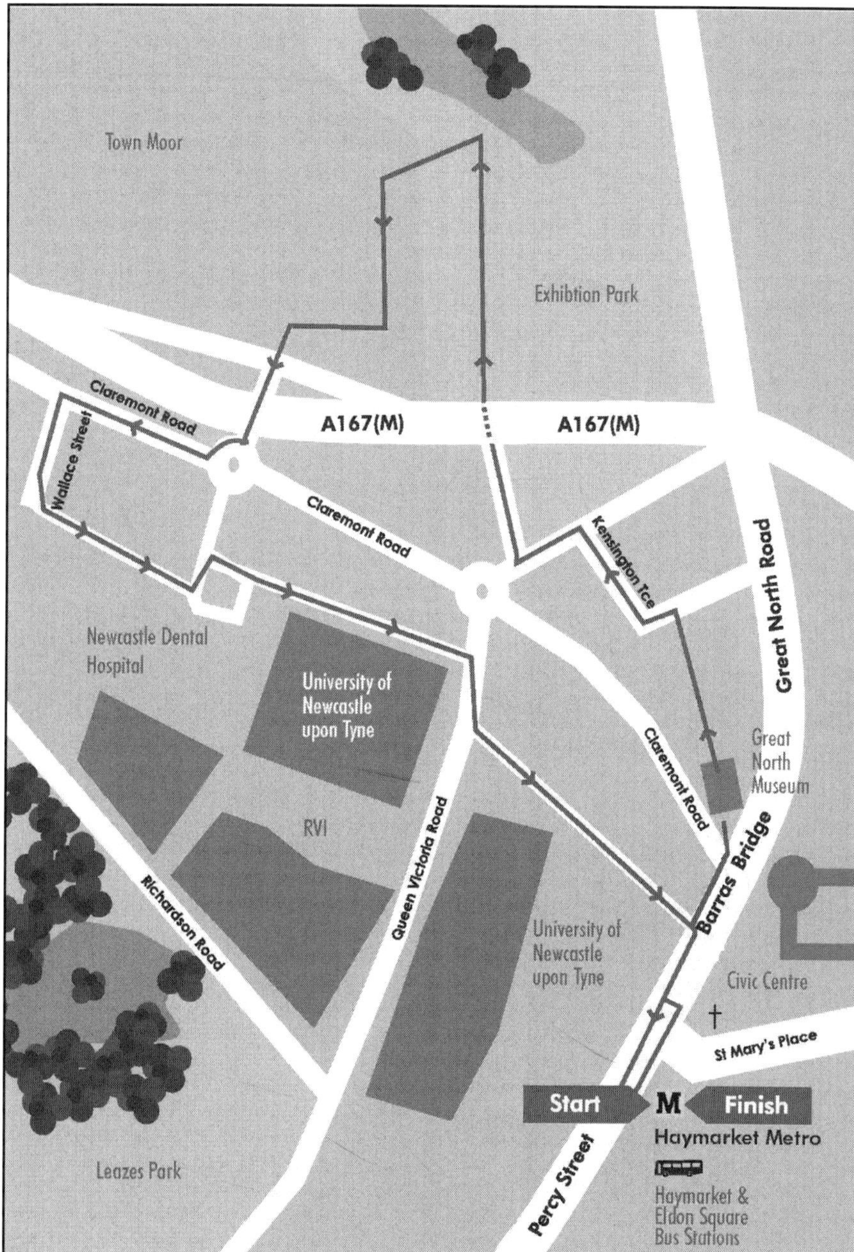
Town Moor
Exhibition Park
Claremont Road
A167(M)
A167(M)
Wallace Street
Claremont Road
Kensington Tce
Great North Road
Newcastle Dental Hospital
University of Newcastle upon Tyne
Claremont Road
Great North Museum
RVI
Queen Victoria Road
Barras Bridge
Richardson Road
University of Newcastle upon Tyne
Civic Centre
St Mary's Place
Start
M
Finish
Haymarket Metro
Haymarket & Eldon Square Bus Stations
Percy Street
Leazes Park

Haymarket

Although the name may conjure up a medieval scene, a market was only established here in the late 1820s on what had been levelled as a parade ground for the Newcastle Volunteer Militia at the time of the Napoleonic War (1803-15). This became a thriving market area not only for hay but also for a variety of farm and other produce. Traders, customers, labourers seeking work and visitors could also enjoy the lively atmosphere of the numerous pubs that sprung up in the vicinity. As Newcastle continued to expand northwards the Grand Hotel (1889) and the Crows Nest Hotel (1902) added perhaps a little more decorum to the area. The name of the former remains engraved above the premises, now the booksellers Blackwells, while the latter is a popular pub. A bus station replaced the market in the 1930s and now the area is also the focus for its revamped bus station, Haymarket Metro Station and access to the city's educational and civic areas.

Tyne and Wear Metro

This ambitious engineering project to provide a light rapid transit system was started in 1974 and officially opened by the Queen in 1980. Initially covering both sides of Tyne, it was further extended to Sunderland and Wearside in 2002. Now its 60 stations, carrying 40 million passengers a year, provide an ideal way of discovering more of NewcastleGateshead and its immediate environs. In December 2009, in order to secure a multi-million pound capital investment from the government, the owners Nexus agreed to subcontract the operation of the system to the German railway company DB Regio from 2010 for a set period of time. Hopefully this will lead to continued modernisation and efficient services.

On 24th March 2011 in celebration of 30 years of the Metro, a short film *Metro the Musical* was premiered at the Sage, Gateshead, and simultaneously shown on the BBC *Look North* programme.

South African War Memorial

The figure of the Goddess Victory, (Nike in the original Greek as scholars and sports enthusiasts will know!), stands on top of this memorial to those who fell in the South African (Boer) War campaign of 1899-1902. This has been a local landmark since its erection here in 1907 (incidently the year self-government was granted to South Africa). On one side is inscribed the regimental motto of the Royal Northumberland Fusiliers *Quo fata vocant* (Whither the Fates call) above the dramatic relief depicting soldiers in conflict. Beneath are the words *Dulce et decum est pro partia mori* (It is sweet and glorious to die for one's country). While on another side poignantly inscribed beneath the dramatic figure clutching an unfurled flag is *Steadfast in life Valiant in death.* Four plaques carry the names and regimental battalions of those whose ultimate sacrifice is recalled.

Barras Bridge

There is no sign nowadays of the bridge with its toll bar that once crossed the now underground Pandon Burn that flows down to the River Tyne. Barras is said to derive from the 'barrow' or burial mound which would be associated with the ancient leper hospitals of St James and St Mary Magdalene both located well outside the city walls. The former site of the Chapel and Hospital of St James, once known as Sick Men's Close, became the location for the Hancock Museum in in the late 19th century. The Hospital of St Mary Magdalene became the site for the Church of St Thomas the Martyr located on the right.

After admiring the war memorial, taking your bearings and observing the bottleneck of traffic that can arise at this important junction, use the pedestrian lights to cross towards the Church of St Thomas the Martyr.

Bear immediately left to a further set of traffic lights and cross over the dual carriageway. Ahead you will see the splendid archway entrance to the quadrangle of Newcastle University (see below).Turn right to pass a large glass-fronted building, housing a visitor centre, the main student services and a range of the University's administrative services **(Qu 2)**.

Continue ahead with the Civic Centre over to your right, to arrive at the bottom of a road (Claremont Road) with the monument of **Lord Armstrong** on the opposite corner. Use

Lord Armstrong (1810-1900)

Lord Armstrong was born in Newcastle. He became a partner in a local law practice, but continued to devote much of his time to his engineering interests. To this end he carried out experiments at the engineering works of his friend Henry Watson on High Bridge. In 1845 he was closely involved in setting up a new water company to supply Newcastle and shortly afterwards he invented the world's first efficient hydraulic crane. In 1847 he gave up the law and founded his engineering firm, W. G. Armstrong and Company. The company initially specialised in hydraulic machines and the Swing Bridge (1876) is still driven by its hydraulic engines. Later the company gained a world-wide reputation for armaments. He was created the 1st Baron Armstrong of Cragside in 1887.

Lord Armstrong

He built Cragside (1864-66), near Rothbury, now owned by the National Trust, described as 'the palace of the modern magician' (Cole, 1996). In addition, in 1894, he acquired and substantially restored Bamburgh Castle.

Apart from his industrial and domestic activities, he was a noted benefactor. In the 1880s he presented the town with land for Armstrong Park in Heaton and Jesmond Dene. Lord and Lady Armstrong were generous supporters of local amenities in health, education and culture, including the Hancock Museum (now incorporated into the Great North Museum). It is fitting that a statue of Lord Armstrong is located near the Museum in recognition of someone who 'was perhaps the greatest benefactor that Newcastle has ever had' (Middlebrook, 1950).

the pedestrian lights to cross to the monument and then take some time to study the panels at the sides **(Qu 3)**.

Now take the shallow steps directly behind the monument that lead to the main entrance to the **Great North Museum.** (Alternatively for smoother accessible entry to the museum turn left and proceed up Claremont Road. After about 50 metres look out for a doorway on your right. This was an entrance made to the 19th-century wagon-way, the Victoria Tunnel, to enable it to be used as an air raid shelter during World War II. Continue for a further 100 metres or so and then turn right to follow the ramp to the main entrance).

Once you have passed through the reception area and enter the museum proper don't forget to look up! **(Qu 4)**.

Great North Museum

In 2009 the Hancock Museum was reopened after a three year multi-million pound extension and refurbishment as 'Great North Museum: Hancock'. The museum opened on this site in 1884 and was given the name 'Hancock' after the local naturalists, the brothers Albany and John Hancock on the death of the latter in 1890. The name remains engraved in the stone façade and many locals will undoubtedly continue to refer to it as 'The Hancock'. A plaque near the reception desk provides information about the two brothers.

The imposing 19th-century structure still predominates but has been enlarged with a rear extension by Sir Terry Farrell & Partners. The contents now incorporate the collections of the Society of Antiquaries and Newcastle University from their joint Museum of Antiquities as well as the contents of the University's Shefton Museum of Greek Art and Archaeology. The 'new' museum is consequently extremely varied and comprehensive, including 'Living Planet' with a large collection of stuffed mammals and animals, 'Fossil Stories', 'Ancient Egyptians', 'Ancient Greeks' and 'Anglo-Saxons'. Of particular local interest will be the imposing 'Hadrian's Wall' as well as 'Natural Northumbria'. There are sight and sound touch-screen information and games to please both children and adults. And do try to experience 'Journey to the afterlife'! There are two cafés: Hancock Café on the first floor and Street Café on the ground floor. Entry is free except to the Planetarium and some special exhibitions. In July-October 2010, 'In the Long Run', an exhibition about the first thirty years of the Great North Run with interactive exhibits and memorabilia, including examples of fancy-dress costumes, proved to be very popular.

For further information see: www.greatnorthmuseum.org

Some Great North runners

From the main entrance to the museum, return to Claremont Road and walk as far as the building that straddles the road (Claremont Tower) to take the path to the right of the pedestrian lights. Walk the short distance to the junction at Devonshire Walk. You are going to turn left but before you do so walk some 15 metres to the right to discover, set in a brick wall, a carving said to be from the former St Mary Magdalene Hospital. Now resume the walk by proceeding left with the Devonshire Building on your right.

(Alternatively, leave the museum by the Street Café exit, turn left and ahead you will see set in a wall, the carving said to be from the former St Mary Magdalene Hospital. Turn immediately right to the Devonshire Building).

This futuristic-looking building houses the Institute for Research & Environment & Sustainability. In the entrance lobby you may notice, *Unity*, a trio of sculptures by the Ugandan artist Lilian Nabulime who gained her PhD at Newcastle University.

Proceed ahead, with on your right a 19th-century terrace of dwellings (Kensington Terrace), now university offices, to the road junction. Turn left and follow the path past the curved Stephenson Building (School of Mechanical & Systems Engineering). Before reaching the end of the road, turn right and cross the road to enter the **Exhibition Park**.

Hidden carving

Exhibition Park

Exhibition Park acquired its name in 1887, when a former recreation area was improved to provide an appropriate site for an exhibition to celebrate Queen Victoria's Golden Jubilee. At the same time a bandstand (located beyond the café) was built and the present lake was created from a small pond which was all that remained of a former reservoir. Some fifty years later a much grander event was planned and the efforts of an enthusiastic committee were rewarded with the opening of The North East Coast Exhibition in 1929.

The Exhibition covered 125 acres and lasted for six months. The underlying idea was to stimulate and revive trade in the area by a celebration of the North East heritage in industry, science and art. Judged by the attendance figures of nearly 4½ million it was a huge success.

Apart from industrial and engineering exhibits there were lots of other attractions, including musical concerts, flower gardens and fountains, a Prayer Hut and many sporting events. Perhaps the most unusual 'exhibit' was an African mud-hut village, occupied for the duration of the Exhibition by a group of native Algerians. A baby was born there and, sadly, one of the dancers in the group died.

Today, the Palace of Arts building, which later housed a science museum and a military vehicle museum, is the only physical survivor, but we can still enjoy the many other pleasures of the Exhibition Park. From time to time there are special events such as the annual Mela Festival, celebrating Asian arts, music and culture.

Work began in June 2011 to change the rather sterile nature of the lake and to transform it into a nature haven via The Lakeside Explorer Project and the park in general is set to be redeveloped following a £2.4m grant from the Heritage Lottery Fund.

You pass the Newcastle Skate Park usually popular at weekends with young daredevil skateboard and BMX bike enthusiasts. The broad roadway descends beneath the Central Motorway before rising quite steeply (the only real incline on the whole walk) to give access to a general view of the park. Follow the wide tarmac track as far as the children's play area. Ahead lies the lake beyond which stands the somewhat forlorn former Palace of Arts building **(Qu 5)**.

To your right is the Sensory Garden and a café (with seasonal opening times). Now, depending on the weather and the time available, you might like to explore the park and see if you can find, for example, the bandstand and the Tyneside Croquet Club's pavilion and croquet lawn.

However, to continue on the walk, proceed ahead past the children's play area to the lakeside. Bear left and then turn left up a broad tarmac path to exit the park via a gate. You are now on the **Town Moor** in the administration of which the **Freemen of Newcastle** play an important role

Town Moor

Looking at Newcastle on any map, the most noticeable feature is the vast open space in the middle of the city. This open area consists of a number of 'moors' which, since the 17th century, have usually been known collectively as the Town Moor. It is recognised as being unique for an industrial city, "Fortunate among towns is Newcastle that she possesses, so near at hand, these open expanses of land..."(Charleton, 1890).

One unusual aspect is its dual ownership, whereby the land is owned by the City Council but the grazing rights are vested in the Freemen. This situation has been governed by a number of statutes, the most recent being The Newcastle upon Tyne Town Moor Act 1988. It is largely as a result of this dual control that the Moor has retained its openness, unencumbered by inappropriate developments, as a place to be freely enjoyed by the citizens of and visitors to Newcastle.

Horse racing was a popular reason for large assemblies from the early 18th century until 1881 when the racecourse was transferred to its present venue in Gosforth Park. Grandstand Road is now the only indication that a grandstand, erected in 1800, once stood on the moor. 'Temperance' meetings attracting large numbers for games and sports replaced the race meetings and these eventually led to the Moor annually hosting, in June, the 'Hoppings', reputed to be Europe's largest travelling funfair.

In the 19th and early 20th century huge crowds regularly gathered in support of political causes. Nowadays athletes of all abilities enjoy training and racing on and around the Moor and the regular Saturday Parkrun proves very popular. Other events, for example exhibitions and circuses, are held with the approval of the City Authorities and the Freemen.

From the Moor you can see urban and suburban sights but you might also encounter cattle, grazing within a few hundred metres of the city centre.

Freemen of Newcastle

Freemen are either hereditary or honorary. Newcastle City Council may confer honorary freedom on individuals such as former council leaders or local celebrities; Alan Shearer being a recent example. Entrance into the hereditary 'Freelage' is open to a freeman's son or time-served apprentice and, from 2009, to a freeman's daughter.

There is uncertainty about the origins of the hereditary freeman. Roman, British and Anglo-Saxon influences have been suggested. Lack of written evidence before the Norman Conquest presents difficulties in establishing a traceable history. After the arrival of the Normans it became fairly common for a town to receive from the king a charter whereby trading and other privileges were conferred or, where appropriate, confirmed. Newcastle's first recorded charter was from Henry II in 1175.

Initially merchants (for example, drapers) and then craftsmen (for example, bakers), grouped themselves into companies (sometimes referred to as gilds) to maintain control over their particular trade or craft. In common with other towns, there were disputes between Newcastle's merchant and craft companies, often to do with the trade guilds trying to gain monopolistic control. The freemen's exclusive rights to carry on trades and crafts died out during the 18th century. However, a few freemen families retained de facto control over local government until the passing of The Municipal Corporation Act 1832. This created 178 municipal boroughs, governed by councils which were elected by ratepayers.

Today's hereditary freemen administer a number of charities and take a lead part in ensuring effective management and maintenance of the Town Moor. They retain their historic grazing rights, usually sub-let to local farmers. During much of the year up to 550 cows may be seen feeding on the Moor's grass.

For further information see: www.freemenofnewcastle.org

Continue ahead to a junction of paths and stop to take time to appreciate the views across this wide green oasis amid an urban landscape. Note the two artificial hills created from waste when the Central Motorway was built in the 1960s and which present a delight to those who bring out their sledges at the least sign of snow. Beyond the park you will also notice a range of rooftops that include part of St James' Park **(Qu 6)**.

Now turn left at the junction of paths. Follow the tarmac path as it bears right, and then left, to leave the Moor by a gate. Keep to the right-hand side and take great care to cross over the motorway slip roads, pausing only to imagine some 50,000 runners assembling below at the start of the annual **Great North Run**.

Turn right to walk up North Terrace (Claremont Road). At a convenient moment cross over the road to a popular pub, The North Terrace with its neat 'terrace' sign.

Proceed ahead to St Luke's Church. St Luke's became a separate parish towards the end of the 19th century in order to serve what was then the distinct village community of Spital Tongues. Note the memorial stone in the wall **(Qu 7)**.

Saturday Parkrun

You pass some relatively modern dwellings on the site of the former Northern Coachbuilders (1920-1970s). A short distance further on is the base of a windmill, originally **Chimney Mill**, with a commemorative plaque beside it **(Qu 8)**.

Continue ahead and turn left at the first road on your left, Wallace Street. Walk

Great North Run

This run from Newcastle to South Shields is said to be the world's largest half-marathon and attracts elite athletes, club runners, wheelchair competitors and fun runners who raise millions of pounds for their chosen charities.

It was first run in 1981 when there were 12,000 participants. As the race grew in popularity numbers increased, so that by 2011 there were some 54,000 entrants. It takes place in September and for the last 18 years has been sponsored by BUPA. Usually, the start of the race is accompanied by a fly-past by the Red Arrows, the RAF display team. One particular feature enjoyed by all participants is the enthusiastic support given by the crowds lining the whole route.

The Great North Run was founded in 1981 by Brendan Foster, champion international athlete and, at the time, Gateshead Council Sports and Recreation Manager. Brendan has been a BBC commentator since 1980 covering all the major athletic competitions and he remains an out-standing ambassador for his native North-East.

Chimney Mill

This building merits one of the city's commemorative plaques, not only being in use for over a hundred years (1782-1892) as a working windmill but also apparently for being the first five-sail windmill in the country. It is the only surviving evidence of the several mills that operated in Spital Tongues, an area of character with some interesting history (Walk 5).

The mill was designed by the noted civil engineer John Smeaton (1724-1792) who was responsible for the innovative Eddystone Lighthouse and various canals and bridges, including the bridge over the River Tyne at Hexham, built to his design the year after his death. The windmill subsequently served as a club-house for the City of Newcastle Golf Club (1892) and then Newcastle United Golf Club (not connected with the football club!). Look for some evidence of its golf club connections on the door surrounds. After several conversions, it is currently in use as a dental practice.

ahead to the end of the road, passing a short section of stone wall on the left which is all that remains of the school that served Spital Tongues for nearly a hundred years, until it finally closed in 1977. Turn left to enter the grounds of the northern part of the vast fifty-acre campus of **Newcastle University**.

Walk along the service road. On your right are the Richardson Road student flats. On your left, you soon pass the University Sports Centre, opposite which older buildings house a laundry and some squash courts. You arrive at a junction of paths just beyond the futuristic-looking Baddiley-Clark building. The Forum Café occupies part of the ground floor.

Turn left to follow a brick wall on your right. In a few metres, on your left, is an elegant 18th-century brick building, the Brewery House, formerly part of W.B. Reid's Leazes Brewery from 1837 until the late 1960s. Excavations in this area have found evidence of a water-power driven snuff mill designed by John Smeaton in 1781 (see above) together with evidence of housing for its workers. Next on your left is the modern Paul O'Gorman building, housing the Northern Institute for Cancer Research.

Turn right to follow the paved path. Immediately on your right is one of the mid-19th-century dwellings of this one-time haven for professionals and wealthy tradesmen. Originally called Leazes Villas, it was built for Emerson Muschamp Bainbridge (1817-1892), founder of the famous Newcastle department store, Bainbridge's (eventually taken over by

Newcastle University

The current university owes its origins to the School of Medicine and Surgery which was established in 1834 and the College of Physical Sciences established in 1871.

Both of these colleges subsequently formed part of the federal University of Durham. The two colleges merged in 1937 to become King's College (known locally simply as King's'). In 1963 the Newcastle component separated from Durham University to become an independent institution as the University of Newcastle upon Tyne (now with the snappier title of Newcastle University).

In the academic year 2010-11 the University had more than 20,000 students and 5,000 staff. It is a member of the Russell Group of leading UK research-based universities. Currently it is engaged on £200m programme to adapt its campus for the twenty-first century, a process that is gradually transforming the Haymarket and other areas of the city.

One of the key players responsible for planning the incorporation of university buildings within the cityscape is the internationally acclaimed architect Sir Terry Farrell, himself a graduate of the University's School of Architecture and former pupil of St Cuthbert's Grammar School, Newcastle.

For further information see: www.ncl.ac.org

the John Lewis Partnership in 1952). It was later used for nursing education and it is now divided into private apartments **(Qu 9)**.

As you progress further you are likely to encounter an increasing number of students many of whom will be attending the Faculty of Medical Sciences that you pass on the right. A variety of foreign languages gives evidence of the international appeal of Newcastle.

As the roadway turns left, leading back to Claremont Road, continue straight ahead into a pedestrian zone. The path narrows as it retains some of the charm of what is still referred to as 'Lovers' Lane'. Here a pleasant carriageway once ran alongside the now culveted Pandon Burn as it made its way from Spital Tongues to the River Tyne. It now serves as an important thoroughfare for university staff and students. At the end of the lane you arrive at a main road (Queen Victoria Road).

Unusual pub sign

Cross the road via the pedestrian lights, turn right and walk some 150 metres to the imposing towered-frontage of the **Armstrong Building**. On the opposite side of the road you will see some of the 21st-century buildings of the Royal Victoria Hospital (RVI).

Bear left to go through a narrow archway on the left of the Armstrong Building to enter the **University quadrangle** where you will find the **Hatton Gallery**.

As you proceed through the quadrangle, you will see some benches along the path that leads to the Architecture Building. One of the benches bears a dedication to a head gardener who served the university for many years **(Qu 10)**.

Proceed ahead to the end of the quadrangle to pass beneath one of the twin arches where generations of anxious students have gathered to see their examination results. Once through the archway you need to stop and look back to admire the impressive fortified-looking frontage. This red brick entrance dates from 1911 a year after the death of King Edward V11, a statue of whom can be seen in the niche just above the two arches. The royal theme was, of course, in the university's title 'King's College' (1937-1963) and so it is not perhaps surprising that after passing through the arches you are standing on King's Road and are now about to descend ahead down King's Walk to the King's Gate building.

On the right you pass another older red brick university building, the Union Society Building (1923), with its student-run clubs and entertainment facilities. You may well be offered some campaigning literature from the student activists who often set up stalls in this area.

Armstrong Building

The Armstrong Building was originally built in stages from 1887, until the completion of its imposing entrance in 1906, to house the College of Physical Sciences (see above, Newcastle University). The foundation stone was laid by Lord Armstrong one of the benefactors and in 1904 the College itself was renamed Armstrong College in honour of Lord Armstrong who had died in 1900. The splendid exterior is matched internally by the attractive King's Hall, a venue for concerts, examinations and graduation ceremonies. Several school offices and subject areas are located here as can be seen from the board at the main entrance and also the side entrance that you will pass shortly.

University quadrangle

The quadrangle was laid out in its present form in 1949 in memory of the members of the Newcastle Division of Durham University who gave their lives in both World Wars. It is surrounded by some older areas of the University. The Armstrong building occupies the right-hand side while the Old Library Building is in the top left-hand corner. This building now houses most of the computer services used by staff and students.

The ivy-covered building further down on the left, is the Architecture Building. However, older generations of students would know this as the Department of Agriculture and two plaques at the entrance indicate that the foundation stone was laid in 1913 by Sir Clement Stephenson and that this noted veterinary surgeon contributed half of the cost of the building.

Hatton Gallery

The Hatton Gallery, now part of the Great North Museum, is in the bottom left-hand corner. The Gallery prides itself on its fine exhibition space which caters for both its highly regard permanent collection as well as regular special displays that appeal to a wide variety of interests. It also organises a comprehensive learning and out-reach programme.

For further details of exhibitions and activities see: www.twmuseums.org.uk/hatton

On your left is the more recently renovated Northern Stage theatre building (2006), previously known as University Theatre, then Newcastle Playhouse. It boasts three performance areas and two bars. In 2010 the theatre group celebrated its fortieth birthday. You may like to pick up a list of current productions from the theatre or pause for refreshments in its welcoming glass-fronted McKennas bar and restaurant.

Finally, you descend via the steps or the ramps towards St Thomas's Church. On your right, you will see the Grand Assembly Rooms (1889), formerly part of the Grand Hotel and not to be confused with the Old Assembly Rooms of 1776 in Fenkle Street. After fulfilling various University roles, including that of Sports Hall, the interior of this fine building has recently been restored to some of original elegance and perhaps for an appropriate use as the Culture Lab, dedicated to the intersection of art and science

University arches

Meanwhile, on your left, at the access to the University from the Haymarket, is the aptly-called King's Gate, opened in 2009 as the Student and Administrative Services Building. Turn right to pass Blackwells Bookshop, formerly the Grand Hotel (1891), and the Crows Nest pub (1902). Pedestrian lights will enable you to return to the Haymarket Metro and Bus Stations and the end of this walk.

Quiz questions

1. **Which two objects is the Goddess Victory holding?**
2. **What is the name of this building?**
3. **What aspects of Lord Armstrong's work are shown on his monument?**
4. **Looking up, immediately after passing through the glass doors beyond the shop and the Welcome Point, which is the tallest animal on display?**
5. **Which museum previously occupied the red-domed building on the other side of the lake?**
6. **How many high-rise blocks of flats can you see from this point ?**
7. **Where is the original war memorial of St Luke's Church?**
8. **When did Chimney Mill cease to be used as a golf clubhouse**
9. **What is the name of this building now?**
10. **What was the first name of the former head gardener?**

4. East of the Haymarket: Civic Centre and Northumbria University

Start/finish: Haymarket Metro Station
Distance: 2.75 miles
Route: Haymarket, Newcastle University Library, Sandyford Road, Civic Centre, Northumbria University Library and Art Galleries, Northumberland Road, City Hall, Laing Art Gallery, City Library, Haymarket
Accessibility: Mostly on pavements with some ascents and descents via ramps
Refreshments: Cafés and pubs in Haymarket area and on the route. Cafés in Laing Art Gallery and City Library

Start from the top of the pedestrianized Northumberland Street and walk towards the church. Go into the church grounds (a favourite place for local workers to relax on a warm summer day) where you will see a plaque, on the left-hand gatepost, referring to its charitable status. We will be looking at three war memorials in the church grounds. The first is just before you reach the church where, on your right, is a sculpture of St George and the Dragon set in a curved wall (John Reid, 1924) **(Qu 1)**.

Walk to the magnificent glass doors at the entrance to **St Thomas' Church (Qu 2)**.

Response to the call

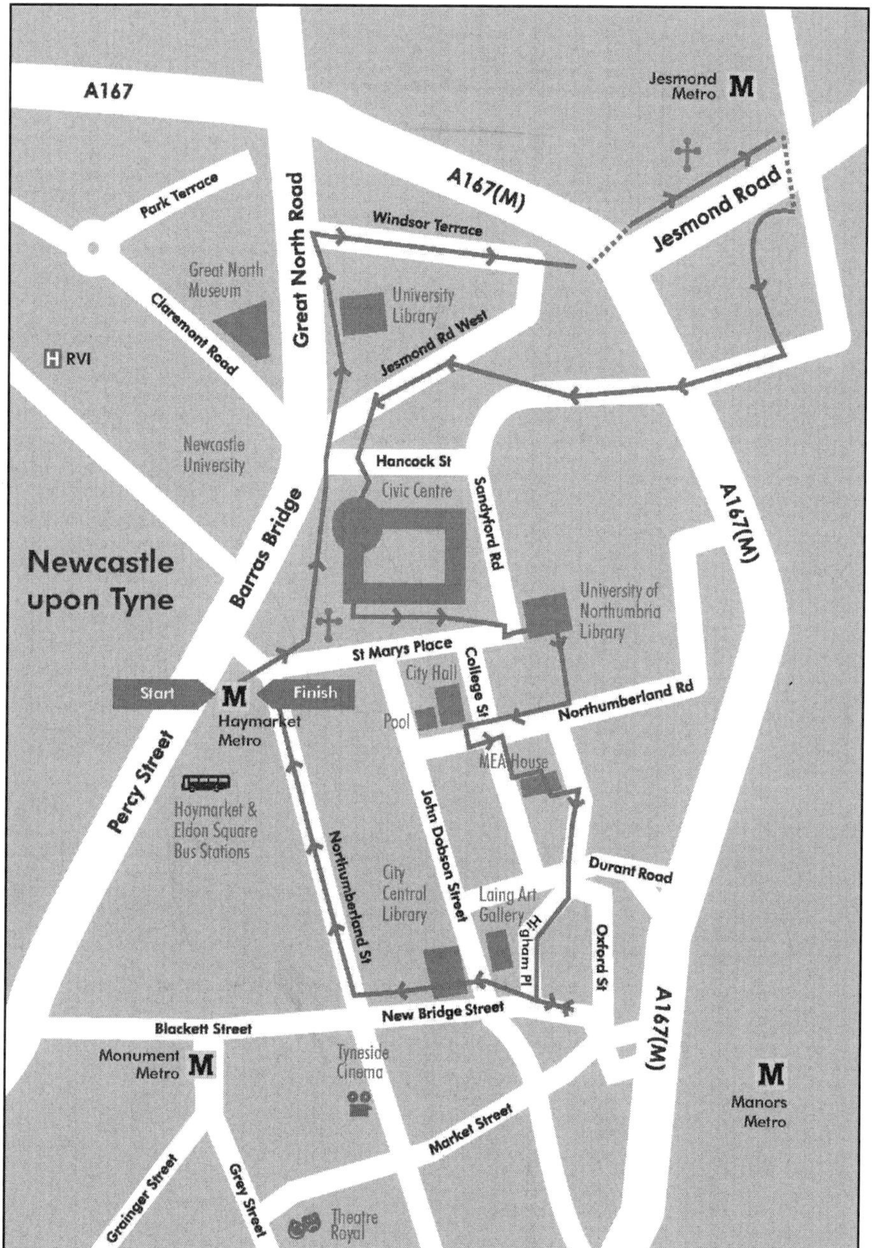
A167
Jesmond Metro
M
A167(M)
Jesmond Road
Park Terrace
Great North Road
Windsor Terrace
Great North Museum
University Library
Claremont Road
Jesmond Rd West
RVI
Newcastle University
Hancock St
Civic Centre
Sandyford Rd
A167(M)
Barras Bridge
Newcastle upon Tyne
University of Northumbria Library
St Marys Place
College St
City Hall
Start
M
Finish
Haymarket Metro
Northumberland Rd
Pool
MEA House
Percy Street
Haymarket & Eldon Square Bus Stations
John Dobson Street
Northumberland St
Durant Road
City Central Library
Laing Art Gallery
Higham Pl
Oxford St
A167(M)
New Bridge Street
Blackett Street
Monument Metro
M
Tyneside Cinema
M
Manors Metro
Market Street
Grainger Street
Grey Street
Theatre Royal

`You will be passing a number of buildings by John Dobson on this walk and you might like to count up how many you see, to help you to answer Question 10.

A short distance after the church entrance is a First World War memorial ***The Response.***

Walk behind *The Response.* Take the path which heads towards the back of the church, then turn left and walk 30 metres to come to the small **Burma Campaign Memorial**, which is about five feet high and is a sandy colour.

St Thomas' Church

The Church of St Thomas the Martyr, which was one of the earliest churches designed by John Dobson, was completed in 1830. Opinions differ as to its architectural merit but one commentator thought it one of the regions "real gems in a national context" (Ian Curry in Pickering ed, 1981). It has an interesting history: St Thomas Becket, Archbishop of Canterbury was murdered in 1170 and one of his murderers is reputed, as a penance, to have built the Chapel of St Thomas, located on the Newcastle riverside. In 1611 the chapel became part of a single institution together with the St Mary Magdalene Hospital for lepers, located in Barras Bridge. By the early 19th century the hospital buildings were in ruins and the corporation demolished the riverside chapel and replaced it with the present building on the site of the hospital.

St Thomas' is neither a parish church nor a 'peculiar' (i.e. a church which is located within a diocese but is outside the authority of the diocesan bishop), but is, uniquely, governed by Acts of Parliament. The Master (equivalent to a vicar) usually serves as Newcastle University Anglican Chaplain.

Inside in the foyer, on your left are two small plaques, one celebrating the centenary of the local Insurance Institute and the other commemorating the bi-centenary of the birth of John Dobson. On the floor the metal object, inscribed I P Paine London 1835, is the church clock's pendulum weight, redundant when the mechanism was digitised. In the nave, the first stained glass window on the left-hand side (Helen Whittaker, 2000) presents a touching reminder of the bravery of the people of Malta as well as members of the armed services and the Merchant Navy during World War II. At the top of the nave are a number of regimental flags and other military memorials.

The Church is heavily involved in social issues. The One World Shop inside and the inscription on the imposing glass doors 'Do justice at the Gate' are reflections of these interests.

The Response

This is an eye-catching memorial which reflects the response to the call to arms in 1914. It carries the patriotic message: *Non sibi sed patriae* (Not for self but for country). It is said to be based on excited friends and families greeting proud volunteer soldiers of the Northumberland Fusiliers marching in 1915 to the Central Station on their way to war. But aren't they going in the wrong direction? It is perhaps unusual to see such a joyful memorial to such a dreadful conflict. Is it merely a coincidence that Sir George and Lady Renwick donated this fine monument to celebrate among other things the safe return of their five sons from the war? An information board provides full details of the designer (Sir W. Goscombe John, 1923) and the background to the work. Don't neglect to see the figures on the back of the monument where the date 1674 refers to the original raising of the regiment in Ireland.

Turn left and walk along the broad path to the exit from the church grounds. Over to your right is the Civic Centre, which we will come back to later in the walk. On the left over the road is the glass-fronted Newcastle University building Kings Gate. Just before the exit, over to your right on the paved area, there is a stone surmounted with a small green plaque. This is a boundary stone defining the limit of the Town Moor.

Now exit the grounds, turn right and proceed up the pedestrian/cycle path. Over the road on your left you can see a statue of Lord Armstrong and you have a good view of the Great North Museum. To your right, on Jesmond Road West, you can see some of the nineteenth-century houses of Carlton Terrace. You arrive at the **Robinson Library** which displays a Charter Mark on the wall.

Bear right, past the library, with a second Charter Mark displayed on the wall, to a service road **(Qu 3)**.

Turn left and walk to the T-junction. Turn right and proceed along the street (Windsor Terrace). The new student halls of residence, Gurney House and Fife House on the left, blend in quite nicely with the 1870s terrace on the right which is mainly now University property. At the end of the terrace before the road bears right, cross the road to a path with four bollards. Go ahead and walk between the trees and after a few metres turn left to walk under the dual carriageway and carry on to arrive at a road (Jesmond Road West). Turn left, walk ahead and pass **Jesmond Parish Church** built as a memorial to the **Revd Richard Clayton**.

Burma Campaign Memorial

The smallest and most recent of the war memorials was erected by the Burma Star Association to commemorate those from the north-east who fell in the Burma Campaign (1941-1945) against Japanese forces. Note the soldier's battle dress. Here young and old are left to ponder that most moving of verses:

> ***When you go home***
> ***tell them of us***
> ***and say for your tomorrow***
> ***we gave our today***

Robinson Library

The Robinson Library is the main library of Newcastle University; there are also two specialist libraries: the Walton Library, covering medicine and dentistry, and the Law Library. The Robinson Library was financed in 1988 by a bequest of £8m from Philip Robinson, a Newcastle antiquarian bookseller who had a long association with the University. His widow, Marjorie, later donated the Robinson Collection of 14th to 19th century books, now among the Robinson Library Special Collections. These consist of over a hundred collections of material ranging from rare books and archives to wood blocks and illustrations, described as a'unique and diverse resource which supports academic research and teaching'.

Continue ahead to the entrance to Jesmond Metro Station. Turn right and proceed by steps or ramp through the underpass. You pass mosaics, somewhat rather worn, depicting scenes from Newcastle's history.

Walk ahead for a few metres to meet a service road. We are going to turn right but before doing so if you look ahead you can see The Carriage pub, originally Jesmond Railway Station (1864) on the former Blyth and Tyne Railway. The station closed in 1978 with the construction of the Metro system.

Now turn right and ascend to reach the main road (Jesmond Road). Turn left and carry on to the large red-brick building (1870). This originated as a private dwelling but from 1916

Jesmond Parish Church and the Revd Richard Clayton

Jesmond Parish Church, the last church designed by Dobson, was completed in 1861; his daughter thought it was her father's masterpiece but opinions differ about that. Its alternative name 'Clayton Memorial Church' reflects that it was built as a memorial to the Revd Richard Clayton. Clayton, the brother of John Clayton, Town Clerk of Newcastle, was Chaplain of St Thomas' Chapel (the predecessor of St Thomas' Church) from 1836 to 1856. He was a much respected minister, both by his congregation and in the town, who was rooted in the evangelical tradition. The design of the church, one of the last Anglican churches to incorporate galleries, reflected the evangelical churchmanship of its founders. This remains the ethos of the church today.

was occupied by a number of institutions until being bought and extended by the Quakers, who moved from their previous meeting house in Pilgrim Street in 1961. They remained there until their move to Gosforth in 2011.

Continue past the building and go through the covered archway then bear left and proceed ahead, passing the Mr Lynch pub on your right. At the junction with the main road, turn right. You pass under a bridge and after 25 metres reach steps on your right.

(To avoid the steps, carry straight on until you come to Link Road. Walk up Link Road to the junction ahead where you rejoin the walk.)

Climb up the steps and go along the row of attractive terrace houses now dominated by the busy motorway **(Qu 4)**.

At the end bear left and carry on to Carlton Terrace at a junction with a road (Link Road). Walk ahead. The blue plaques on several of the houses give details of this John Dobson project.

At the end of the road bear left into Great North Road. A blue plaque on the one of the houses indicates that this was once the home of **Albany and John Hancock** whose collections of natural history specimens formed the basis of the Hancock Museum, now incorporated into the Great North Museum **(Qu 5)**.

Go through the gap in the railings on your right then turn left on to the path parallel to the road and walk about 50 metres to the pathway on the left with a tree on the corner. Go along this path and just before The Hancock pub on your left, bear right down the ramp. At the bottom turn sharp right and follow the entrance road which bears left round the **Civic Centre**, which was started when **T. Dan Smith** was leader of the City Council. You arrive at the circular grand entrance.

Walk ahead under the building. To your right, at the edge of the water feature, the large stone block commemorates the visit of US president Jimmy Carter in 1977. The President and Mrs Carter had promoted the then recently-established Friendship Force which aims to

Albany and John Hancock

Albany Hancock (1806-1873) and his brother John (1808-1890) were born in Newcastle upon Tyne and attended the Royal Grammar School there. Later in life they lived with their sister Mary, who shared their interest in natural history, in which they had been influenced by their father.

Albany qualified as a solicitor with an office in the town and later worked for a local manufacturing company. However, from childhood his main interest was in natural history, in particular in molluscs and marine animals, and from the age of thirty he devoted himself to the subject, publishing some seventy papers and lending support to Charles Darwin with whom he corresponded.

John's interest lay particularly in ornithology and taxidermy, he was later referred to as the 'father of taxidermy'. He edited Thomas Bewick's 1847 edition of *Birds* and in 1874 he published *Catalogue of the Birds of Northumberland and Durham.* In addition he practised as a landscape architect.

The brothers were founder members of the Tyneside Naturalists Field Club. They both built up collections of natural history specimens, many of which were donated to the local natural history museum which, in the 1890s, was renamed the Hancock Museum in their honour and which is now part of the Great North Museum.

build bridges between the US and the rest of the world by involving exchange visits between citizens; the Newcastle - Atlanta exchange in 1977 was one of the earliest such ventures.

Bear left and walk past the *River God Tyne* fountain (David Wynne, 1968) and up a few steps (or the nearby ramp) to the large windows. These have a series of etchings which include some classical allusions as well as reminders of giants of local industry, including an electric lamp bulb for Joseph Swan and the Stephensons' Rocket. Carry on and at the top of a further small flight of steps (or nearby ramp) you will see the Wren Stone and an inscription outlining its interesting history **(Qu 6)**.

Turn right and make your way to the *Swans in Flight* sculpture (David Wynne, 1968) which is said to represent Newcastle's connections with five Scandinavian countries (Denmark, Faroes, Iceland, Norway, Sweden). Although this connection could not have applied to another edition of the sculpture (1968) located in the grounds of a North American college.

Now turn right to meet the Ceremonial Way, a vehicular road leading to the formal entrance to the Civic Centre. (Occasionally the direct route through is screened off and you have to retrace your steps and go round the grand circular entrance to reach the Ceremonial Way.) Note, on your right, the tall gas torchlight holders which line the roadway and which are lit to mark special events **(Qu 7)**.

Now turn left and proceed to the end of the building and turn left. The Registry Office is through the entrance on the left and you might encounter a group of people celebrating after a recent wedding ceremony. Walk alongside the Civic Centre on your left and the lawn on your right. Ahead to the right you can see the unusual tower and spire of St James' United Reformed Church.

Exit onto a road (Sandyford Road). Opposite is the main city centre campus of **Northumbria University**.

Civic Centre

This large, bold building, clad in Portland stone, was designed by George Kenyon, City Architect, and constructed in 1960-1968. Plans for a new building to replace the old Town Hall were first mooted in the 1920s and an open competition to design a new Town Hall at Barras Bridge was held in the late 1930s. However, the advent of World War II and post-war restrictions on building work meant that progress on a new project was not possible until the early 1960s. It was formally opened in 1968 by His Majesty King Olaf V of Norway. Newcastle's citizens are reminded of the city's close ties with Bergen, Norway with the annual presentation by that country of a giant Christmas Tree. This stands near the Civic Centre in Barras Bridge during the festive season.

Bergen's Christmas present

Newcastle Civic Centre is planned round a quadrangle and, as can be expected, it not only has administrative accommodation but also reflects civic pride in its Grand Entrance, Council Chamber, Banqueting Hall and an elaborate tower which houses a carillon. Apart from the *River God Tyne* fountain there are several notable works of art which are located in the Civic Centre grounds.

T. Dan Smith

Thomas Daniel Smith (1915-1993) was born in Wallsend. After a period of unemployment in the 1930s, he started a painting and decorating business. Politically he was initially a Trotskyist but joined the Labour Party in the 1940s. He quickly made a name as a member of Newcastle City Council and became Chairman of the Housing Committee in 1958 and was leader of the Council from 1960-1965. His engaging, charismatic personality together with his enthusiasm and visionary zeal for massive slum clearance programmes and city centre projects led to his becoming complimented by some as 'Mr Newcastle', although it has to be said, others preferred different, somewhat pejorative, epithets. Newcastle was, in his own words, to become a 'Brasilia of the North' which, in addition to high-rise apartment blocks replacing former slum areas, would embrace inner-city motorways and developments in retailing, education, leisure and arts and café culture. One aspect of this was the authorisation for the demolition of a large part of the city centre to make way for the huge Eldon Square retail shopping complex. From 1965-1970 he sat on regional and national bodies and wrote two books.

However, his political career came to end with his spectacular fall from grace following accusations of corruption, particularly in his dealings with the disgraced architect John Poulson. As a result he received a six-year jail sentence. Following his release, after serving three years, he became involved in penal reform and worked on a drama-documentary film *T. Dan Smith* in which he played himself. Latterly he lived, perhaps appropriately, in a high-rise apartment block overlooking an inner-city motorway, in the Spital Tongues area of Newcastle.

Bear right and go to the traffic lights. Cross the road. Turn left and go straight ahead, passing, on your left, the *Pillar Man* (Nicholas Widerberg, 2004), part of the 'Hidden Rivers' art project. On your left is Northumbria University's **City Centre Campus Library** and in the same block **Northumbria University Art Gallery and Gallery North and Gallery Studio Northumbria**.

Carry on for 40 metres alongside Northumberland Building on your right and then turn right at the University shop and follow the path under the building to exit onto a pedestrianized road (Northumberland Road). Turn right and proceed ahead. After a few metres you pass Brady and Martin Court, a housing development which incorporates the

Northumbria University

Northumbria University came into existence in 1992 with the conferment of university status on Newcastle Polytechnic. The Polytechnic was formed in 1969 by the amalgamation of three existing Newcastle colleges: the College of Art and Industrial Design, the Municipal College of Commerce, Rutherford College of Technology. The technology college was named after Dr J. H. Rutherford. In the early 1970s the range of disciplines was extended by the merger with two local colleges of education. Northumbria University started off with the name 'University of Northumbria at Newcastle' and the acronym UNN. Eventually this was shortened to the 'University of Northumbria' or, more familiarly 'Northumbria University'.

Northumbria operates on two campuses, the City Centre campus and Coach Lane campus, the latter came from its merger with Northern Counties College of Education. Recently the City Centre campus has been enlarged with the addition of the City Campus East.

The university has around 25,000 students. It has an extensive portfolio of undergraduate and postgraduate courses and has consistently performed with top or near top ratings in league tables of new universities.

City Centre Campus library

This is the main university library. There are also two specialist libraries: the Coach Lane Campus Library covering health, community and education, and the Law Practice library. The main library has a number of specialist collections relating to cultural policy and also houses the European Documentation Centre, which is a reference collection of official documents from the European Union Institutions and Agencies.

Northumbria University Art Gallery

The gallery was established in 1977 'as a teaching gallery and the University's link between town and gown'. Apart from a permanent collection of over 350 works the gallery holds touring and other exhibitions as well as a Saturday arts club for 8-12 year olds.

Gallery North and Graduate Studio Northumbria

These were set up in 2009 and are located in the building to the left of the Art Gallery. Gallery North seeks to provide 'an important contemporary exhibition space', and is closely linked with the University's teaching and learning environment, including, for example, undergraduate and post graduate degree shows. Graduate Studio Northumbria offers studio resources to around thirty graduate artists.

Pedestrianized Northumberland Road

attractive bow-fronted properties, originally occupied by the local firm of Brady and Martin, wholesale chemical manufacturers. A little further on, on the left, is the former Trinity Presbyterian Church (1895) now owned by Northumbria University, as are most of the properties in this section of Northumberland Road.

On your right you pass St James' United Reformed Church (1884) and the attractive, red brick College House (1883). High in the wall, in a niche, is a statue of Dame Eleanor Allan. She was the daughter of a city goldsmith and widow of a wealthy tobacco merchant who, in 1705, founded the school which bears her name. From its beginning in the west end it moved to this building but is now located in purpose-built premises in Fenham. Carry on past the **City Hall and Pool**.

Cross to the other side of Northumberland Road, turn left, walk back along the road. You pass another Dobson building, originally a riding school (1847) of the Northumberland Yeomanry and later a drill hall. It is now owned by Northumbria University as is the adjacent Burt Hall (1895). Burt Hall was formerly home of the Northumberland Miners' Association and commemorates **Thomas Burt**. The statue on the top represents a miner going home and is based on the painting *Going Home* by Ralph Hedley in the Laing Art Gallery collection. A plaque refers to a miners' leader who was 'a true Northumbrian' **(Qu 8)**.

City Hall and Pool

When the Victorian baths, designed in 1837-39 by John Dobson, were demolished in the 1920s to make way for more modern facilities, the site was large enough to accommodate not only swimming baths but also Newcastle's first dedicated concert venue, the City Hall. While the name 'Northumberland Baths' remains set in stone above the doorway, the entrance is now a few metres to the right under the more modern title of 'City Pool'. Here city-centre workers and others can enjoy the 25 metre pool as well as the Turkish bath and sauna suite. The City of Newcastle Swimming Club based here prides itself on its competitive coaching scheme that has placed swimmers on Olympic and Commonwealth Games teams over a long number of years. If you step inside the automatic door you may find, on your right, information about the first customer to use the swimming pool!

Since its opening in 1927, the adjacent 2000+-capacity City Hall has played host to many important social, political and religious meetings as well as a very wide range of entertainment, including national and international orchestras, classical artists and pop stars and groups as well as stand-up comedians. Local choirs are pleased to entertain their loyal followers here, while proud family and friends delight in coming to witness the annual graduation ceremonies of Northumbria University. With so much on-going demand the City Hall continues to thrive despite the arrival of more recent concert venues such as the Arena, the Sage and the O_2 Academy.

Thomas Burt

Thomas Burt (1837-1922) was born in a tiny pit village in South Northumberland. Following in his father's footsteps he worked in a number of pits, starting at the age of ten as a trapper-boy, working for twelve hours a day, mostly in pitch black conditions, and responsible for opening and closing ventilation doors. He became a hewer at 18 and continued working as a miner until the 1870s.

However, from around the age of 14, he set about making up for his limited formal schooling by embarking on a programme of self-education. As a result, he was soon made secretary of a number of local bodies and became involved in miners' association activities. In 1864, following his proposal for a separate organisation for Northumberland miners (breaking the link with Durham), he became secretary of the Northumberland Miners' Association. 'By 1872 his moderation, integrity and skilful leadership had established a strong union and had won for the Northumbrian pitmen a better position than that enjoyed by any other group of English miners' (Middlebrook, 1950).

Thomas Burt's increasing local influence culminated in his election to Parliament in 1873 as one of its first working-class members. He stood as a Radical candidate with backing form local Liberals. He had an impressive record as an M.P. and in 1892 became secretary of the Board of Trade. He retired from Parliament in 1913.

Apart from the recognition given to him by naming the union headquarters 'Burt Hall', he was given the freedom of Newcastle and the freedom of Morpeth and awarded with the honorary degree of Doctor of Civil Law by the University of Durham.

At the crossroads, turn right. Over the road is Northumbria University's red-brick Sutherland Building (1887) formerly part of Durham University, as is evidenced by the lettering DUCM (Durham University College of Medicine) just above the first floor windows. Proceed to the end of the street, turn left and carry on along Ellison Place. You pass a house with a plaque, where the religious leader Cardinal Hume was born.

You reach MEA House, over the road on the right. This was opened by H.M. The Queen in 1974, and was the first British building to be purpose-built to provide modern office accommodation and meeting rooms for registered charities. MEA are the initials of the first names of the three people who initiated the project to build the property: Mungo Campbell, **Esther McCracken**, Alistair Fyfe.

Esther McCracken (1902-1971)

Esther Helen Armstrong was born in Newcastle and attended the Central Newcastle High School. She married Angus McCracken, an accountant and a first-class rugby player (Northern Rugby Club's McCracken Park is named after him). He died in action in 1943 and in 1944 Esther married the shipping magnate, Mungo Campbell.

She found fame as an actress and a playwright. Her plays *Quiet Wedding* (1938) and *Quiet Weekend* (1941) being early successes. From 1940 to 1956 she compered the very popular local radio show *Wot Cheor Geordie*.

Esther, her husband, Mungo Campbell, and their friend, local solicitor Alistair Fyfe, initiated the MEA house project and the work continues through the Rothley Trust, named after the Northumbrian hamlet where she lived.

Carry on to an entrance to Ellison Building on your left. If this is open and you pop in, you will see a stained glass window in memory of Dr John Hunter Rutherford. A picture of the window is used as the front cover of *Rutherford's Ladder* (Allen and Buswell, 2005) which is sub-titled 'The Making of Northumbria University, 1871-1996' and which pays tribute to Dr Rutherford's contribution to the development of technical education in Newcastle.

Cross the road, turn sharp right and walk up the wide ramp. Below on your left is the Church of the Divine Unity (1940), Newcastle's only art deco church and the adjacent Durant Hall, the church's meeting room. Follow the signs to the Library. Just before you reach the tall Bewick Court, turn left and continue down the ramp. At the end of the ramp walk ahead for a few metres then turn right to come to a road (Higham Place).

Walk down Higham Place. On the left you pass the Grainger Rooms, aptly named as this was an early work by Richard Grainger. From 1908 it became the meeting place of the **Pen and Palette Club**. You will find a plaque about the Northern Architectural Association **(Qu 9)**.

On the opposite side of the road is the ornate, original entrance to the Laing Art Gallery.

At the end of the street turn left. After 30 metres you reach a house built in 1823 by John Dobson who lived and died there. On its east side the house was extended but 'spoilt, alas, by nasty alterations' (Pevsner and Richmond, 1992). Since Dobson's death the house and later extensions have hosted a number of activities, including the Oxford Galleries a very popular ballroom, particularly with young people, during the fifties and sixties. Currently it is occupied by the Liquid/ Envy night club.

Turn back and walk across the area of *The Blue Carpet* (Thomas Heatherwick, 2001) an art work which was supposed to consist of blue-coloured stones; although, now, only traces of the blue can be seen. On the left is the former Lying-in Hospital (1826) by John Dobson; financed by charitable subscription, it provided suitable accommodation for expectant mothers -but only for married ones! It closed in 1923. Later it became the North East headquarters for the BBC until their move to Fenham in 1987 and is currently used by the Newcastle Building Society **(Qu 10)**.

Pen and Palette Club

The club, founded in 1900 as a venue for local literati, artists and musicians, held its meetings in the Higham Place building from 1908. From its earliest days well-known personalities were invited to speak at its dinners. The building was owned by the Fenwick family (owners of the famous Fenwick's store), who allowed the club to use the premises. In 1940 the club bought the building from the family and continued to meet there until 2011. For some years the property was let to restaurant tenants, and the club continued to hold dinners there. However, unable to find new tenants the decision was made, reluctantly, to move elsewhere. At the time of writing, the club is holding its monthly meetings in Newcastle's Mansion House in Jesmond.

Former lying-in hospital

Laing Art Gallery

The Laing Art Gallery was opened in 1904. It was financed by Alexander Laing, a Scottish wine and spirit merchant and hotel proprietor, whose wealth had accumulated through his business activities in Newcastle. Another wine and spirit merchant, A. H. Higgonbottom, later donated his collection of Japanese art to the gallery. John Dobson's daughter Margaret bequeathed some architectural drawings and fine pieces of furniture, which had been left to her by her father, at her death on 1905.

C. Bernard Stevenson was the first curator, charged with the task of building a collection from, effectively, a zero base. Initially, he borrowed items from friends and acquaintances to get things going. Remarkably, he remained curator for 53 years. He was succeeded by his son B. Collingwood Stevenson who extended the collection and established the Friends of the Laing Art Gallery. The Friends are an active group whose activities include running an information desk and offering free talks on the stories behind some of the gallery's best-loved paintings. They made a generous donation to enable the restoration of the arts and crafts stained glass window by J Edgar Mitchell (1904) which was reinstated in its original position by the stairs to the first floor in 2004.

Today, there is much to appreciate in the gallery; apart from its splendid interior it has an extensive permanent collection. In October 2010 a new permanent display *Northern Spirit* 'celebrating the achievements of artists, manufacturers and makers from the North East' was opened. In addition complementary, temporary exhibitions are a regular feature. In common with many similar institutions, the gallery has diversified by offering facilities for conferences and functions. There is a special room for small children as well as a shop and a café.

For further information see: www.twmuseams.org.uk/laing; Tel 0191 2327734

City Library

Opened in June 2009, this six story glass-walled building replaced the former library which stood on the same site. There are two entrances, one on New Bridge Street and the other, one level up on the recently renovated Princess Square. The building, which is named after Charles Avison, the 18th century Newcastle composer, is very much of the 21st century and provides an interesting contrast with its nearby neighbour, the early 20th-century Laing Art Gallery. Inside, the building is state-of-the art, completely self-service and with all the facilities expected of a modern library, including a comprehensive local studies and family history collection. An important asset is 'The Newcastle Collection' consisting of extensive collections of rare books and heritage materials built up since the opening of the original reference library in 1884.

Library and Art Gallery

A particularly interesting feature, best seen from inside, is the *Four Questions* art work which is printed on the glazing facing John Dobson Street. The answers to the four questions provide four compositions which take on different appearances depending on the time of day or night when they are viewed. From inside the building they are best viewed from the three upper floors. The library is open seven days a week.

For further information see: www.newcastle.gov.uk/libraries
Tel 0191 2774100

Charles Avison (1709-1790)

Charles Avison was born in Newcastle and, apart from a period in London to study music, he remained in the town for the whole of his life. Subsequently, he turned down several opportunities to take up prestigious positions elsewhere. Both his parents were musicians and presumably were an early influence on his growth as a musician.

In 1735 he was appointed organist of St John the Baptist Church in Newcastle and a year later became organist at St Nicholas' Church (which became Newcastle Cathedral in 1882). He married his wife Catherine in 1737 and two of their surviving sons became organists at St Nicholas.

Locally his fame grew, as a composer, conductor and organist, and he was recognised as the major influence in Newcastle and district's musical scene. However, it was a book rather than a musical composition which made his name known at a national level, with the publication of his *Essay on Musical Expression*, the first work on musical criticism published in English.

According to the *New Grove Dictionary of Music and Musicians* he was 'the most important English concerto composer of the 18th century'. Sadly his music remained largely neglected after his death. Happily, since 1994, with the formation of the Avison Ensemble who perform his music on period instruments, his work is being brought back to a wider public. Two of Avison's *Workbooks*, which provide valuable sources for the performance of his work, have been restored by specialists at Northumbria University and are kept in the City Library.

Charles Avison is buried in the grounds of St Andrew's Church.

Ahead on the right is the **Laing Art Gallery**.

From the gallery you reach the **City Library** across the road. The Library building is named after **Charles Avison**. If you look back you will see some interesting murals on the side of the Laing Art Gallery. You can enter the library by the first door on the right.

You can exit the library from the entrance on the second floor, near to where the café is situated. If so, walk ahead and proceed along the pedestrianized street (Northumberland Place), which is on the left of Northumberland House, to exit onto Northumberland Street. Turn right and walk to the Haymarket Metro Station and the end of the walk. (Otherwise, leave the building through the door by which you entered, turn right and walk to the crossroads. Turn right to proceed along Northumberland Street to the Haymarket Metro Station.)

Quiz questions

1. Which groups are named on the pillar of the St George and the Dragon memorial?
2. Apart from 'Do Justice at the Gate', what else is inscribed on the doors?
3. What do you think is the significance of the blue Charter Mark displayed on the wall of the Robinson Library?
4. What is the name of this terrace?
5. What was the address of the Hancock brothers?
6. Who made a gift of the Wren Stone to the City of Newcastle?
7. How many torchlight holders are there on the Ceremonial Way?
8. Which miners' leader was referred to as 'a true Northumbrian'?
9. What does the plaque in Higham Place celebrate?
10. How many John Dobson buildings have you passed on this walk?

5. Spital Tongues and Leazes Park

Start/finish:	**Haymarket Metro Station**
Distance:	**2.75 miles**
Route:	**Haymarket, Percy Street, St Thomas' Street, Royal Victoria Infirmary (RVI), Spital Tongues, Barrack Road, Leazes Park, St Thomas' Crescent, Haymarket**
Accessibility:	**On pavements and tarmac tracks**
Refreshments:	**Cafés and pubs in Haymarket, a pub in Spital Tongues and a seasonal café in Leazes Park**

Again we begin our walk at the Haymarket. Leave the Metro Station via the Percy Street exit and bear right to use the pedestrian crossing located at the west side of the Metro Station. At the traffic lights, cross over the road (Percy Street) which is named after the Percys (Earls and Dukes of Northumberland based at Alnwick Castle since 1309). Once you are over the road turn left and in a few metres you arrive at an imposing building, known as the **Bruce Building**. Above the stout wooden door you will see a clue to one of former owners **(Qu 1)**.

A few metres further on, you pass The Hotspur public house. Just before you reach the corner of the block, look carefully at the wall above Walton Robinson Property Consultants and you will see a small plaque. This indicates that this building, now known as the Bruce

A young Queen Victoria

Building, was once the site of the Percy Street Academy founded by John Bruce in 1806 and operated by his son, **John Collingwood Bruce** from 1834 to 1860.

Now before you turn right up St Thomas' Street you might like to glance ahead to see Percy Street seemingly dominated by bus stations and car parks. An Oxfam shop and other temporary-looking outlets stand on the corner of the site once occupied by the Palace Theatre until its closure in 1958. Further on you will see a glass-covered bridge linking the Eldon Square shopping centre with its late-1980s annex Eldon Gardens and its multi-storey car park. Sadly this replaced the Handysides Arcade, a splendid cast iron and glass structure containing several treasured commercial outlets including second-hand book and record shops as well as the avant-guarde 1960s-Club a'Gogo, an early venue for The Animals, Newcastle's answer to The Beatles.

Turn right and walk up St Thomas' Street. On the left you will see the arched entrance to St Thomas Street Business Centre, site of the former stables of Newcastle Breweries **(Qu 2)**.

On the right you pass old and new university buildings, the final one of which is the former Medical School (now the King George VI Building). At the road junction (Queen

Bruce Building

The current building by Joseph Oswald was completed in 1900 to accommodate the offices of the Newcastle Breweries Ltd. It was built on the site of Bruce's Academy (see below) which had closed in 1881. Here the most famous ex-pupil was probably Robert Stephenson, the engineer who attended at the age of eleven, from 1814 to 1819.

The brewery company had acquired several local breweries, including John Sanderson and Sons which had had a brewery on the site since 1850. In 1872 John Sanderson had named his pub, The Hotspur to recall Henry Percy (1364-1403), son of the Earl of Northumberland, nicknamed Harry Hotspur (referred to in Shakespeare's, *Henry IV, Part 1*).

The newly-formed Newcastle Breweries company came into operation in 1896 with a five-pointed blue star, representing the five constituent breweries, as its landmark emblem. It was able to extend and develop a substantial brewery complex in the surrounding area, based on Sanderson's premises.

King's College, now Newcastle University, acquired the building in 1950 as it began to plan its future expansion. University departments which include Heritage Studies have been able to enjoy some rather splendidly tiled rooms, stained glass windows and an elegant staircase.

John Collingwood Bruce (1805-1892)

Dr Collingwood Bruce taught at the school founded by his father and led it from 1834 to 1860. He qualified in medicine and divinity was a Fellow of the Society of Antiquaries. He had intended to become a medical missionary before he found he needed to continue his father's educational role in Newcastle. However, after handing over the management of the school to others, he was able to devote himself more fully to his wide research interests which resulted in the publication of works on a variety of subjects, including local history and folk music. His fame rests largely on his work on the Roman Wall and he is credited with leading the first organised study tour along its course. His *Handbook to the Roman Wall* still remains a standard classic. He is honoured by a splendid effigy in St Nicholas' Cathedral.

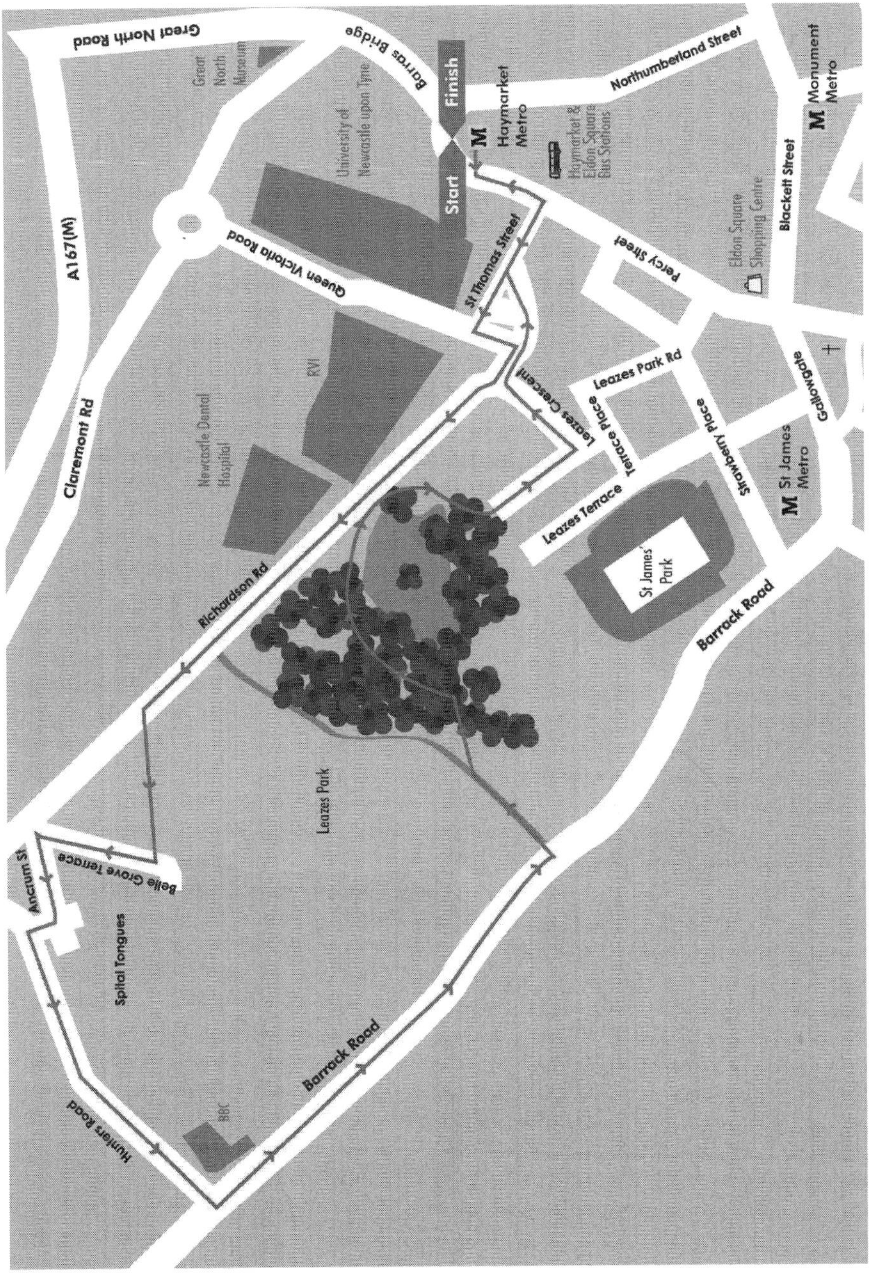
Great North Road
Barras Bridge
Great North Museum
University of Newcastle upon Tyne
Finish
Start
Haymarket Metro
Northumberland Street
Haymarket & Eldon Square Bus Stations
Monument Metro
Blackett Street
Eldon Square Shopping Centre
Percy Street
St Thomas Street
Queen Victoria Road
A167(M)
Claremont Rd
RVI
Newcastle Dental Hospital
Leazes Crescent
Leazes Park Rd
Terrace Place
Leazes Terrace
Strawberry Place
Gallowgate
St James Metro
St James' Park
Barrack Road
Richardson Rd
Leazes Park
Ancrum St
Belle Grove Terrace
Spital Tongues
Hunters Road
BBC
Barrack Road

Victoria Road) cross ahead via the pedestrian lights to what was once the main entrance to the **Royal Victoria Infirmary (RVI)**.

Turn left, then right to walk up the road (Richardson Road) with the tree-lined park on your left. After about 100 metres, on your right, in the grounds of the hospital is the oldest remaining section of the hospital in front of which you may be able to see a statue of someone closely associated with the hospital **(Qu 3)**.

Continue up the road to pass the access to the Accident & Emergency Department and other modern hospital buildings on the right and some park entrances on the left. When you eventually reach the access road to the Dental Hospital use the traffic island to cross the road and then go through the metal gate into the green space of Castle Leazes. Turn right and follow the path nearest to the road. Over to the left are the University's Castle Leazes Halls of Residence, while to the right are its Richardson Road Students' Flats.

Now continue ahead ignoring paths off to the left and right. Exit Castle Leazes to arrive at **Spital Tongues**. We are going to turn right, but before doing so, notice to your left Belle Grove Villas, beyond which is the site of the lunatic asylum created in 1766. This was later more delicately renamed the Belle Grove Retreat before becoming private housing in the late 1850s. Apparently it was this initial use of 'Belle Grove' that led to many of the local streets being prefaced with the same name.

The heart of Spital Tongues

Royal Victoria Infirmary (RVI)

The hospital is always known locally as the RVI. The Infirmary made its modest beginning in a house in Gallowgate in 1751, pending the construction of a purpose-built hospital in Forth Banks, just south of the current Centre for Life. The Infirmary in Forth Banks, which opened to patients in 1753, obtained the title of Royal Infirmary in 1887, the year of Queen Victoria's Golden Jubilee. The hospital had expanded considerably but the proximity of the increasingly busy railway, road and cattle market was proving to be a drawback, so a plan was put in motion to commemorate the Queen's Diamond Jubilee by building a new hospital on Castle Leazes.

The Prince of Wales laid the foundation stone in 1900 and returned as King Edward VII, six years later, to officially open the newly-named Royal Victoria Infirmary and to unveil a statue of his late mother. Since then the hospital has been expanded and modernised to the extent that only the façade of the original entrance through Peacock Hall remains intact. The Dental School and Medical School moved onto the main site in 1978 and 1985 respectively and the state-of-the-art Leazes and Claremont Wings opened in 1992 and 1996 respectively. The appearance of the hospital on Queen Victoria Road has been dramatically changed with a new Victoria Wing, Main Entrance and the Great North Children's Hospital.

Spital Tongues

This unusual name is apparently comes from 'spital', being derived from 'hospital', and 'tongue', referring to an outlying piece of land. The Hospital of St Mary Magdalene, said to have been founded in the 12th century to care for lepers, was originally located in the area now occupied in Barras Bridge by St Thomas' Church . Two additional 'tongues' of land granted to the 'hospital' by Edward I in 1291 included what is now known as Spital Tongues.

Various Acts of Parliament have regulated the management of the not inconsiderable St Mary Magdalene estates under various trustees for charitable purposes. This had its impact on Spital Tongues in 1884 when the Charity opened a Home for Incurables at Moor Lodge (see below). This was to have several changes of name and usage. It became the St Mary Magdalene Home in 1931, the Hunters Moor Hospital in 1948 under the NHS and it ended its days as the Regional Neurological Centre in 2008.

In 1936-7 the Holy Jesus Hospital moved to Spital Tongues following its closure on City Road. The property holdings of both of these defunct hospitals are now managed by the St Mary Magdalene & Holy Jesus Trustee Company. Nowadays the Joint Charitable Trust manages sheltered accommodation, support services and a social care home on 'Mary Magdalene' land in Spital Tongues. An allocation of the sheltered housing is available to the Freemen of Newcastle.

Coal was mined here at the Spital Tongues (or Leazes Main) Colliery for a relatively short period of time from 1835. In order to transport the coal down to the River Tyne, a 2.5 mile tunnel was opened in 1842. The tunnel, although a success in itself, ceased being used when the colliery closed at the end of the 1850s. However, the Victoria Tunnel, as it was called, was reopened as an important World War II air raid shelter. In recent times a section in the Ouseburn Village area has been restored and has become a popular tourist attraction.

The coal miners were followed by furniture workers with the establishment of Robson's Cabinet Factory in 1880. This engaged some 200 employees who lived in streets named after the popular furniture makers Sheraton and Chippendale and others named after the Scottish Border towns of Ancrum and Oxnam where many of the workers were said to have come from. This family firm was first established in 1835 on Northumberland Street where its retail outlet traded for nearly a hundred years. The company was responsible for the furnishing of churches, stately homes and ocean liners and its products are still highly valued at auctions today. However, Robson's came to an end when it was taken over by the national chain of Maple's in 1953.

'The character of the 'village' has undoubtedly changed over the years. The hospitals, the furniture factory, the school, the post office and most of the shops have closed. Happily, nevertheless, this area, virtually surrounded by the Town Moor, still gives the appearance of an oasis amid the city boundaries. At the same time, a new vibrancy has been introduced with the large influx of students following the steady expansion in this direction of Newcastle University. However, a change not to everyone's satisfaction.

Ralph Hedley (1848-1913)

Ralph Hedley painter, woodcarver, sculptor and illustrator was a pupil of William Scott Bell (see below) at the Government School of Design in Newcastle. He founded his own wood carving firm and some important examples of his work can be found, for example, in St Nicholas' Cathedral.

His oil and watercolour paintings, which reflect many aspects of local life, feature prominently in the Laing Art Gallery and they are also highly prized by private collectors. The statue of the miner on top of Burt Hall in Northumberland Street is believed to have been modelled on one of his paintings

His two sons continued with the business long after his death. In 1948 his younger son Roger was invited to make the replacement head for Earl Grey whose original head on the top of Grey's Monument had been struck by lightning!

Turn right to pass, on your left, the attractive houses of Belle Grove Terrace once home to T. Dan Smith, City Council Leader, 1960-65. Several high-rise residential blocks were erected during his term of office and it is interesting to note that T. Dan Smith was to spend the last years of his life in Mill House, the fifteen- storey tower block that rises above the rooftops ahead to the right.

At the end of the terrace, immediately before the Belle Grove Hotel, a once popular pub (sadly boarded up at the time of writing) there is a heritage plaque indicating that the renowned local artist **Ralph Hedley** lived here for several years before his death in 1913 **(Qu 4)**.

Turn left after the Belle Grove Hotel into Ancrum Street and in a short distance, on your left, you will pass The Apostolic Church, formerly the Benson Memorial Church (1867), and, on your right, Magdalene Court housing complex. At the crossroads turn right into Belle Grove West. Near this junction was the entrance to the Victoria Tunnel. The Spital House pub lies ahead on the other side of the main road. To the right of the pub is where Robson's Cabinet Factory once stood. A short distance further to the right are the bungalows of the sheltered housing complex known as St Mary Magdalene Hospital.

You are at Hunter's Road named after William Hunter a coal owner who surrendered his lease of Moor Lodge which was to become the Home for Incurables and then many years later to bear his own name as the Hunters Moor Hospital (as detailed above). Turn left. A few metres further, on the right, the former hospital site is being used to build a nursery and junior school for Dame Allan's Schools. The school, which is planned to open in 2012, will add to the capacity of the school originally founded by Dame Eleanor Allan which has been based in nearby Fenham since its move from city centre in the 1930s.

Continuing ahead you pass Huntsmoor House, built as a soldiers' home in 1899 for the nearby Fenham Barracks, and more recently used as a warehouse for the booksellers Thornes before being converted into student accommodation. Notice the carved shields.

The next road on your left is Fountain Row. It is here that the Pandon Burn began as a stream, originally the Bailiff Burn, flowing all the way to the River Tyne which necessitated the construction of a bridge at the area of Barras Bridge. The bridge is no longer visible but the burn, now culveted, still runs its full length through the city to the Tyne. The green on the left after you cross Fountain Row was once the site of the pit head of Spital Tongues Colliery.

The Pink Palace

Proceed further to a major crossroads. To the right, Ponteland Road leads to the suburb of Fenham and beyond, ahead Brighton Grove leads to Newcastle General Hospital and the west end of the city. To the left, is the aptly-named Barrack Road, site of Fenham Barracks built in 1806 and functioning as home for many generations of soldiers until 1962. On your left is the BBC Broadcasting Centre, nicknamed 'The Pink Palace', housing various departments of the BBC transferred from other locations including the former Lying-in-Hospital building near the Laing Art Gallery.

Turn left and proceed down Barrack Road. On your right, the green space is part of Nuns Moor (itself part of the Town Moor). At one time it included the Garrison Ground, an enclosed sports ground for the army and, for a time, the home of the athletics club Elswick Harriers and later, Benwell Cricket Club.

You cross Holland Drive, the entrance to a number of business and service units. Here you will find a sign for Fenham Barracks and you will notice that the army still has a presence here **(Qu 5)**.

Continue ahead passing the stone gatehouse of the barracks **(Qu 6)**.

Shortly, on your right, you pass some housing association properties generally known as Sutton's Dwellings. In 1900, William Sutton a London businessman left money to establish a trust to provide 'model' low cost housing in London and other major cities. On your left is the tree-lined perimeter of Castle Leazes. Further ahead, on the right, are the high-rise dwellings of Queen's Court. The football stadium becomes increasingly evident ahead as you arrive at a road junction. On your right is The Black Bull where there is a heritage plaque to Alex Burns (1907-2003). A member of Elswick Harriers, he won many national championships and represented his country at two Olympic Games.

Turn left through a stone gateway. Here you will find an information board about **Leazes Park.**

The path rises quite steeply until you reach the Jubilee Gates on the right **(Qu 7)**.

Pass through the gates into the park and follow the path ahead as it bears left to pass a bust of Sir Charles Hamond, one of the people responsible for establishing the park and who officially opened it in 1873. You are now on the terrace. From here you can appreciate some of the delights experienced by the early visitors with the bandstand and the lake lying ahead behind the trees.

Now walk down the steps (alternatively, to avoid the steps you need to retrace your steps to just before the gated exit, turn right and then turn right again to resume the walk at the bottom of the steps). At the bottom of the steps if you look left and right, on the grass you will see two stone animals which you would not expect to meet in this park **(Qu 8)**!

Walk ahead for some 40 metres and turn left. An information board provides some insights into the terrace and bandstand areas. Now follow the main path as it bears right. Ignore the first crossing of paths and in 200 metres or so you arrive at a junction of paths.

Stop here and you will find some stainless steel flowers set into the path. These are part of the 'Hidden Rivers' public art works project designed to recall small rivers now underground, such as the Pandon Burn, that flow into the River Tyne. In this case, *The*

Leazes Park

Jubilee Gateway

Government concern with public health and sanitation resulted in the setting up of the 'Health of Towns Commission' in 1843. Dr Reid, who was appointed to head the enquiry into Newcastle's response, published his report in 1845. The Reid Report recognised the advantage of public open spaces and recommended that parks should be opened in the east and west ends of the town; his suggestion was not taken up.

Some years later, in 1858, a petition, signed by nearly 3,000 working men from the west end of the town, asking for a park to be made available was also, initially, ignored. Nevertheless, the idea took root and after a long lead time Leazes Park, the first public park in Newcastle, was opened in 1873.

A symbol of the Lort Burn

Several attractions were later added: in 1879, a bandstand and a long terrace where Victorian ladies could 'promenade in their finery'; in 1897, magnificent Jubilee Gates to celebrate Queen Victoria's Diamond Jubilee. Subsequently, there have been many small changes and improvements.

However, the most important development has been the extensive restoration of the Grade II listed park, thanks to a £3.7 million grant from the Heritage Lottery Fund in 2000. Today's visitors can thus enjoy the delights of the park almost as it was in its Victorian heyday.

Flowering of the Lort Burn (Tom Grimsey, 2005) depicts the flow of the Lort Burn into the lake before it continues its passage to emerge at the Tyne near the Guildhall. On your left, low ornate blue pools suggest the source of the stream and wave-like slabs lead to a wave-like railing indicating where the burn enters the lake.

The path on the left leads beyond the artwork to a children's play area.

Turn right to walk to the lakeside. Now depending on the time you have available and the weather conditions you may like to explore the park, sit and watch the swans go by, see the fishermen casting their lines, observe the rowing boats in use or visit the children's play park.

To continue with the walk you need to go in a clockwise direction, passing the Richardson Road Lodge with its information point and the Café by the Lake (seasonal opening times). About three-quarters of the way around the lake, take the broad path off towards the terrace of houses and the football stadium. You soon come to a junction of paths and to the right you will see the bandstand and the terrace. Turn left, bear right and continue ahead with the tennis courts on your left **(Qu 9)**.

On your right is the splendid rectangular Leazes Terrace said to be 'probably the grandest terrace on Tyneside' (McCombie, 2009). This, together with the neighbouring Leazes Crescent, was designed by Thomas Oliver for Richard Grainger. This was before Grainger embarked upon his ambitious plan for the centre of the town, now referred to as 'Grainger Town'. Before Leazes Terrace was restored in 1959 for Newcastle University, mostly as student housing, it was not uncommon to see people sitting on the rooftops watching the match at the football ground below. Nowadays, the west side of the terrace itself is sadly somewhat overshadowed by the redevelopment of the football stadium.

Shortly after the path bears left, turn right to exit from the park. Turn left and walk a short distance to the end of Leazes Crescent. Turn right and then cross the road with care to the self-proclaimed 'World Famous' Trent House! Continue ahead into St Thomas' Crescent, a 19th-century area of architectural merit. Here the Crescent and the adjacent street, somewhat misleadingly called St Thomas' Square, form a charming oasis, away from the hustle and bustle of the Haymarket area. A heritage plague on the right identifies the residence of the artist and poet **William Bell Scott (Qu 10)**.

William Bell Scott (1811-1890)

Although this Scottish born artist only resided for a few years in St Thomas' Crescent his association with the north of England was much longer. He was Director of the Government School of Design in Newcastle for 20 years (1843-1863) and as such was a major influence on many important local artists. He portrayed several Northumbrian coastal and street scenes some of which can be seen in the Laing Art Gallery. Among his most noted local works are the large canvases in the former home of the Trevelyan family, Wallington Hall (now owned by The National Trust) which show aspects of Northumbrian history. He was also an engraver, etcher, writer and illustrator of books as well as a leading poet of his day. It was through poetry that he became friendly with the British painter and poet Dante Gabriel Rossetti. Rossetti is believed to have visited Bell Scott's studio located behind his house. Subsequently Bell Scott's work is said to have reflected the fidelity to nature and realistic colouring of the Pre-Raphaelite movement of Rossetti and his associates.

J.Edgar Mitchell (1871-1922)

Like William Bell Scott, J. Edgar. Mitchell is believed to have been born in Scotland. However, he came to live and work in Newcastle at the turn of the century. He painted many local scenes including, *The Village Tailor* and *The Old Cabinet Maker* both of which were exhibited at the Royal Academy. The latter is believed to depict a scene in the workshop in North Shields of the furniture maker Hedley Chapman, the founder of Chapman's, the family furniture firm. He also worked in stained glass and designed glazing for many important buildings. Thanks to a generous donation from the Friends of the Laing Art Gallery, the beautiful Arts and Crafts window that he designed for the gallery when it opened in 1904, was restored and re-installed a hundred years later in its original position at the top of the main stairs. At the time of his death, J. Edgar Mitchell was art master at the Queen Elizabeth Grammar School, Hexham,

Another noted artist, **J.Edgar Mitchell** is believed to have resided later in No 19 St Thomas' Crescent.

At the end of the crescent you arrive again at St Thomas' Street. Turn right and pass St Thomas Street Business Centre where you might glance through the cobbled entrance to see how the former brewery stables have been converted into a variety of business units. At the junction you are once again at Percy Street. Ahead of you is the bus station which Marks and Spencer had to provide in return for planning permission to extend their premises from the Eldon Square shopping centre. Unfortunately the roof of the bus station had to be replaced in 2006 when pieces of glass began to descend on waiting passengers! It was again subject to further work in 2010/11. The domed turret on the right of M&S provides a sympathetic replica of the domes on the Bruce Building opposite. Now you are back in the Haymarket and the end of the walk.

Quiz questions

1. **Which company did this building once belong to?**
2. **Why would the brewery have stables?**
3. **Who is represented in this statue?**
4. **When did Ralph Hedley begin to live in Belle Grove Terrace?**
5. **What part of the army is now based here?**
6. **What do you now find behind the gatehouse of Fenham Barracks?**
7. **Which anniversary is recalled in the Jubilee Gates?**
8. **What are these two animals?**
9. **What other game is played within the tennis courts area?**
10. **At what number in St Thomas' Crescent did William Bell Scott live?**

6. Through Grainger Town

Start/finish: Monument Metro Station
Distance: 1.75 miles
Route: Grey's Monument, Central Arcade, Grainger Market, St John's Church, Plummer Tower, Tyneside Cinema, Grey's Monument
Accessibility: On pavements throughout
Refreshments: Tyneside Cinema and cafés and pubs throughout the route

The walk begins at the Monument Metro Station next to where **Earl Grey** is honoured in the form of **Grey's Monument.**

Grainger Town Regeneration Project

In 1991 the City Council designated an area of the city centre as 'Grainger Town', in recognition of the work of the property developer Richard Grainger in the 1830s and 40s. The designated area contains some 420 buildings although not all are the work of Grainger and some historic parts of the city such as Blackfriars and the Bigg Market are also included. An initial study in 1992 found that a third of the floor area of the buildings was unused. After further detailed studies, The Grainger Town Project, a partnership of public, private and community interests, embarked in 1997 on a major regeneration scheme. The six year project has brought about significant improvements and 'a real economic, cultural and quality future has been firmly secured for the wonderful townscape of Newcastle's Grainger Town' (Lovie, 2001). Street names in the designated area carry the title 'Grainger Town' and the logo of the Grainger Town Partnership in the form of one of the domes of the Central Exchange Buildings (see below). This walk covers the area's main streets while other parts of Grainger Town, such as Blackfriars, are included in Walk 6.

Richard Grainger (1797-1861)

Richard Grainger was born in High Friar Lane in relatively modest circumstances. However, he progressed from jobbing builder to entrepreneur-developer and came to play a major role in the regeneration of Newcastle. In the 1820s he began to make his mark with the construction of dwellings in the Leazes area, St Mary's Place and Higham Place and in 1831-32 he constructed in the splendid Royal Arcade (sadly demolished in the mid-1960s, see below).

However, it is his work in the heart of the town in the 1830s and 40s for which he is most acclaimed. In addition to his technical skill he had a persuasive ability to raise funds and to negotiate with vested interests. He also gained the support and cooperation of key people such as John Clayton, lawyer and Town Clerk (see below), to put into effect plans to demolish older properties and to build a series of streets in the centre of Newcastle. It is amazing now to think that he was able to achieve so much fine work in the short space of some seven years. The effect would not have been so visually satisfying had he not enlisted the architectural skills of men like Thomas Oliver, John and Benjamin Green, John Dobson and his 'in house' architects John Walker and George Wardle.

Earl Grey (1764-1845)

Charles 2nd Earl Grey came from an old-established family from Howick Hall in Northumberland. He succeeded his father, who had been created 1st Earl Grey following his illustrious military career, in 1807. After completing his education at Eton and Cambridge he entered parliament as a Whig in 1786 at the age of twenty-two. In 1794 he married Mary Ponsonby (1776-1851). It was a happy marriage and Mary bore sixteen children. However, in his absence on parliamentary business Grey indulged in a series of affairs, the most infamous being with the Duchess of Devonshire.

In Parliament he rose through the ministerial ranks, becoming First Lord of the Admiralty, Foreign Secretary and, in 1830, Prime Minister. He argued passionately for parliamentary reform, in particular to get rid of some of the rotten boroughs (which, for example, might send two members to parliament from a population of ten) and to enable representation in the House of Commons for the newly emerging industrial towns.

After a tremendous struggle with the opponents of reforms, the Representation of the People Act (the first Reform Act) was passed in 1832. Opinions differ as to the importance of this Act on the development of British democracy but most agree that, at the least, it was a valuable first step. Other far reaching legislation effected during his premiership included the Abolition of Slavery Act 1833, and laws restricting rhe employment of children.

Apart from the tea which bears his name (reputedly from a diplomatic present of bergamot flavoured tea he once received), he is commemorated in the names of Grey College, Durham University and Grey Street, Newcastle and in Grey's Monument in the city centre.

Grey's Monument

This imposing, 147 feet tall monument, a focal point in Grainger's redevelopment, was built in 1838. It was designed by the well-known Newcastle architect, Benjamin Green. The Portland stone statue of the earl is by Edward Hodges Baily (1788-1867) whose work included the statue of Lord Nelson on Nelson' s Column in London. There is a long inscription on the pedestal at the foot of the monument which details Earl Grey's achievements.

In 1941 the statue's head was struck by lightning. A replacement by Roger Hedley, son of the artist Ralph Hedley, was installed in 1947.

The monument is open on specified occasions. Details are obtainable from the Tourist Information Office. The view from the top of the column is well worth the effort of climbing the 164 steps to reach it.

Earl Grey surveys the town

Here at the junction of Blackett Street, Grey Street and Grainger Street, you may come across political, religious and cultural gatherings of various types, often enlivened by music. Take a few moments before you set out, to admire the splendour of the gentle sweep of the city's finest street, Grey Street. Walk a few metres down Grey Street and turn right to enter the **Central Exchange Buildings and the Central Arcade (Qu 1)**.

Leave the Central Arcade by the exit on the right that leads into Grainger Street. On your right, set into the pavement, you will find an artwork *Grainger Dedication* by Charlie Holmes and Ian Ness (2002) in honour of Richard Grainger, with the apt inscription 'The past is my present to your future'.

Cross over into Nelson Street. Immediately on the wall of the first building on the left, you will find a plaque referring to three foreign visitors, **Guiseppe Garibaldi, Louis Kossuth, William Lloyd Garrison** who were received by the radical campaigner, local member of parliament and newspaper owner Joseph Cowen **(Qu 2)**.

Continue along Nelson Street. After a few metres, on the right-hand side, you pass the Green Market entrance to Eldon Square. The construction of the shopping centre reduced the

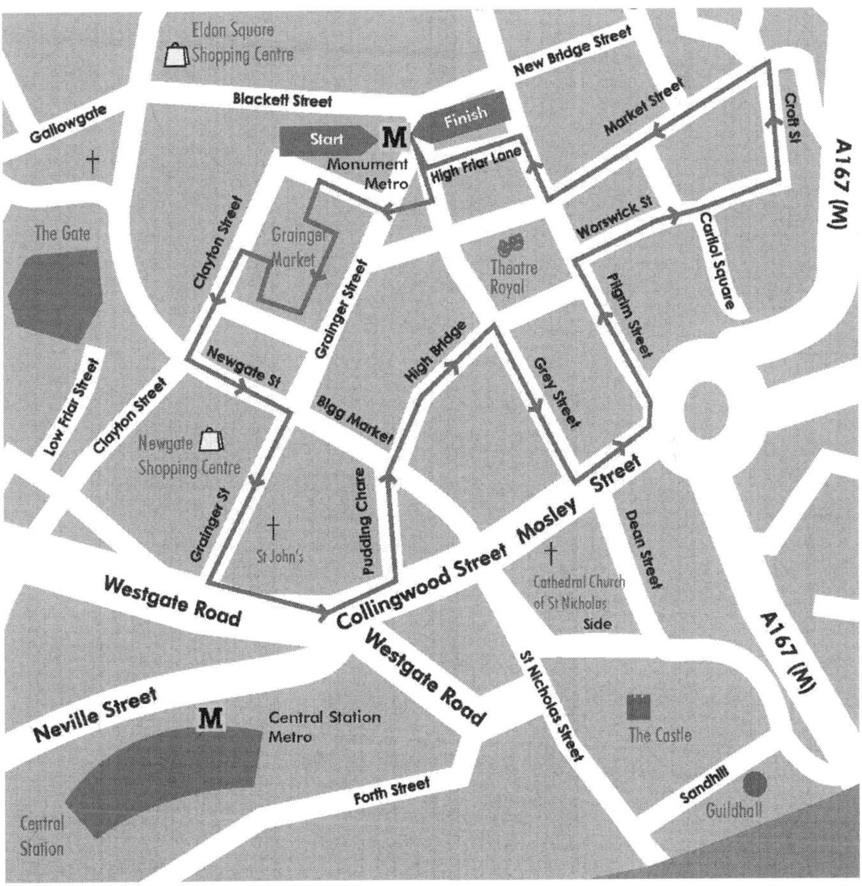

Central Exchange Buildings and the Central Arcade

This elegant three-sided building with its end domes was originally built in1837 by Richard Grainger, to the design of Wardle and Walker, as a corn market. However, faced with opposition from businesses, the Town Corporation withdrew its approval thus obliging Grainger to change tack. The result was the conversion of the trading floor into a news room. Such was its success that its membership rose to some 1600 users who, in addition, enjoyed the benefits of the surrounding coffee rooms. Over the next sixty years, as fashions changed so did the use of the news room area as it came to serve at various times as an art gallery, a concert hall and a theatre. Unfortunately, in 1901, a disastrous fire brought this period to an end. However, a new chapter in the history of the building was created when it was reconstructed after the fire to re-open in 1906 in the form in which you find it today with its Central Arcade.

Central Arcade

The beautifully tiled Central Arcade with its glass roof and flower-decked balconies provides an attractive shop-lined passageway from Grey Street to Market Street with an exit to Grainger Street. The Arcade is lined with retail outlets that include J.G. Windows who have been there since 1908. A Tourist Information Centre is situated at the Market Street end. Floors two and three of the building are occupied by apartments, some of which are the result of conversion under the Grainger Town Project, while the fourth floor consists of offices. On the Market Street side of the building there is a sign referring to 'Goods Entrance Central Exchange Hotel and Central Arcade', evidence of the previous existence within the building of an hotel.

Guiseppe Garibaldi (1807-1882)

Italian nationalist and patriot he was a key figure in the struggle to free Italy from foreign control and establish an independent kingdom. He spent periods in exile when he travelled to raise resources to further his military campaigns. He stayed for a month in Newcastle when the ship he was sailing in from New York to Genoa docked in the Tyne in 1854.

Louis (Lajos) Kossuth (1802-1894)

Hungarian statesman and leader of the failed Hungarian Revolution of 1848-49. He spent the rest of his life in exile travelling widely to promote the cause of Hungarian nationalism including a visit to Newcastle in 1865.

William Lloyd Garrison (1805-1879)

A leading American anti-slavery campaigner and advocate of women's rights. Like Joseph Cowen, he was a journalist and one time newspaper owner. Although the plaque gives the date of his visit to Newcastle as 1876, the year his wife died, it is more likely to have been 1877 when he came to London.

rear area of the properties on this side of Nelson Street. The adjacent Café Royal, once a noted bar, is now a pleasant coffee shop. The next building once served as the Music Hall (1838), the New Tyne Concert Hall (1879) and The Gaiety Music Hall (1884 and finally as the Gaiety Cinema which closed in 1949. The facade bears a plaque referring to visits made by the famous novelist Charles Dickens **(Qu 3)**.

The last building on the right bears a stone panel above the second floor on which is engraved the name **Cordwainers Hall**. Ahead you will see what was the Lord Collingwood pub (currently Victory Amusements) built for Grainger in the late 1830s and appropriately located adjacent to the street named after Nelson.

On the left-hand side of the street there are five entrances to the **Grainger Market**. Go into the Grainger Market via the middle entrance. Here you will find a Plan

Cordwainers Hall

This was once the meeting place of the Cordwainers' Guild. The cordwainers were shoemakers who derived their name from the fact that they originally made shoes from the soft leather (cordwain) from Cordoba in Spain. In 1556 they founded one of Newcastle's important trade guilds and they occupied several premises, including Blackfriars before moving to this site in the late 1830s. Today with membership generally based on inheritance they remain as one of the incorporated companies of the Freemen of Newcastle.

Grainger Market

Richard Grainger's development of Grey Street necessitated the demolition of the open air Butcher Market so he entrusted John Dobson with the design of this splendid alternative. The opening ceremony in 1835 was marked by a dinner attended by some 2000 people, presumably the great and the good of that time. There is a painting of this occasion by Henry Perlee Parker in the Laing Art Gallery. Apparently at the time it was claimed to be the largest indoor market in Europe, and the Evening Chronicle went as far as to describe it as 'the most magnificent in the world'! It was originally divided into two sections, the flesh market with some one hundred and eighty butchers' shops and the vegetable market with fifty-five or so outlets. A fire at the turn of the 20th century destroyed part of the roofing and in 1901 this was replaced by the current latticed-steel glazed roof. More recently, under the auspices of the City Council and the Grainger Town Project, the interior has undergone a general facelift and the restoration of some of its original features.

Although the market is still noted for its meat, fruit and vegetables, it appears to have something for everyone from handicrafts to headstones. There are plenty of opportunities to enjoy refreshments and from time to time you may find arts and craft markets and entertainment in the Events Space. You might come across some metal floor covers, between the Plant Stalls, that conceal the entrance to a World War II air raid shelter.

This attractive market is certainly very well worth a visit but note that it is closed on Sundays.

Grainger Market

of the Market and you will see that the area is neatly divided into numbered alleys with lateral crossings and entrances/exits to the three other surrounding streets: Grainger Street, Nun Street and Clayton Street. After visiting the Market, the walk continues from Clayton Street, to the right of the building as you enter, so eventually you need to make your way to that side of the building. Strolling roughly in a clockwise direction is therefore recommended.

One of the first outlets to spot is Marks and Spencer Original Penny Bazaar, in Alley 3, where you will find some photographs of the development from 1895 to 1976 of 'the world's oldest and smallest M&S store'. Make sure you visit the Weigh House (accessible from both Alleys 1 and 2), if not to get weighed then at least to pick up a brochure about the market (with a plan of the layout) as well as some tourist information **(Qu 4)**.

Exit from the Grainger Market at Katherines Florist onto Clayton Street, named after **John Clayton**, the Town Clerk who assisted Grainger.

On the right is a pavement plaque about the Market. To the right, at the end of Clayton Street, you will see a further entrance into the Eldon Square Shopping Centre. This blocked the previous access that Clayton Street once enjoyed to Grainger's original Eldon Square.

Turn left and proceed ahead passing a pavement plaque about John Clayton. On the right is the entrance to the extension to the Eldon Square Shopping Centre that opened in February 2010 (St Andrew's Way) and a pub where you need to look at the sign hanging outside **(Qu 5)**.

On your left is Nun Street which has a fine terrace of facades. This street, with accesses to the Grainger Market, is so named because of the 12th-century nunnery of St Bartholomew that once stood in this area.

John Clayton (1792-1890)

John Clayton spent much of his childhood on the Chesters Estate which his father had acquired. It was here that he developed his great interest in Hadrian's Wall and in later years as an enthusiastic antiquarian he bought land in order to preserve the Wall. In 1822 he succeeded his father as Town Clerk, a post he held for forty-five years. During his long term of office he gave his support in particular to Richard Grainger's ambitious scheme to redevelop the centre of Newcastle. 'His sympathetic assistance, influence and wealth were decisive in persuading the corporation to sanction the plans and invaluable in helping to raise the £2,000,000 which the full scheme is said to have involved' (Middlebrook, 1950).

Continuing ahead along Clayton Street, you soon reach the crossroads with Newgate Street, the name a further reminder of the gated nature of the town walls. Continue ahead via the traffic lights and turn immediately left to walk down Newgate Street.

In a few metres, stop at the functional-looking Newgate Hotel, formerly the Swallow Hotel. The hotel stands above a shopping mall that extends into Grainger Street. This was once the site of the Empire Theatre, a popular venue for variety acts before closing in 1963, and where acts such as Morecambe & Wise performed before becoming TV stars.

Look across the road at the façade above Yummies. This former dwelling was built in the 1820s on the site of the gatehouse of St Bartholomew's Nunnery. This raises the question: was this house, in the aptly named Nuns Lane, designed in this ecclesiastical style "to evoke its medieval predecessor?" (Pevsner and Richmond, 1992).

You soon rejoin Grainger Street at the point at which Grainger's design ended. The street was only continued southwards after Grainger's death in order to give better access to the Central Station.

With the Bigg Market ahead, cross over to the other side of Grainger Street, turn

Chateau-like premises

immediately right and proceed down Grainger Street towards the Central Station. There are impressive Victorian buildings on both sides of the street. On the right, look for the Chaucer Building, No 57, where at its top you will see emblems indicating its early use in the 1870s by the Freemasons. Later you will see evidence of another masonic establishment. The last building (Yates) on the left before the church looks like a French Chateau. Once the offices of the Newcastle and Gateshead Gas Company, it was also occupied by the well-known local store, Wengers. The elegant building on the other side of the road at the corner of Grainger Street and Westgate Road was once the Trustees Savings Bank **(Qu 6)**.

Before you visit the **Church of St John the Baptist**, notice that beyond the traffic lights, as Grainger Street continues ahead to the Central Station, there are three bronze painted figures, *Man with potential selves* (Sean Heany 2003). At the same time, on the left, the rather unimaginative edifice, which in the 1970s replaced the Douglas Hotel, contrasts rather unfavourably with the elegant 1870s County Hotel on the right.

Church of St John the Baptist

This venerable building provides an interesting contrast with its Victorian and modern neighbours. There is evidence of a twelfth- century church on the site but most of what we see today dates from the fourteenth and fifteenth centuries. It was first mentioned in a charter of 1196 and is one of the four original parish churches located within the Town Wall.

Inside, there are many William Wailes stained glass windows and other noteworthy features, which can be easily identified from the explanatory leaflet provided. Just beyond the entrance, in the baptistry, the sixteenth-century carved font cover is a splendid example of local woodwork. In the vaulted ceiling above this there is a coat of arms with the inscription *Orate pro anima Robarti Rodis*. Robert Rhodes financed the extension to the south aisle and other additions. He owned land on which Bessie Surtees house was built and was a benefactor of St John's and other Newcastle churches in the mid-fifteenth century. Near the altar, in the north wall of the chancel is a cross-shaped opening through which an anchorite, a religious hermit, could observe the Mass without being seen.

In 1927 St John's led the way in the Church of England in making the main Sunday service a parish communion, i.e. a central act of worship for the whole parish, instead of the then pattern of worship (typically, a splendid mid-morning service of matins with perhaps a weekly or less frequent early morning holy communion).

Worship at St John's is firmly rooted in the Anglo-Catholic tradition.

For further information see: www.stjohnthebaptistnewcastle.com

With the church on your left, walk down Westgate Road to the end of the church railings, noting on your right, at the corner of the Long Bar, a listed building in the form of a stone pillar! This once stood nearby at the Hospital of St Mary the Virgin which in turn became the first site of what is now the Newcastle Royal Grammar School.

Dominating the traffic island on your right is the monument to the railway pioneer George Stephenson, beyond which you can see a range of important buildings: the Station Hotel, the Institute of Mining, the Literary and Philosophical Society (Lit & Phil) and Bolbec Hall.

At the end of the church railings turn left and walk a few metres down Rosemary Lane. You will find a plaque commemorating the fact that Charles Avison, said to be the foremost concerto composer of his time, lived and worked here in the 1730s **(Qu 7)**.

Retrace your steps to the main road and turn left. The splendid-looking building on your left, the Union Rooms, an exclusive gentleman's club for about 100 years, has become a popular Wetherspoons pub. The entrance hall contains information and pictures relating to its origins and, in addition to sampling its fine fare, it is worth viewing the elegant staircase and the stained glass windows with their literary connections.

A short distance ahead, as Westgate Road bears to the right at its junction with Collingwood Street, you arrive at Pudding Chare, one of Newcastle's numerous narrow alleyways. Before you turn left, stop to admire the former Barclay's Bank building, now Revolution. It is worth considering taking further nourishment here if only to admire the splendid pillars and ceiling of the former banking hall!

Proceed up Pudding Chare which provides a dismal response to the elegance of the two previous buildings. You pass the aptly named Bar Fleet St adjacent to the premises of the local newspaper group, NJC Media.

Continue ahead across the road and over the Bigg Market towards the Beehive. Pass the Beehive with its ornate tiling and walk along High Bridge. This is another of the references to the bridges that were once needed to cross the small streams or burns that run down to the River Tyne. In this case it was over the Lort Burn, now concealed beneath Grey Street a short distance ahead.

You pass the Duke of Wellington pub where a former landlord, William Campbell (1856-1878), was ' Once the heaviest man in the country ...At his death aged 22 he weighed 53 stones and was 6ft 3ins tall' (Morgan, 2000). Apparently his funeral was a spectacular event. His coffin had to be winched from a third floor window and some 40,000 sightseers packed the streets before he was buried in Jesmond cemetery.

A few metres further, on the left-hand side of the street, next to High Bridge Studios and Gallery, you will find a plaque celebrating the two hundredth anniversary of the birth of Lord Armstrong, 'inventor, engineer, scientist, businessman'. It was on this site that he carried out some of his earliest experiments before he decided to give up his career as a solicitor and devote himself to engineering.

You soon reach elegant Grey Street. Turn right and immediately on the wall of Blakes Coffee House you will find a plaque, perhaps rather surprisingly dedicated to a Portuguese diplomat and writer, **Jose Maria de Eca de Queiros**.

Continue down Grey Street taking time to admire the facades of what is generally regarded as Grainger's finest street. The side you are walking down was mainly the work of Grainger's own architects John Walker and George Wardle, while the section opposite was that of John Dobson. The elegant building with high columns, now occupied by Barluga, was at one time an appropriate setting for the Bank of England. Shortly you will have the opportunity to compare it with the building to which the bank moved in the late 1960s.

Jose Maria de Eca de Queiros (1845-1900)

Ian Ayris humorously gave Newcastle's 'Most Exotic Plaque Award' to someone whose name clearly does not resonate in Newcastle! (Grundy et al, 2006). However, de Eca de Queiros is regarded as one of Portugal's foremost 19th-century writers. After qualifying in law he lived in London for a while working as a lawyer and a journalist before becoming a local government administrator in his home country. He joined the diplomatic service in 1873. And after a short spell in Havanna he returned to England in 1874 to undertake consular duties in Newcastle and Bristol. He moved to Paris in 1878, made his home there and died there twenty-two years later. He was given a state funeral in his native Portugal.

Newcastle's most exotic plaque

It is said that his most productive time as a writer were the four years he spent in Newcastle. It was during this period that one of his most famous novels, *The Crime of Father Amaro* was published in Portugal amid much controversy. It was a challenging work questioning the role of Faith and like much of his literary output tackled issues such as greed and corruption in Portuguese society. It did not appear that he had much regard for English society either and his *Letters from England* were very critical of the English abroad. Interestingly enough he wrote of Britain's inability to subdue Afghanistan at the time. His works have been translated into some twenty foreign languages. It is not clear what impact living in Newcastle made upon him but perhaps it give him time and space to be creative!

At the crossroads, with Dean Street ahead, turn left into Mosley Street, named after Alderman Mosley who played an important part in improving the town in the second half of the 18th century. The grandeur of the buildings here, together with those in the opposite direction, is largely due to the fact that at one time this was the main location in the city of the regional headquarters of the major banking and insurance companies.

After a few metres, next to Corbitts (dealers in stamps, coins and medals), there is a plaque referring to the fact that the pharmacist **John Mawson** was once located at No 13 where **Joseph Swan**, inventor of the incandescent light bulb, joined the firm and carried out experiments. There is a hotly disputed claim that Mosley Street was the first street in the world to be illuminated by electric light!

Now you will see a large traffic island, often still referred to as the Swan House roundabout, using the original name of the building. This was first constructed as part of T. Dan Smith's 1960s redevelopment scheme and caused considerable controversy particularly as it involved the demolition of Grainger and Dobson's impressive Royal Arcade (1832). Described as 'the most serious of Newcastle's architectural losses in the1960s' (McCombie, 2009).

At the time there were suggestions that the building would be reconstructed elsewhere and so the stones were marked accordingly. It appears that this was done in chalk and,

John Mawson (1815-1867)

John Mawson a chemist and druggist opened his shop in Mosley Street in 1843 and subsequently employed Joseph Swan with whom he later formed a business partnership. He also came to own a dispensary on Hood Street part of the site of which was later to become the premises of the booksellers Mawson, Swan and Morgan (see below). In 1867 he became Sheriff of Newcastle and it was in this role that he was killed in a dreadful accident shortly afterwards. In order to dispose of some canisters of nitro-glycerine used for blasting in mines and which had been found in a cellar in the Cloth Market, Mawson led a group of men to the Town Moor. Unfortunately their attempt to dispose of the material in an old mine working from the Spital Tongues Colliery resulted in a huge explosion and the death of John Mawson and his six companions.

Joseph Swan (1828-1914)

Joseph Swan, who like John Mawson had served an apprenticeship as a druggist, moved to Newcastle from Sunderland and was employed by Mawson at his Mosley Street shop. There he was encouraged to continue to carry out experiments in the small laboratory that his employer set up above the shop. This resulted in many inventions relating to photography,including the carbon process for permanent photographic prints.

However, it is with regard to his development of the incandescent light bulb that Swan is best remembered. He demonstrated the effectiveness of his electric light bulb to an enthralled audience in the Literary and Philosophical Society in Newcastle in 1879. Controversy arose regarding competing claims to the invention by Swan and the American Thomas Edison. However, this was largely resolved by their merging their interests in the Edison and Swan Company in 1882. Swan ensured that the home in Low Fell that he shared with his second wife, the widow of John Mawson, was illuminated by electric light. He was knighted in 1904.

For many local people the names of both Mawson and Swan became inextricably linked through the establishment of the well-known booksellers and stationers Mawson Swan and Morgan in 1878. Thomas Morgan being the name of the manager. The company traded until 1973 when it was replaced by Waterstone's. The building is currently occupied by the fashion store H&M although the line of electric lamps outside serve as reminder of Joseph Swan.

whether by accident or design, the rain made any such project impossible! In 2004 Swan House was refurbished and the original occupants such as BT and Social Service departments were replaced by trendier apartments and 'The world famous' (!) Linekers and the Metro Radio station. The construction of the Central Motorway under Swan House also led to the enclosure of the historic Holy Jesus Hospital within a rather dismal setting .

To the right from here you will be able to see the tower of All Saints Church and the Tyne Bridge, beyond which lies Gateshead. Turn left to enter Pilgrim Street traditionally the main entrance to Newcastle. No 98-100 is **Alderman Fenwick's House**, said to be 'the best and most complete historic house in Newcastle' (McCombie, 2009). Almost opposite are the now deserted regional offices of the Bank of England, built for the bank in 1968-71 when it moved from its premises in Grey Street. You may like to make your own comparison between the two buildings.

Alderman Fenwick's House

Towards the end of the 17th century the house came into the possession of the Fenwick family and it remained in their ownership at least until the 1750s. It seems to have owed its name to Nicholas Fenwick who was Mayor and Member of Parliament as well as an Alderman of Newcastle. At the beginning of the 1780s, after having had several owners, it was altered to become an important coaching inn, the Queen's Head Inn. In 1834 it was purchased by the Town Council at the time Richard Grainger was planning the construction of nearby Grey Street between Pilgrim Street and the Cloth Market. Further alterations took place in 1883 when the property was leased to the Newcastle upon Tyne Liberal Club. It became a highly regarded gentlemen's club with a library, smoking rooms and coffee rooms, a dining room able to seat 150 people, a billiard room, a chess room, together with bedrooms for members and accommodation for servants.

However, changing political and social circumstances in the 20th century eventually took their toll on the ability of the members to meet the rising costs of maintaining the building and in 1962 the Club realised it needed to leave the premises. After years of neglect it was not until 1982 that the Tyne and Wear Building Preservation Trust was invited by the City Council to carry out the restoration of the building. The Trust pushed ahead as best as possible, struggling at times, to raise the funds required to undertake such an enormous task. However, the work was eventually completed in 1997 when it could be said 'the survival and restoration of this house has been like the emergence of a butterfly from a chrysalis' (Heslop, Jobling, and McCombie, 2001).

The beautifully restored building is now divided into prestigious office accommodation. Although it is not generally open to the public, it is possible to gain admittance to the former dining room by contacting the Tyne and Wear Building Preservation Trust as indicated on the notice at the entrance. Once inside it is possible to appreciate the small window dated 1726 in the entrance hall, the elegant staircase, the roof lantern, housing a wind vane against a painted background, and the delightful dining room with panelled walls and embossed ceiling.

A short distance further up Pilgrim Street, The Market Lane public house, although much altered, occupies a building dating from the early 18th century. The pub itself is popularly known as 'The Monkey Bar' said to be due to bricklayers leaving their hods nicknamed 'monkeys' until they were able to pay off any bar money owing.

In a short distance you pass the other end of High Bridge, where you will find the Bacchus pub, a popular meeting place. Immediately after High Bridge you will see that No 54 Pilgrim Street, now a lounge bar and live music venue, has an ornate entrance, with two smaller doorways at either side. To the right, there is an inscribed cornerstone indicating that this building owed its origins to the Freemasons **(Qu 8)**.

You soon reach the corner of Pilgrim Street and Market Street. Before you turn right, look for the sign 'Seymour's Corner' on the Market Street side of the corner. This refers to the fact that this was the site of Seymour's, one of the first sports shops in Newcastle. It was owned by Stan Seymour, at various times player, manager, chairman and president of Newcastle United F C before his death in 1978. His son later also became club chairman.

Turn right at the lights to cross to the other side of Pilgrim Street and thus leave the designated area of Grainger Town for a short while. You are at the Police Station where you turn right to return down Pilgrim Street for a short distance passing the former Fire Station. (At the time of writing, this whole side of Pilgrim Street continues to await much-needed redevelopment).

Turn left down down Worswick Street, named after **Fr James Worswick** who was responsible for the building of St Andrew's RC Church on this site in 1798. A plaque testifies to his high standing. Worswick Street was also well known from 1929 to 1996 because of the bus station opposite the church.

Continue ahead through Carliol Square. The curved building on the right, now a health and fitness club, was once the city's main telephone exchange, built on the site of an earlier police station. You cross a road (Carliol Street). You may then wish to avert your eyes from the building on the right! Ahead you may hear the roar of the traffic on the Central Motorway, beyond which is part of Northumbria University. Turn left into Croft Street to the Plummer Tower, once part of the Town Wall and later to have other uses. An information board provides

Early Police and Fire Stations

Fr James Worswick (1771-1843)

James Worswick who was born in Lancashire began his studies for the priesthood in France. However, he was obliged to flee to England in the turmoil of the French revolution and was eventually ordained in York in 1795. Within months of becoming a priest he was sent to Newcastle where he ministered for forty-five years. Finding Catholic services being celebrated in two inadequate houses in Newgate Street and Westgate Road he purchased a house with a large garden in Pilgrim Street. He then raised the money to build St Andrew's, the first post-reformation Roman Catholic church in Newcastle. In 1830 he extended the church to cope with the influx of Irish immigrants.

He was responsible for the building of further churches in South Shields and Gateshead and was part of the committee that set about building St Mary's Cathedral. Although he is buried there, he died before the cathedral was completed. Redevelopment of the area in 1875 led to the removal of Worswick's original building and the construction of the present church. Some stained glass from the earlier building can be seen in the windows that face you as you enter the small courtyard.

James Worswick's ministry was widely acclaimed and he worked hard not only for his own flock but also to develop good relations with those of other faiths. Unusually perhaps for a Catholic priest, the present street was named after him in 1933 and then in 2006 a commemorative plaque was dedicated to him. Before the unveiling, Councillor Pauline Allen described him 'as a forefather in helping to create our multi-cultural city' (www.newcastle.gov.uk). Fr Worswick would be pleased to know that St Andrew's still plays an active role within the city. It is also interesting to note that some eighty years after his death, another prominent local Roman Catholic, Basil Hume was baptised here.

Chapmans

This long- established Tyneside family firm, now in its fifth generation, was founded in North Shields in 1847 by the cabinet maker, Hedley Chapman (1814-1895). In 1871 he opened his furniture showrooms in Newcastle's Northumberland Street which at that time was not the main shopping area it is today. However, his foresight was well rewarded years later when Northumberland Street did become the city's main focus for shoppers. After the First World War, Chapmans concentrated mainly on their retail business and in 1920 the company registered the trademark 'Siesta' as an exclusive label for all the furniture they were to sell. Further premises were acquired and by 1937 Siesta House occupied a large combined site on Northumberland Street and the adjacent Prudhoe Street.

However, in 1946, they decided it was an appropriate time to make a move, and to that end they leased property from the Mary Magdalene Trust on the Great North Road at the junction of Barras Bridge and Jesmond Road. Opened in 1949, the converted block of Georgian houses, with its attractively landscaped gardens, made 'Chapmans Corner' a well-known Newcastle landmark. Chapmans remained there for twenty years until a further move was made necessary by the development of the Central Motorway. It was then that Siesta House moved into a substantial building in Market Street and Carliol Street that contained a ballroom in which the popular Tilleys Tea Dances of the 1920s were held. The former Northumberland Street site is now occupied by Marks and Spencer and the entrance to Eldon Square Shopping Centre. Sadly after 157 years in business, with the lease of the premises ending, Chapmans announced it was to close mid-2012.

details of this section of the town wall and the extensive open space called Carliol Croft that once lay here within the old town boundaries **(Qu 9)**.

At the end of Croft Street, turn left along Market Street (East) passing the front of the premises of the family firm of **Chapmans**. Proceed across Carliol Street via the traffic lights, then turn immediately right to cross to the other side of Market Street (East) and then left to continue along Market Street (East).

In a short distance, on the side entrance of what is Carliol House, you will find a plaque with further reference to Carliol Croft and the Carliol family. The building itself was completed in 1928 for the Newcastle upon Tyne Electric Supply Co. Ltd and, with some name changes, it has been associated with the electricity industry at least until the departure of Npower to Durham in 2010. Ahead, on the Pilgrim Street side of the building, next to the entrance of what is currently Start Fitness, there is a plaque, dedicated appropriately by the original electricity-related occupants, to Sir Joseph Swan **(Qu 10)**.

The left-hand side of Market Street (East) contains the Magistrates Courts and the Central Police Station (pending redevelopment of this whole area).

Plummer Tower

Cross over Pilgrim Street at the traffic lights to return to the designated area of Grainger Town. Turn right to walk up the left-hand side of Pilgrim Street. You pass Hood Street before you arrive at the narrow High Friar Lane and the entrance to the **Tyneside Cinema**.

Now proceed along High Friar Lane, once the site of the Grey Friars Monastery as well as of the humble birthplace of Richard Grainger, to return to Monument Metro Station and the end of the walk.

Tyneside Cinema

The cinema was first opened as the News Theatre in 1937. It followed the trend of the period, as people all over the country flocked to newsreel theatres to see national and international news on screen for the first time. However the televising of the Coronation in 1953 heralded the end of this period and by the end of the 1960s the news theatre as such came to the end. In 1976, after several years of fits and starts, the Newcastle cinema re-opened as the Tyneside Cinema. Major restoration and expansion was carried out from 2006 until it re-opened once again in 2008 in its present form. Now the cinema welcomes visitors daily and provides a very helpful Self-Guided Tour leaflet as well as free guided tours on specific days.

Architecturally the 1930s largely art deco interior of the building is a real gem. The first floor foyer offers a timeline of the Tyneside Cinema's history together with a video of the history of film. The second floor offers cinema buffs an exhibition of technical equipment while football fans can usually watch footage of Newcastle United's legendary triumphs. On this floor you will also find the Tyneside Coffee Rooms where, in addition to enjoying refreshments, you can also appreciate its fine décor. The third floor has a bar, small screen and special events facilities. The fourth floor contains a third screen.

The cinema's programme offers a wide range of classical and contemporary films, a children's Saturday Film Club, study days for students of film and media studies, screening of films for schools and regular special events.

Details of activities and tours can be found on www.tynesidecinema.co.uk or Tel 0845 217 9909.

Quiz questions

1. What can you buy from J.G. Windows in the Central Arcade?
2. What did Guiseppe Garibaldi visit in Nelson Street in 1854?
3. How many visits did Charles Dickens make to the Music Hall in Nelson Street?
4. How much does it cost to get weighed in the Grainger Market?
5. Whose portrait hangs outside the pub in Clayton Street opposite the entrance to Nun Street?
6. What is the name of this building now?
7. What jobs did Charles Avison get while he lived in Rosemary Lane?
8. When was the cornerstone of the former Masonic Temple in Pilgrim Street laid?
9. What other names are given to the Plummer Tower?
10. Where was Sir Joseph Swan born?

7. In and around Chinatown

Start/finish: **Monument Metro Station**
Distance: **1.5 miles**
Route: **Grey's Monument, Old Eldon Square, St James' Park, Town Wall, Chinatown, Westgate Road, Clayton Street, Newgate Street, St Andrew's Church, Grey's Monument**
Accessibility: **Mostly on the level on pavements**
Refreshments: **Cafés and pubs throughout the route**

From the Metro Station cross to Waterstone's bookshop which occupies the attractive **Emerson Chambers**.

Walk ahead with the glass walls of the Eldon Square Shopping Centre over the road on your left. On your right you come to Fenwick's. The sober and elegant lines of its art deco Blacket Street entrance appear in sharp contrast to the extravagant forms of its next door neighbour Emerson Chambers. On the pavement on your left you will see a red brick sculpture *Parsons Polygon* (David Hamilton, 1985), which not only commemorates the achievements of **Sir Charles Algernon Parsons** but serves to conceal the ventilation shaft for the Metro Station beneath it.

Proceed ahead to come to **Old Eldon Square**

Carry on, under the somewhat garish glass bridge, to the crossroads where you need to go straight across, then turn right and walk the short distance to Leazes Park Road. Turn left and proceed up the road. On the left is the Labour Club, while coincidentally the first building on the right-hand side, at the corner with Percy Street, once housed the Socialist Meeting Room where the Peoples Theatre, now in Heaton, originated in 1911. Continuing up the steep road you pass another connection with entertainment in the form of the booking office for the Hyena Comedy Club.

At the top of the street, opposite the El Coto Spanish restaurant, you will see the

St George slays the dragon

Emerson Chambers

Dating from 1903, this building which once contained shops, offices and an elegant basement restaurant is now occupied by Waterstone's. It was the work of Benjamin Simpson who was also responsible for another fine building, the Half Moon, in the Bigg Market. His imaginative creations even seem to bring a feeling of the Spanish architect Gaudi to Newcastle. Here, note, in particular, the exotic roof with its delightful clock and its windows said to be topped by 'witches' hats'.

Sir Charles Algernon Parsons (1854-1931)

The sixth son of the Earl of Rosse, himself a well-known scientist, Charles Algernon Parsons was brought up in Ireland and attended Trinity College Dublin. After graduating from Cambridge University in 1877 he joined W. G. Armstrong at Elswick, Newcastle as an apprentice (quite a posh one!). Following other employment he became a junior partner in the Gateshead engineering firm, Clarke Chapman. In 1889, when the partnership was dissolved, he set up his own works, C. A. Parsons and Company, at Heaton, Newcastle which made turbine generators to his own design. He maintained his interest in marine applications and in 1897 set up Parsons Marine Steam Turbine Company in Wallsend.

In 1897 Parson's marine company built the Turbinia, the first vessel to be propelled by turbines. There was a somewhat lukewarm reception of this phenomenon until Parsons gatecrashed the 1897 naval Spithead Review, held to celebrate Queen Victoria's sixty years on the throne. The tiny Turbinia achieved speeds of over 34 knots and outpaced chasing vessels. This unorthodox approach succeeded, with the recognition by the naval authorities of the value of this new method of propulsion. Today, the Turbinia sits proudly on display in the Discovery Museum in Newcastle.

C. A. Parsons and Company became extremely successful. Amongst other outputs the company built turbine generators for power stations all over the world and for many years was a major employer in Newcastle. In 1968 it merged with the Hebburn-based switchgear makers A Reyrolle to become Reyrolle Parsons and in a further merger in 1977 the latter company joined with crane makers Clarke Chapman to form Northern Engineering Industries (NEI). Rolls Royce took over the company in 1989 and in 1997 sold the business to the German conglomerate Siemens. Hence, the once-proud Parsons name has been lost. Employment on the Heaton site is now counted in hundreds rather than the thousands of the 1960s.

splendid façade of the former Jewish Synagogue (1880-1978) with the Star of David carved into the brickwork above the upper windows. In 1984 the site was converted into a shopping arcade, the Leazes Arcade, as named above the doorway. However, the interior was gutted by fire in 1990 and the building was subsequently restored. It is now occupied by the Comedy Club, Madison's Bar and a number of flats.

At the crossroads, turn left and walk along the road (Strawberry Place) passing the Strawberry Pub, favourite haunt of football fans. An information panel just round the corner on the side of the building explains the derivation of the name **(Qu 1)**.

As you proceed ahead, you pass the site of St James' Hall, an important boxing

Former Leazes Synagogue

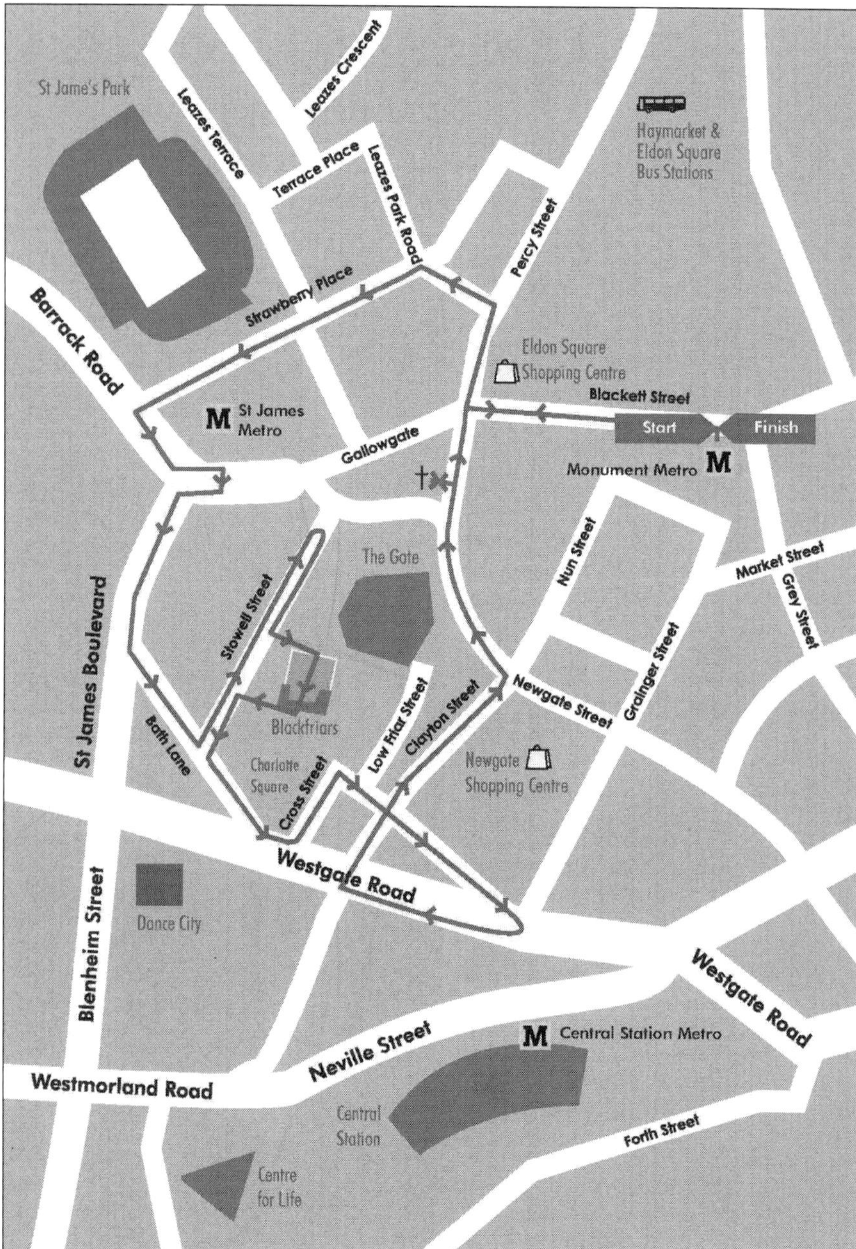
St James's Park
Leazes Terrace
Leazes Crescent
Terrace Place
Leazes Park Road
Haymarket & Eldon Square Bus Stations
Percy Street
Barrack Road
Strawberry Place
Eldon Square Shopping Centre
Blackett Street
St James Metro
Gallowgate
Start
Finish
Monument Metro
Nun Street
Market Street
Grey Street
The Gate
Stowell Street
St James Boulevard
Grainger Street
Blackfriars
Low Friar Street
Clayton Street
Newgate Street
Bath Lane
Charlotte Square
Cross Street
Newgate Shopping Centre
Westgate Road
Blenheim Street
Dance City
Westgate Road
Neville Street
Central Station Metro
Westmorland Road
Central Station
Forth Street
Centre for Life

Old Eldon Square

This is a little green oasis in the city centre. Sadly, the terrace of the fine, former houses on the east side is all that remains of Grainger and Dobson's original Eldon Square (1826), whose north and west terraces were demolished when the Eldon Square shopping centre was built in the 1970s.The splendid First World War Memorial (C. L. Hartwell, 1923) of St George and the Dragon provides an appropriate setting for the City's annual Remembrance Day ceremony. The benches near the Memorial are dedicated to members of various services who gave their lives in conflict. The four stone-plinths that surround the Memorial each carry plaques detailing aspects of the history of Eldon Square itself.

and wrestling venue, demolished in the late 1970s to make way for the St James Metro Station. It was also used for public meetings and Winston Churchill gave an election address there in 1951.

You need to cross to the other side of the road and continue alongside the back of the Gallowgate end of **St James' Park** with the Official Club Store and Shearer's Sports Bar and Lounge built into its base. You will also see the entrance to the Learning Centre, attendance at which provides inspiration to local school pupils. Near here a stadium map will help you get your bearings. You can follow the St James Walkway at least as far as the Players and Official Entrance. Here you can look at the numerous heritage stones with their varied dedications.

From the football stadium (from near the stadium map), cross to the other side of Strawberry Place at the traffic lights. Turn right. Pause here.

Over the road, the tall Sandman Signature Hotel and Newcastle University Business School buildings are on the site of the former Newcastle Breweries complex. Much of the remainder of the former brewery site is being developed as Newcastle Science Central (six English cities were designated by the government as Science Cities in December 2004). An early project here (which commenced in February 2011) by Newcastle and Durham Universities' scientists was to drill a 2000 metre borehole to bring up hot water to supply future energy needs for the site. The team reached hot water in June 2011. In doing so they passed through some of the coal seams which were exploited in previous centuries when coal mining was such an important part of the area's economy.

Follow the pavement as it bears left. After a few metres take the ramp on your left and walk to the concourse of St James Metro Station where you will find posters of individual Newcastle United stars, the late **Sir Bobby Robson** and the original team of 1892 (when moustaches seemed to be very fashionable). From the entrance to the Metro Station bear slightly right and walk towards the yellow Metro sign ahead. After a few metres turn left at an access road, then turn right to walk through the Sir Bobby Robson Memorial Garden. The Garden has five sculpted stones (Graeme Mitcheson, 2011) representing periods in Sir Bobby's life. You arrive at a main road.

Now turn right and walk to the traffic lights ahead. Cross the road and proceed along the dual carriageway (St James Boulevard).

On your left is Citygate (Ryder, 2004). At the crossroads notice, over the road, stands the statue by Susanna Robinson (1991) of J. E. T. (Jackie) Milburn (1924 - 1988). 'Wor Jackie' played for Newcastle from 1943 - 1957 mostly as a prolific goal-scoring centre forward and represented England thirteen times. His initials seemed by many to aptly reflect his speed on the pitch! (It is planned to move the statue to outside St James' Park.)

St James' Park

Football appears to have been played here since at least 1880 although the present club did not come into existence until Newcastle East End and Newcastle West End merged as Newcastle United in 1892. The origin of the name is probably due to the prior existence of neighbouring St James Street (1830s) which, in turn, may owe its origin to the former St James Hospital at Barras Bridge.

Spectators is a result of various redevelopment schemes the most recent of which was completed in 2000. However, the record attendance was, in the pre all-seater stadium era in 1930, when 65,386 fans packed the ground to see former local hero Hughie Gallagher return to play for Chelsea.

Several planning applications from the club met with Council opposition, joined at times with objections from local residents and environmentalists to any suggestion of further encroach-ment into the Leazes area. Threats were even made to relocate the ground to other sites. However, common sense prevailed and St James' Park is now a splendid stadium within a convenient city environment. Nevertheless, the club seems to remain in the news, as much for events off the pitch as on it, as recent plans to rename the stadium have illustrated.

For Stadium tours and match tickets: Tel 08443721892

NUFC at home

Sir Bobby Robson (1933 – 2009)

He was born and brought up in County Durham and started his working life as an apprentice electrician at a local colliery. However, he continued to play football for local teams and, aged 17, he became a player for Fulham. His many accomplishments as a professional footballer include twenty appearances in the England team. Subsequently he embarked on a career in football management with successful spells as manager of English and Continental teams as well as being chief coach for England from 1982 to 1990. His final position as a club manager was with Newcastle United from 1999 to 2004.

He was a much respected player and manager who, from 1990, struggled stoically with recurring bouts of cancer. In March 2008 he founded the Sir Bobby Robson Foundation which plays an important role in medical developments in cancer at Newcastle's Freeman Hospital. As a result of the lead given by Sir Bobby, as well as the affection in which he was held by his many admirers, some £1.6 million had been raised at the time of his death and by July 2011 the total was £3.5million.

Follow the pavement as it bears left and proceed ahead along Bath Lane, so named because of the Public Medical Baths, Newcastle's first, which were established near here as a private venture in 1781. Unfortunately, the water supply dried up and they were demolished in the middle of the 19th century.

Cross the service road and on the left you will see the three-storey House of Recovery which was built in 1804 as a fever hospital, away from the then centre of population

It closed in 1888 when the City Hospital for Infectious Diseases (referred to locally as Walkergate Hospital) was opened. During World War II the basement of the former fever hospital was used as an air raid shelter **(Qu 2)**.

One-time House of Recovery

Revd. Dr. John Hunter Rutherford (1826-1890)

He was born in Jedburgh and educated at Jedburgh Grammar School and St Andrew's University. He joined the staff of his old school but, having decided to become an evangelical minister, studied theology at Glasgow University. After gaining further experience in tutoring and preaching he agreed to conduct services of a church in Kelso where, 'so successful was he that the congregation increased from twelve to sixty in a few weeks' (Maw, 1964). As a result he became Minister of that church in 1845 at the age of nineteen. This was just one indication of the drive and charisma which served him well in his later work in Newcastle.

He was associated with Newcastle from 1849. From 1860, as Minister of the Bath Lane Congregational Church, he regularly reached to congregations of more than 1,200 people all wishing to hear his thoughtful, vigorous addresses.

Dr Rutherford was a keen advocate of temperance and developed interests in education and medicine although it was not until he was forty-one that he qualified as a doctor at the Medical College in Newcastle. He was a remarkable man who contributed much to the well-being of his fellow citizens but it is probably the promotion of education for which he is best remembered.

Bath Lane School opened in 1872 and soon branch schools were established. Eventually, education was provided at infant, elementary and secondary levels. In 1877, a separate School of Science and Arts was opened. A new building, originally planned in 1887 was opened in 1904 and named Rutherford College in honour of Dr Rutherford. From this beginning emerged Rutherford Technical College (later a co-founder of Newcastle Polytechnic and subsequently the University of Northumbria), Rutherford Grammar School for boys and Rutherford High School for girls, all fitting memorials to Dr Rutherford.

Also on your left was the site of Rutherford College, established in memory of **Revd. Dr J. H. Rutherford**. Look out for the foundation stone (it's in front of the trees just before the brick wall) laid by Joseph Cowen (see below), a close associate of Dr Rutherford
It's the sole survivor of the college building, which was demolished in the 1980s **(Qu 3)**.

Around here seemed to be a popular place for educational establishments. Apart from Dr Rutherford's schools, St Cuthbert's Grammar School, a Roman Catholic school founded in 1881, was located here from 1883 until 1922 when it moved to its present site on Benwell Hill.

On the right, the domed-roof building is the former Cooperative Wholesale Society printing works (1890), currently housing a restaurant with apartments above, by **Frank West Rich**.

A few metres ahead there is a path on the left with a nearby panel with information about Bath Lane. Bear left on the path and walk ahead, then bear left and proceed ahead with the high **Town Wall** on your right and the recently-excavated town ditch on your left.

Frank West Rich (1840-1929)

He was born in Yorkshire and moved to Newcastle where he opened an architectural practice in 1872. He was employed as a consulting architect to Lord Armstrong and later carried out a number of commissions for Lord Armstrong's associates. In 1897 he became President of the Northern Architectural Association.

His elaborate style, particularly the domed roof, of the Cooperative Printing Works in Bath Lane, is also seen in the Turnbull Building (1898), formerly a printing works, near the Quayside and the 1893 Ouseburn School. In contrast his Bolbec Hall is much less exuberant. His other work includes the rebuilding of the interior of the Literary and Philosophical building in 1893/4 after a fire and in Jesmond a real tennis court which is still in use.

Both of his sons, Roland and Edmund, followed in their father's footsteps and became architects.

You pass the remains of three towers. The first immediately on your right, is the Heber Tower which, like several of the Town Wall towers, was later used by the members of Trade Guilds as meeting places; this tower being used by the Company of Armouriers, Curriers and Feltmakers. About half-way along is the **Morden Tower**, which for a time was used by the

Town Wall

When the town expanded beyond the immediate confines of the castle it became necessary to build a new defensive system to repel attempted incursions by Scottish raiders. This consisted of an inner lane, a wall and an outer ditch. To finance its construction, during the 13th and 14th centuries, a special murage tax was paid.

The completed wall was two miles long and included six major gates and a series of seventeen strong semi-circular towers interspersed by lookout turrets, posterns and watergates. It was between 7 and 10 feet wide and between 20 and 30 feet high. The ditch was about 15 feet deep and 36 feet wide.

The wall was maintained in good repair but after the 1745 rebellion it gradually fell into disuse, and parts were demolished to make way for new developments. Nevertheless, the sections of wall which still exist, some of which feature on this walk, give a good idea of the impressive defences possessed by Newcastle in medieval times.

Company of Plumbers, Glaziers, Pewterers and Painters. Since 1964 the Tower has been a centre for poetry reading and music. Local poet **Basil Bunting** was an early participant in the sessions.

Before proceeding to the end of this section of the Town Wall notice, on your left, an information panel which gives details of Gallowgate Lead Works which was located here for around 150 years until its closure in 1933 **(Qu 4)**.

Continue on the path to pass the remains of the Ever Tower, used in the 19th century by the Company of Paviors, Colliers and Carriagemen.

Exit onto St Andrew's Street at the colourful Chinese arch (Yonglai Zhang, 2005), indicating that you about to enter Newcastle's Chinatown **(Qu 5)**.

Apart from its Chinese symbols, including two lions at the base, the elaborate arch includes seven panels showing North East scenes **(Qu 6)**.

Turn right and then bear right to Rosie's Bar, named after Rosie O'Shea who

Multiculturism

Morden Tower and Basil Bunting (1900-1985)

Apart from its historic significance, the Morden Tower gained a new lease of life when Ron and Connie Pickard organised the first poetry reading there in 1964. Since then local and internationally-known poets have given readings of their works, which have been much appreciated by the audience in the intimate atmosphere provided in the Tower.

Basil Bunting, a modernist poet, was born of Quaker parents in Newcastle. He had a varied career and travelled in Europe and Persia. Throughout his life, poetry and music were abiding interests. His poetry became known in the 1920s and from that time he was a friend of, and influenced by, the American poet Ezra Pond.

Bunting returned to Newcastle and from 1952 was a journalist on the local Evening Chronicle. His poetry was largely forgotten until his rediscovery in the mid-1960s by the young local poet Ron Pickard. In 1965 Bunting gave the first public reading of his new epic poem *Briggflatts* in the Morden Tower. Subsequently his importance as a modernist poet has been increasingly recognised. Durham University's Basil Bunting Poetry Centre encourages study and research into Bunting's work. In 2009, an annual Basil Bunting Poetry Award was established by the Newcastle Centre for the Literary Arts of Newcastle University.

There is a memorial to Basil Bunting in Durham University Botanic Garden and he is buried in the Quaker graveyard at Briggflatts, Cumbria.

Blackfriars

In the13th century, various religious orders of friars were established throughout western Europe to assist in ministering to the growing populations as towns expanded. Newcastle was no exception to this process and, during the 13th century, four friaries came into being within the town and another was established in 1360. Although the friars took vows and wore the same sort of habits as monks, they did not live in monasteries cut off from the hustle and bustle of everyday life. Instead, they assisted the local parish priests in preaching and teaching and other social work. One of Newcastle's five friaries was established by the Dominican Order.

The Dominican Order was founded in France by St Dominic in 1216, as the Order of Preachers, later known simply as Dominicans or, because of the black cloak they wore over their white habit, as the Black Friars. They set up centres in England and established a friary, within a precinct of seven acres, in Newcastle in 1239. The five Newcastle friaries, together with the nunnery of St Bartholomew, were dissolved by Henry VIII in 1536. By then, it seems that numbers in the six religious houses had dwindled to sixty; the Dominican Black Friars, with a prior and twelve brethren, had most.

The friary church did not survive but the cloistered buildings were bought by the mayor and burgesses of Newcastle who, in 1552, leased them to nine of the town's craft guilds.

The guilds adapted the premises to suit their own requirements and remained in occupation for 250 years or so but most moved to other premises early in the 19th century.

There followed a period of neglect and consequent deterioration until the site was acquired by the City Council which instituted a restoration programme culminating in 1981.

Today, the restored buildings have a number of craft workshops, offices and a restaurant.

opened a tavern on this site in the late 19th century, and famous for its 'moving heads' in the back bar. Cross to the other side of Stowell Street, named after Lord Stowell, Lord Eldon's brother and, hence, brother-in-law of Bessie Surtees. She became famous when she eloped from her parents' house in Sandhill in 1772. Notice that, apart from restaurants and shops the Chinese theme is underlined in the street furniture and lighting. If you happen to be here for the Chinese New Year, you can witness the annual celebrations which always include a fearsome dragon and lots of firecrackers.

Walk ahead along Stowell Street. In a short distance, over the road, high above the entrance to a building, you will see an embossed sheaf of wheat, a sickle and a spade, beneath which is the motto 'Labor and wait'. This building was constructed at the beginning of the 20th century as a Cooperative Society warehouse. We are going to turn left, immediately before No 41 on the left-hand side, but before doing so look over the road where there is a small terrace of brick-built cottages, all that remains of the original Stowell Street built around 1824.

Blackfriars

Proceed through the alleyway to arrive at **Blackfriars** on your right and enter the grassed area. Lots of details are available on the information panels. After exploring this delightful little place exit through the archway near the Blackfriars Restaurant that claims to have 'The oldest dining room in the UK', and turn right.

Walk to Stowell Street and turn left. Over the road on the right you have another view of the Heber Tower. Carry on for a few metres and turn left to walk alongside another section of the Town Wall, with the wall on your left. At the junction with Westgate Road you come to the stainless steel *Ever changing* (Eilis O'Connell, 2005) which is designed so that the location's continual changes are reflected in the sculpture's surface. Opposite is the Tyne Theatre. Turn left, then take the next left and walk along Cross Street. At the junction turn left into Charlotte Square, built in the 1770s in the Black Friars precinct, and 'Newcastle's only C18 square in the London style' (McCombie, 2009). A plaque on No1 informs us that this was the home of the architect **William Newton**.

Retrace your steps to Cross Street then carry straight on down Fenkle Street crossing Low Friar Street. Notice the elegant curved corners on these 18th-century properties. Cross Clayton Street and continue along Fenkle Street to reach, on your left, The Assembly Rooms, sometimes called **The Old Assembly Rooms**, often affectionately referred to as 'The Old Ass'.

On the right, you will see the white stone-clad Cross House (1911), designed by Cackett and Burns Dick who used the then innovative reinforced concrete system. There was a disastrous fire in the building on 23rd

William Newton (1730-1798)

He was said to be the most successful Newcastle architect of his time and worked mainly in Newcastle and the North East. His notable buildings in Newcastle include his 1764 design of St Ann's Church, constructed using stone from a recently demolished section of the Town Wall as well as Charlotte Square (1776) and The Assembly Rooms (1774), both seen on this walk. With fellow architect David Stephenson he worked in the 1780s on interior renovation of St Nicholas' Church (later Newcastle Anglican Cathedral) and in the 1790s on alterations to the Guildhall.

In addition to his work in Newcastle he designed several country houses including Backworth Hall (1780), now Backworth Miners' Welfare Hall, and Howick Hall (1782), which remains the residence of the Grey family.

William Newton married Dorothy Bell with whom he had twelve children. He is buried in St Andrew's churchyard in Newcastle.

Cross House

The Old Assembly Rooms

In 1776, at a time when Newcastle's educational and cultural activities were being developed, a group of 129 local notables financed the construction of The Assembly Rooms. Hence, Newcastle had a prestigious building for recreation and the entertainment of important visitors. Designed by William Newton it was located in what was then one of the most pleasant parts of the town.

From its opening it was visited by many of the great and the good and hosted many entertainments and events, ranging from a concert by Johann Strauss in 1838 to a dinner in 1910 to celebrate winning the English Championship by Newcastle United Football Club (who haven't had many opportunities for such celebrations in recent years!).

Following its requisition by the military during the First World War, and subsequent refurbishment, it was acquired by a new company. From the 1920s through to the 1950s it was a popular venue for functions such as dances and dinner dances. However, as fashions for entertainment changed, its use declined and its owner went into liquidation in 1967. There followed a period of neglect and deterioration, including pigeons flying in through the vandalised roof and nesting in its magnificent chandeliers.

Happily, in 1974, it was bought and splendidly restored by members of the Michaelides family. Today it is once again a prestigious venue run by them in accordance with their stated aim to give 'meticulous attention to the maintenance of the building'.

December 1919 caused when stocks of celluloid film ignited. Many people were rescued but sadly there were eleven deaths. Sixteen of the rescuers received bravery awards. One good thing to come out of the incident was the passing of an Act of Parliament to control the use and storage of such film material.

Below the gable-end of this triangular building there is a statue of **Joseph Cowen**.

Carry on towards the traffic lights. On your left you pass Gibb Chambers, named after Dr Gibbs of *Blaydon Races* fame. A plaque indicates that he lived here for a number of years **(Qu 7)**.

Lord Taylor of Gosforth (1930-1997)

Peter Taylor was born in Newcastle and attended the Royal Grammar School there. He was one of those people who could have succeeded in a number of fields, including music; he remained a highly proficient pianist throughout his life. After Cambridge he became a barrister. During his career at the Bar he was involved in a number of high profile cases including the prosecution of the Leader of the Liberal Party, Jeremy Thorpe, and the subsequently disgraced architect John Poulson.

As a judge he became very well-known to the public with the publication of his report into the Hillsborough disaster in 1989; its recommendations included having mandatory all-seater football stadiums.

He was made a life peer as Lord Taylor of Gosforth following his appointment as Lord Chief Justice of England in 1992. During his period as Lord Chief Justice he did not avoid political controversy. His early death was a sad loss for the justice system of the country.

Joseph Cowen (1831-1900)

Joseph Cowen was born and died at Stella Hall, Blaydon. His father, Sir Joseph Cowen, was the Liberal Member of Parliament for Newcastle from 1865 to 1874 and was knighted in 1871 for his efforts in making the River Tyne an important navigable river, with a consequent impact on Newcastle's industrial growth. Sir Joseph's wealth derived partly from a brick business in Blaydon.

Thus the young Joseph came from a fairly privileged background. However, he soon developed radical ideas and, while furthering his education at Edinburgh University, became interested in European revolutionary movements. This continued when he joined his father's brick works, where, it is said, he smuggled seditious documents abroad in consignments of bricks. His friends included European radicals such as Louis Blanc, Guiseppe Garibaldi, Lajos Kossuth and Guiseppe Mazzini.

In 1874, he succeeded his father as Member of Parliament for Newcastle and served until 1885. In his dress, speech and manner he identified himself with North East miners and supported many local causes. He was not one to toe the party line and could be vitriolic when opposing a motion. However, both locally and at Westminster he became a respected and well-known public figure.

Although re-elected in 1885, he soon retired from public life owing to his utter disenchantment with local party political intrigues. He had already resigned as an alderman and took no further part in municipal or national politics, instead devoting himself to his newspaper, the Newcastle Daily Chronicle and his mining and brick-making businesses.

At the traffic lights, turn right to cross the road then turn right and walk back up Westgate Road. On your left, a plaque on No 51 informs us that this was the former chambers of the Lord Chief Justice, **Lord Taylor of Gosforth**.

A little further on you will see Newcastle's original Assembly Rooms where a plaque gives details about Charles Avison, the Newcastle composer **(Qu 8)**.

Shortly you come to **Newcastle Arts Centre** occupying 67-75 Westgate Road. The 18th-century No 67 was the town house of Sir Matthew White Ridley of Blagdon Hall, Stannington.

Newcastle Arts Centre

From beginnings in the late 1960s and 1970s, two photographers, Mike Tilley and Norma Pickard, developed multi-media arts projects, moving eventually from a base in Whitley Bay to Newcastle. In 1981 they formed Newcastle Arts Centre Limited. A group of listed but derelict 18th, 19th and 20th century properties in Westgate Road was acquired in September 1981 which, with financial support from a number of government agencies, was extensively restored and adapted to accommodate a multiplicity of arts activities. The Arts Centre won a RIBA/Times Community Award and was formally opened by Prince Charles in 1988. A substantial upgrade followed and the Centre reopened in January 2000.

The centre's attractions include an art gallery, which presents new exhibitions featuring both historic and contemporary work with a regional connection, arts and music studios and the region's leading arts materials store. It has a café and a cellar bar as well as providing space for conferences and workshops.

A few metres past the Centre's main entrance there is a Heritage Plaque which gives details of the discovery that a Hadrian's Wall milecastle was located here **(Qu 9)**.

Turn immediately left into Black Swan Court, a fascinating little area, which is part of the Arts Centre. Musical and other events are held here. Outside the pottery, you will find further information about the excavations during which traces of the milecastle were discovered. A huge metal sculpture *The Iron Man* dominates the left-hand corner. This was used in a production of *The Iron Man: A Children's Story in Five Nights* by Ted Hughes (1968) at a local theatre but lack of space there led to it being housed in the courtyard.

Leave the courtyard and turn left to continue along Westgate Road. You pass Isaac Walton, tailors; one of Newcastle's better known trade names since 1887. Now downsized from its heyday in large premises in Grainger Street, it remains as a tailor specialising in gentlemen's made to measure wear.

At the crossroads turn right into Clayton Street. The corner site occupied by the 02academy, a rock and pop music venue, has been the location for entertainment ventures since the opening of The Picture House, one of Newcastle's earliest cinemas, in 1912. It was rebuilt in 1927 and carried on as a cinema, under various names until, as the Gaumont, it closed in 1958. In 1959 the building became the Majestic Ballroom but, unable to complete with the new Mayfair Ballroom (see below), restarted life as the Gala Bingo club.

Walk a few paces, and cross Fenkle Street. The property occupied by Clayton News was once well-known as the chemist's shop called **Dirty Dick's**.

Proceed along Clayton Street named after John Clayton, Town Clerk, who helped to raise the finance to build Clayton Street in 1837 as part of Richard Grainger's ambitious plans for the redevelopment of this area. The upper floors of these 19th-century properties help to remind us of their original appearance, but, sadly, several of them present an uncared for picture. When convenient, cross to the other side of the road. At the crossroads proceed ahead then turn left into Newgate Street and walk ahead.

Here, in complete contrast with 19th-century Clayton Street, you see bold, aggressive modern developments: Debenhams store and an extension to the Eldon Square shopping complex on the right and, on your left, Sam Jacks and then the glass-fronted The Gate, a leisure and entertainment complex of bars, restaurants, shops, a casino and the 12-screen Empire Cinema, which, apart from the Tyneside Cinema, is the only public cinema in the city centre. The Gate occupies the site of the former Mayfair Ballroom. The tall, steel and glass sculpture *Ellipsis Eclipses* (Danny Lane, 2005) underlines the in-your-face modernity of this spot. Opposite The Gate you will see on the pavement two plaques referring to the White Cross and Newgate Street. Another contrast comes with the art deco building on the left-hand side, the **Newcastle Cooperative Society department store**.

Dirty Dick's

In 1867 James Crozier (1813-1888) a qualified chemist, having travelled the world, opened a chemist's shop in Clayton Street. Following a burglary he installed window shutters which he never opened. This, together with his neglect of his own appearance, he wore the same suit day and night, led to the nickname 'Dirty Dick's'.

Apart from selling various remedies, he gave personal consultations. His consultation fees and prices for medicines varied according to the customer's ability to pay; in genuine cases of hardship he made no charge. Hence, in spite of the epithet he became extremely popular and was very successful as a pharmacist and herbalist.

St Andrew's Church

Your first impression of the church might well agree with the description in St Andrew's guidebook of it as 'a friendly old stone building with a stubby tower, set amongst trees and grave stones in the bustling heart of Newcastle City'. It is said to be the oldest church in Newcastle and is one of the four ancient parish churches within the Town Wall. It is possible that a Saxon church occupied this site. However, although the present building was begun in the late 12th century what you see now is some 13th and 14th century work with later additions.

The tower was damaged in the Civil War and was further weakened from the ringing of a heavier set of 18th-century bells which, consequently, could not be rung. These were recast and re-hung in 1966 and now chime with clappers moved electronically rather than by ropes and bell ringers.

Today, St Andrew's remains a parish church, with traditional services and a missionary outreach to the City. It is also the headquarters of the City Centre Chaplaincy as well as providing a place of worship for the Greek Orthodox community and a base for the Northumbria Deaf Mission.

Among the interesting features inside, there are several plainly-glazed windows in the Northumbrian style by the notable designer Leonard Evetts. In the left-hand side of the chancel (formerly the outside wall) there is a hagioscope, or squint, which provided an angled view of the altar for those excluded, such as lepers. The window in the Lady Chapel shows a child signing the *Lord's Prayer* in deaf language. Two moving examples of means of communicating with disadvantaged people.

Leonard Evetts (1909-1997)

Leonard Evetts was described in his obituary in The Times in October 1997 as 'the most prolific stained-glass artist of this century'. He was born in Newport, Monmouthshire. His father was a respected local builder who passed on to the young Leonard, his interest in sign writing, painting and a love of architecture. He won one of only four National Scholarships to attend the RCA from 1930 to 1933. Here he studied calligraphy under the famous Edward Johnston and stained glass under the influential stained glass artist Martin Travers. He joined the Department of Fine Art at Kings College, Newcastle, as a lecturer in design. Apart from war-time service, he remained there, ultimately becoming Head of Department, until he retired in 1974. From the 1940s he undertook stained glass and other commissions and carried on with these after his retirement.

Although mostly known for his magnificent stained glass windows, Evetts produced a wide range of artistic output. In a 'Catalogue of Works' in *Leonard Evetts Master Designer* (published privately 2001) his work is categorised as: I Ecclesiastical Stained Glass; II Lettering; III Heraldry; IV Miscellaneous, which includes much ecclesiastical work. In addition he was a talented and much-respected water colourist.

Evetts completed some three hundred church windows throughout Britain and abroad, including over one hundred in Northumberland and Durham. There is an Evetts window in St Nicholas Cathedral. The outstanding contribution of his artistic work for the Church of England was recognised in 1995 when he was awarded a Lambeth Doctorate by the Archbishop of Canterbury.

Newcastle Cooperative Society department store

Designed by L.G. Elkins, the Cooperative Wholesale Society in-house architect, the building was completed in 1932. Apart from its external appearance, there are interesting art deco and other components inside the building. After 75 years as a department store this iconic building closed, except for the ground-floor food section, in 2007. Discussions are taking place with a view to the redevelopment of the former store possibly retaining shops on the ground floor and converting the remainder to a hotel. The Grade II listing, conferred in 1987, should result in the retention of its art deco features.

Sadly this was not the case with another building from the same era, the 1931 Odeon Cinema (originally the Paramount) in Pilgrim Street, which was controversially delisted in 2001. Although the façade might be saved, the glories of its 1930s' opulent interior have been lost.

Cross to the other side via a pedestrian crossing, turn right and cross St Andrew's Street, its interesting alterative name 'Darn Crook' is said to derive from the 'dark crooked lane', which it used to be, to arrive at **St Andrew's Church**. Go into the first entrance where an information board gives details of some famous people, including Charles Avison, buried here (the church and grounds are open between 9.00am and 3.00pm). Before going inside the church, it's worth walking to the end of the path where you can see a well-preserved remnant of the Town Wall. Inside, among many things of interest, are windows by **Leonard Evetts (Qu 10)**.

Leave the church grounds and turn left. Walk to the crossroads. Before turning right to complete the walk, you can see on the other side of the road, to your left, the former General Electric Company (G.E.C.) building (1936) with cast iron motifs showing men at work. Now turn right and proceed back to Grey's Monument and the end of the walk.

Quiz questions

1. **How did Strawberry Place get its name?**
2. **How can you confirm that the fever hospital was built away from the then centre of population?**
3. **On what date was the foundation stone of Rutherford College laid?**
4. **Why are mill stones placed by an information board near the Town Wall ditch?**
5. **Who, apart from Chinese people, have a meeting place near the Chinese arch?**
6. **On what is the right-hand lion's paw resting?**
7. **For how many years did Dr Gibbs live in his house on Westgate Road?**
8. **Why is Charles Avison commemorated by a plaque on the original Assembly Rooms building?**
9. **In what year were traces of a Hadrian's Wall milecastle discovered in Newcastle Arts Centre?**
10. **How many sections of Newcastle's Town Wall have you seen on this walk?**

8. West to Westgate

Start/finish: **Central Station**
Distance: **2 miles**
Route: **Central Station, Centre for Life, Discovery Museum, Summerhill Grove, Westgate Road, Tyne Theatre, St Mary's Cathedral, Central Station**
Accessibility: **On pavements with ramped access to buildings**
Refreshments: **Central Station, Centre for Life, Discovery Museum, St Mary's Cathedral**

We begin this walk on the concourse of Newcastle's only railway station, the **Central Station**. Before you leave the main concourse via one of the three archways of the entrance lobby, notice the commemorative plaques **(Qu 1)**.

Turn left in the portico to leave the station and proceed ahead with the elegant line of lamps on your left. On the right you will see the statue of the noted religious leader Basil

Central Station

Designed by John Dobson, the Central Station was opened by Queen Victoria, accompanied by Prince Albert, in August 1850. Dobson's design, especially with the introduction of the wrought iron and glass arched roof, was much acclaimed and subsequently copied. The three glass canopies allow natural light to illuminate the three parallel bays of track below. Dobson was also responsible for the adjacent Station Hotel of 1850 which became the Royal Station Hotel when Her Majesty and the Prince Consort returned to open it 1858. However, financial constraints prevented him from building the station's portico and the seven-arched bay frontage was added by Thomas Prosser in 1862-63.

Above the main concourse exit are medallions of the Queen and Prince Albert with the date 28 September 1849 which is rather curious as it appears they attended in 1850 at the official opening! There is also a medallion of King Edward VII who visited the station in 1906 when he came to open the nearby railway bridge which bears his name. Among several later additions and modifications was the addition in 1893 of a waiting lounge for first class passengers. Closed as such in the 1960s, it was used among other things as British Transport Police cells until it was carefully restored to its former elegance in 2000 when it reopened as the Centurion Bar. Refreshments for all tastes can be enjoyed in the beautifully tiled interior-bar and the adjoining glass conservatory Café and Deli. The underground Central Station for the Tyne and Wear Metro was opened in 1981.

Gracious curves of the Central Station

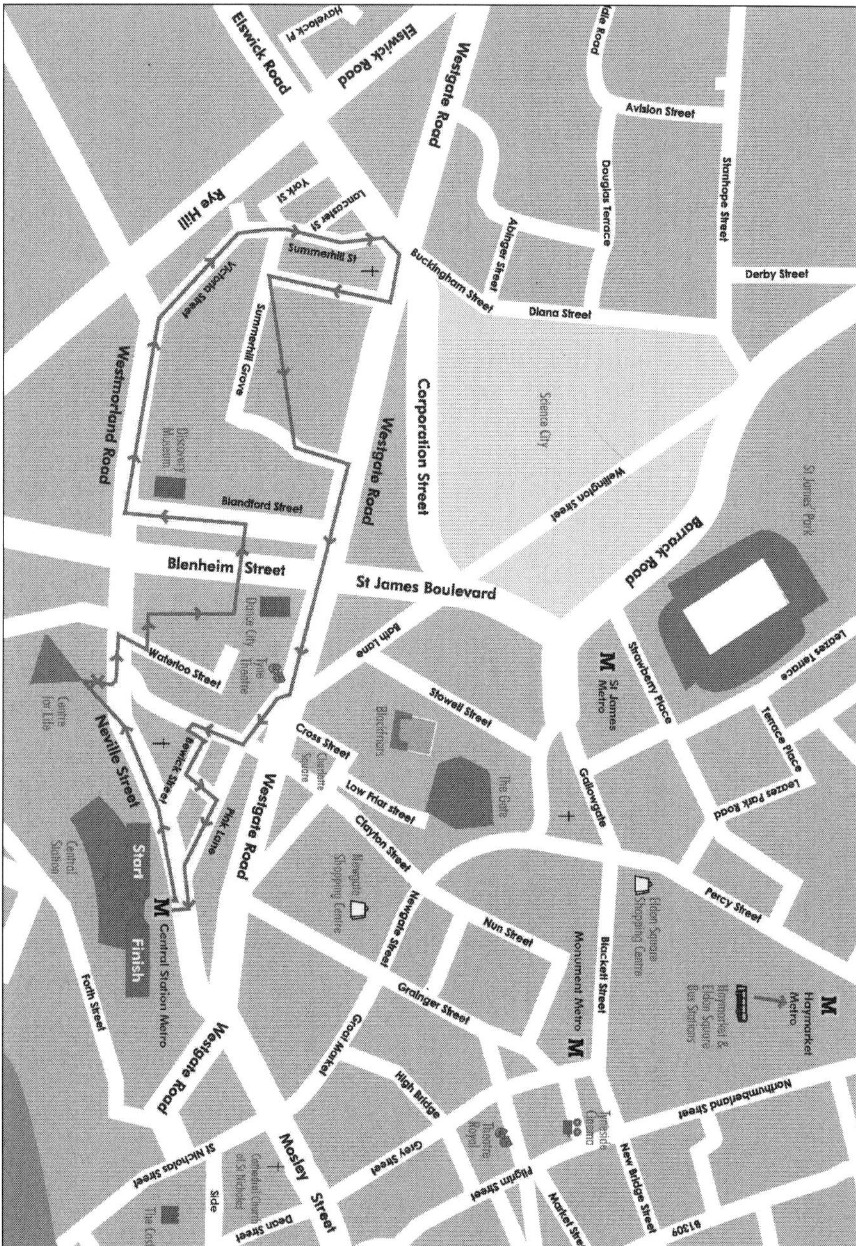
Havelock Pl
Elswick Road
Elswick Road
Westgate Road
Avison Street
Douglas Terrace
Stanhope Street
Derby Street
Rye Hill
York St
Lancaster St
Summerhill St
Victoria Street
Summerhill Grove
Abinger Street
Buckingham Street
Diana Street
Westmorland Road
Discovery Museum
Blandford Street
Westgate Road
Corporation Street
Science City
Wellington Street
Barrack Road
St James' Park
Blenheim Street
St James Boulevard
Dance City
Bath Lane
Waterloo Street
Tyne Theatre
Centre for Life
Stowell Street
St James Metro
Strawberry Place
Leazes Terrace
Terrace Place
Leazes Park Road
Blackfriars
Cross Street
Charlotte Square
Bewick Street
Neville Street
Low Friar Street
The Gate
Gallowgate
Pink Lane
Westgate Road
Clayton Street
Newgate Shopping Centre
Central Station
Start
Finish
M
Central Station Metro
Newgate Street
Nun Street
Monument Metro
M
Blackett Street
Eldon Square Shopping Centre
Percy Street
M
Haymarket Metro
Haymarket & Eldon Square Bus Stations
Forth Street
Westgate Road
Grainger Street
Groat Market
High Bridge
Tyneside Cinema
Northumberland Street
Theatre Royal
Grey Street
St Nicholas Street
Mosley Street
Cathedral Church of St Nicholas
Side
Dean Street
The Castle
Pilgrim Street
Market Street
New Bridge Street
B1309

Centre for Life

The whole complex stands in an area that has had many previous uses including an important medical connection in the shape of the original Newcastle Infirmary. This was opened here at Forth Banks in 1753 where it remained until its replacement by the Royal Victoria Infirmary in 1906 on a site obtained from the Freemen and the Town Corporation at Castle Leazes.

A cattle market was held here from 1830 which explains the existence in Time Square of the Cattle Market Office and Toll House designed by John Dobson in 1831 and now commercial offices. The Marlborough Crescent Bus Station was also in this area from the late 1920s to the early 1980s.

One of the country's fourteen landmark Millennium projects, this dramatic-looking building which opened in 2000 was designed by the locally-educated and internationally-renowned architect Sir Terry Farrell. It has facilitated the establishment of a science village bringing together various organisations and people involved in life sciences. Over five hundred people from some thirty different countries are employed in partner organisations such as the Institute of Human Genetics, the Life Bioscience Centre, the North East England Stem Cell Institute and the Newcastle Fertility Clinic. With state-of-the-art research facilities the Centre has gained a world-wide reputation for its work into stem cell technology. It also contains conference, exhibition and banqueting suites and its schools programme plays an important role in promoting scientific education. The Life Science Centre referred to above is the major public attraction within the complex with both permanent and temporary attractions and exhibitions. In May to October 2010 its Doctor Who Exhibition attracted a record number of visitors.

For further information see: www.life.org.uk or Tel: (0191) 2438223

Hume in front of the east walls of St Mary's Catholic Cathedral (these two landmarks are visited later on the walk). Continue ahead to the blue walls of the **Centre for Life**, which are proudly inscribed *Life A Centre for World - Class Science.*

Enter the large open space, Newcastle's own Times Square! Here on your left you will find a pub and a couple of night clubs. Continue ahead to pass the steel art work *Double Helix* (Charles Jencks, 2000). To the right is the Cattle Market Office and Toll House. In the winter an outdoor skating rink adds to the attractions. Ahead you arrive at the Life Science Centre. There is an admission charge if you wish to enjoy the exhibitions, demonstrations, interactive displays and games as well as a planetarium and a popular motion ride. Happily, entry to the adjacent café and shop is free **(Qu 2)**.

Cattle Market Office and Life Science Centre

Now retrace your steps back to the

entrance to Time Square and use the traffic lights to cross the road (Westmorland Road) straight ahead. Turn left, walk a short distance and then turn right at the first road (Waterloo Street). Continue ahead for about 50 metres and on the right you will see a memorial fountain bequeathed by Rachel Burns in memory of Richard and Rachel Grainger. It may seem a pity that a monument associated with a figure of such importance as Grainger is sited here. However, we need to bear in mind that this tribute was located only a short distance from the family house, which we shall pass near the end of this walk **(Qu 3)**.

With the fountain behind you, cross with care to the other side of the road and walk up the paved access into the two-level Waterloo Square. Turn right and use the steps or ramped pathway to climb gently into the upper square. Both the upper and lower parts of the square are surrounded by several new and revitalised buildings. On your left is the Barn Asia restaurant and on your right, Centralofts. Continuing ahead via the steps (or the ramp on the right) you soon reach Dance City, opened in 2005 with facilities for dance performances, classes and workshops at all levels for all abilities. It includes the Urban Café.

Discovery Museum

The building itself, known as Blandford House, was opened in 1899 as the headquarters, warehouse and distribution centre for the Co-operative Wholesale Society. As such it served more than one hundred local Co-ops until it was finally supplanted by direct delivery services in the 1970s. If you go to the sixth floor you can admire the splendid Great Hall used by the Society for dances and events. There is also a plaque honouring those employees who lost their lives in the First World War.

The Museum of Science and Industry, located in the Exhibition Park since 1934, was transferred to Blandford House in 1978 as the Museum of Science and Engineering. The artefacts held in the Joicey Museum (previously bequeathed by John George Joicey of the colliery owning family) were also moved here from the Holy Jesus Hospital building and the Museum was renamed Discovery Museum in 1993. A major refurbishment culminated in 2004.

Revolutionary vessel

Open seven days a week with free entry, this is a popular family venue. It provides a wonderful insight into numerous aspects of local life including sections such as 'Newcastle Story', 'Story of the Tyne' and 'Tyneside Challenge'. Shipbuilding, fashion and military life are well covered and there is a variety of interactive models to attract both young and old. July 2010 saw the installation of the BFI Mediatheque, described as 'a digital jukebox of film and television programmes' providing free access on a wide range of topics.

There is a programme of regularly-changing exhibitions, a café and a shop and flat access into the museum and lifts to all floors. The Tyne and Wear Archive Service, of interest to family-history enthusiasts, is also housed within the building.

For further details see: www.twmuseums.org.uk/discovery or Tel: (0191) 2326789

Turn left to the main road (St James Boulevard), turn left and use the traffic lights to cross the busy dual carriageway. Continue ahead up the slip road, turn left and after a few metres turn right to the blue arched entrance to the **Discovery Museum (Qu 4)**.

After visiting the museum, turn right and walk to the main road (Westmorland Road) and turn right again. The road rises quite steeply. Over to the left you will see some of the buildings on the main campus of Newcastle College, a significant higher and further education establishment. You arrive at The Villa Vic pub where you bear right into Victoria Street with older properties on the right and modern dwellings on the left. You are now in a conservation area with contrasting levels of property and garden upkeep. Ahead at the junction you will see a rather desolate-looking building designed by John Dobson, this was once the **Barber Surgeons' Hall.**

Bear right to pass the gates of St Anne's Court (formerly St Anne's Convent and School) on the right. The Sisters of Mercy moved here 1870. Their school closed in 1983 and the convent was converted into independent flats in 1993. A small community of nuns still lives in one of the adjacent properties. The work of the Order in Newcastle is acknowledged in one of the windows in St Mary's Cathedral (see below). At the junction (Summerhill Grove) turn left, walk a short distance and then turn right into Summerhill Street.

You soon reach the imposing Church of St Matthew which was commenced in 1877, had the tower added in 1895 and was completed in 1905. The adjacent church hall, contains a long- established clothes store which has been a useful asset to the community. The wife of a previous vicar was reputed to know the waist measurements of all the men in the parish! **(Qu 5)**.

The church stands in a commanding position, high both in stature and in liturgical practices. The noticeboard adds 'Big Lamp' to the name, a reference to the fact that this area apparently claimed to have one of the first electric street lamps in Newcastle. The building next to the church, once an undertakers, gained fame as the premises of The Big Lamp Brewery noted for its real ale (located now further up the Tyne at Newburn). A few metres ahead is the Big Lamp junction. To the left is the convergence of Westgate Road and Elswick

Barber Surgeons' Hall (1851-1857)

This unusual name was a throwback to the medical practitioners of medieval times who among other treatments used blood-letting, drawing teeth and cutting hair. Today red and white barbers' poles still symbolise blood and the white cloth used to clean it up. The two professions were formally separated in 1745! The barber-surgeons have remained as a constituent company of the Freemen of Newcastle since 1442. The Newcastle hall opened as a Medical College in1851 to replace a much older hall, probably that of the original barber-surgeons, near Manors, where medical education in Newcastle had first begun but which had to be demolished to make way for the advent of the railway.

Shortly after the opening of this second Barber Surgeons Hall in Newcastle, disagreement in the medical school led to a larger group establishing themselves in what is now Orchard Street, near the Central Station. However, the two rival teaching establishments merged in 1857 to form the basis for the current Newcastle University Faculty of Medical Sciences.

In the late 1880s the Hall was altered, as evidenced in the name on the stonework, to became St Paul's Church School until it was replaced by the modern building just visible to the left. Still visible on the upper section, the motif of the medical profession in the form of the serpent entwined around a staff, bears witness to better days for this building.

Road. Trees indicate the whereabouts of the now sadly neglected Westgate Hill Cemetery. This, the first non-parish and inter-denominational cemetery in Newcastle, opened in1829 and served until 1967. The impressive building, on the corner to the right, housing The Prudhoe Street Mission, is Westgate Hall.

Turn right to follow what was once the line of Hadrian's Wall and descend Westgate Road, or Westgate Hill as it is commonly called. As you look at the commercial outlets ahead, you will soon appreciate that this is an important area for motor bike enthusiasts. After about 200 metres turn right into Ravensworth Terrace. On the left, the houses of High Swinburne Place reveal some well-preserved Georgian features. The railway engineer Robert Stephenson lived further down this road from 1829 to 1833. On the right, the cobbled Ravensworth Terrace contains modern-looking office accommodation. Above the entrance door you will see the Star of David as this was once the Ravensworth Terrace Synagogue (1925-1969) which, in turn, had replaced three houses on the site.

You are now in Summerhill Square, a delightful oasis of largely early-19th century dwellings whose occupants included noted families such as the Pumphreys, famed for their coffee house in the Bigg Market. Proceed ahead along the narrow lane with the childrens' play area on the left occupying a corner of the parkland. On your right, hidden behind the wall, is the bowling green and pavilion of the former Summerhill Bowling Club. The club closed in 2011 after being in existence for nearly a hundred years and the land was acquired by the 'Friends of Summerhill' who hope to see it used for community activities. The wall itself is believed to have been at the bottom of the garden of the house that gave its name to this area, the owner having come from a tiny place called Summerhill near Dublin.

Stop just at the junction before you take the narrow tarmac path that leads diagonally across Summerhill Park. To the right is the St Anne's Convent building with its former chapel on the end corner. Ahead to your left, a plaque on No 7 (Summerhill Grove) indicates that **Dr William Rea** a prominent Victorian musician once resided here **(Qu 6)**.

Now take the diagonal path across the park from where you can appreciate the elegant housing that surrounds this pleasant space. Leave through the gateway, turn left, and on the right you pass No 1 Summerhill Terrace. A plaque indicates that Mo Mowlam, respected MP

Dr William Rea (1822-1903)

William Rea was born in London where he began his musical education as an organist and pianist. He subsequently broadened his horizons by spending several years in European cities with strong musical traditions such as Leipzig and Prague. In 1860 Newcastle Corporation recognised his talent when it decided to appoint him as the Council Organist in preference to local candidates in what proved to be an inspired choice. He was responsible for raising the profile of classical music and making it more accessible to ordinary people through weekly concerts in the Town Hall. It is interesting now to imagine the sound of Mozart, Strauss and Wagner echoing up the Bigg Market! He also inaugurated a very successful series of 'Promenade Concerts' with distinguished guest orchestras and soloists long before Henry Wood founded his Albert Hall Proms in 1895. He taught and lectured on music and Durham University conferred a musical doctorate on him in 1886. Although he still remains relatively unknown in Newcastle, at least this commemorative plaque serves to bring to our attention a man who in the words on his tombstone in Old Jesmond Cemetery, 'devoted more than 40 years to cultivate a love of good music amongst the people of this city' (Morgan, 2000).

for Redcar and Northern Ireland Secretary at the time of the Good Friday Peace Agreement, lived here at one time **(Qu 7)**.

Continue ahead a short distance to exit back onto Westgate Road. Turn right, proceed ahead and cross St James Boulevard. On the left is Nexus House, headquarters of the Tyne and Wear Transport Executive, responsible for the provision of Metro, bus and ferry services in the region. On the right, you will see the gable ends with the signs for The Robert Sinclair Tobacco Co Ltd, occupants of Blenheim House from 1919 to 1986. The cream and green building is a retirement home for the city's Chinese community while further to the right is Dance City which we met earlier on the walk.

Nexus House

Once over the busy boulevard, you pass the former Salvation Army Temple on your left and then the **Tyne Theatre** a little further down on your right.

Almost opposite the theatre is the bottom of Bath Lane where you will see a section of the Town Wall and the steel sculpture, *Ever-changing* (Eilis O'Connell, 2004). The building on the left-hand corner of Bath Lane was once the meeting hall of the Company of House Carpenters, a constituent group within the Freemen of Newcastle. It was built here in 1812 when the nearby West Gate of the town which housed its earlier premises was demolished (see below).

The street next to the theatre is named after Roger Thornton who is said to have arrived here in the 15th century in a penniless state, before becoming a wealthy merchant, Mayor, MP and generous benefactor to the town. Here, in metal strips in the paving, in the artwork, *Tyne Line of Text Flow* (Sommer, Downing and Herbert, 2005), you may be able to decipher a series of text-style messages relating to the region's history.

Tyne Theatre

A few metres further down Westgate Road, on your left is the entrance to Cross Street with the domed Imperial Building

Tyne Theatre

The Tyne Theatre and Opera House first opened in 1867 on land acquired by the Newcastle M.P. and newspaper proprietor Joseph Cowen. A problem arose initially because part of this area of land had been previously purchased by the town's Jewish Community for use as a cemetery. However, despite appeals by them, the building of the theatre was allowed to go ahead. Nevertheless, the very small section that had already been used for burials was retained. So today, completely enclosed behind the New Tyne Theatre and the adjacent Thornton Street, is a tiny Jewish Cemetery where five graves from the period 1835-1851 are still maintained and visited regularly by a Rabbi.

As the theatre prospered, so it expanded with the purchase of adjacent buildings including The Westgate Music Hall or Old Tyne Music Hall. It is said that at one time it could hold 3000 people! All the leading performers of the time are said to have appeared here. However, in 1917 with falling audiences it was leased to Sir Oswald Stoll who converted it into the Stoll Cinema. The name Stoll Picture Theatre still stands between the columns at first floor level. In 1929 it had the distinction of showing the first talking picture in Newcastle. It survived as a cinema for a further fifty-five years, eventually veering from religious themes such as *The Song of Bernadette* to X-rated films such as *World without Shame* to attract audiences, before it finally closed in 1974.

It was saved from extinction by the enthusiastic efforts of Jack Dixon and the Tyneside Operatic Society with the creation of a charitable trust to renovate the theatre and reopen it as the New Tyne Theatre Trust in 1977. Its new status was clearly acknowledged when the famous Spanish tenor, Placido Domingo accepted an invitation to make a guest appearance in a gala performance of *Tosca* in 1983. He is said to have been particularly impressed by the theatre's splendid acoustics and its unique Victorian understage machinery. Unfortunately a disastrous fire at Christmas 1985 caused a further massive setback. However, after another major renovation, the Trust reopened the theatre eleven months later.

The theatre's progress has long been threatened by financial insecurity but at last it seems to be on a firm setting. The City Council acquired the freehold lease in 2008 and then handed it over to the Tyne Theatre & Opera House Preservation Trust in 2008. To boost the Trust's efforts to preserve and restore the building, in 2010 locally-born international rock stars, Sting and Mark Knopfler accepted invitations to become honorary vice-presidents of the Trust. The theatre is managed by the SMG Europe, owners of the Metro Radio Arena. In January 2012, Mill Volvo replaced The Journal as naming sponsor of the theatre.

Audiences today enjoy a very wide range of performances that include musicals, top comedy and concert artists, tribute bands and the theatre's long established tradition of pantomime. It has even gone from X-films to X-factor auditions!

For further information see: www.millvolvotynetheatre.co.uk

(1895) on the corner. It was at this point that the substantial West Gate allowed entrance to the town through the Town Wall. Once these town gates ceased to have a defensive role they served other functions. West Gate housed a prison and it was also the headquarters of the House Carpenters Company (see above).

On your right, opposite Cross Street, take the narrow lane, Pink Lane, named after the Spynke or Pink Tower that once stood in the Town Wall. At the junction with Clayton Street, stop and look to your left where you will see a 'golden lady' clock identical to the one in Blackett Street because this was also once the site of a branch of Northern Goldsmiths.

St Mary's Roman Catholic Cathedral

Fr James Worswick, who has the distinction of having the street where he built St Andrew's Church named after him, was part of the group which in 1838 proposed the building of a larger church in Newcastle to meet the needs of the influx of Catholics largely from Ireland. The architect Augustus Pugin renown for his work on The Palace of Westminster was commissioned to design the new church. St Mary's was opened as a parish church in 1844 and elevated to the status of a cathedral following the creation of the Diocese of Hexham in 1850 (in 1861 renamed Hexham and Newcastle). James Worswick who did not live to see the project completed is buried in the Cathedral. The tower and spire were only added later in 1872 thanks to a legacy left by Elizabeth Dunn who is remembered in one of the windows (see below).The passage of time has seen many refurbishments and improvements some of which have been in accordance with changes in liturgical practices. In 1985 an annexe was added for meetings and this was redeveloped in 1998 to contain a café and bookshop. The covered link with the church provides a cloister-like enclosure for the interior patio behind which stands Cathedral House, the residence of the clergy. November 2009 to September 2010 saw the re-ordering of the chancel, re-tiling of the floor, the installation of new lighting, the reposition of the baptismal font and the enhancement of the Lady Chapel. A new pipe organ and choir gallery are expected to be operational by autumn 2012.

Unlike its sister-cathedral, St Nicholas, the Cathedral Church of St Mary does not contain memorial plaques and effigies of the great and the good of Newcastle. However, it does offer a number of interesting stained glass windows which include both modern and Victorian windows. To your right on entering, on the south side, is the Private Adam Wakenshaw V.C. Memorial Window. Adam Wakenshaw, of nearby Duke Street, educated at St Aloysius Secondary Modern School, was the only member of the armed forces from Tyneside to be awarded the Victoria Cross in World War II. This window was designed by Cate Watkinson (2004) whose work also features in Grey Street and Sandgate.

There then follows the Industrial Heritage Window celebrating local industrial skill by Joseph Nuttgens (2006).The great east window, the Jesse Window, portraying the genealogy of Christ, was designed by Pugin and made by the noted local manufacturer William Wailes who had premises in nearby Bath Lane. On the north side is the Mercy Window commemorating 150 years of dedicated work by the Sisters of Mercy in Newcastle. In the north-west corner is the Elizabeth Dunn Window, where you can see the lady kneeling in front of the Cathedral with tower and spire which her legacy provided.

For further information see: www.stmaryscathedral.org.uk

Cardinal Basil Hume (1923-1999)

Born in Newcastle in Ellison Place in 1923, the son of a Scottish cardiac physician and a French Catholic mother, Basil Hume was a pupil at Ampleforth College, North Yorkshire for five years before entering the Benedictine Monastery there in 1941. He was ordained priest in 1950, elected Abbot of Ampleforth and much to his surprise made Archbishop of Westminster in February 1976. Three months later as leader of the Roman Catholics in England and Wales, he was elevated to the rank of Cardinal by Pope Paul VI.

He proved himself to be an effective spiritual leader, a distinguished scholar and a skilled negotiator. Humble and approachable he preferred to wear the monk's habit rather than the cardinal's robes. He campaigned for social justice and as President of the charity 'Shelter' he encouraged support for the homeless. In 1986 he founded the Cardinal Hume Centre near Westminster Cathedral which continues to offer assistance to vulnerable and excluded people of all or no faiths, particularly the homeless young.

Basil Hume never forgot his roots in the north east and he found inspiration in its long Christian heritage which he reflected in his book *In the Footsteps of the Northern Saints*. Nigel Boonham's fine statue, appropriately shows his subject wearing a monk's habit, his cardinal's cap and a St Cuthbert's cross standing on a plinth in the shape of Holy Island and the Inner Farne amid boulders from the shoreline. Nor was Basil Hume afraid to confess his allegiance to Newcastle United. His pleasure on being made an Honorary Freeman of the City in 1980 was greatly enhanced by the fact that he was in the company of one of his footballing heroes, Jackie Milburn.

Cardinal Basil Hume

The Cardinal was highly regarded both within and without church circles and he was equally respected in the civil, political and royal establishment. Her Majesty the Queen awarded him her Order of Merit when they met for the last time fourteen days before his death in 1999, and well after his death she habitually referred to him as 'My Cardinal' (Howard, 2005). The Queen was to honour him further when she officially opened the Basil Hume Memorial Garden during her Jubilee Year in 2002. An information panel commemorates the Queen's visit and gives some details of the nearby boulders.

Turn right to pass the elegant former Crown Hotel building, now apartments and a restaurant. Continue as far as Nos 28 and 36 with their plaques indicating that they once served as an office and a home to Richard Grainger, 'visionary and builder'.

Retrace your steps and use the pedestrian lights to cross over to **St Mary's Roman Catholic Cathedral**, its Cloister Café and bookshop. Look out for the Adam Wakenshaw Memorial Window and its corresponding information panel **(Qu 8)**.

After visiting the Cathedral, turn right and walk a few metres to take the first street on your right (Bewick Street). Proceed ahead, noting the small stone heads near the top of each of the Cathedral windows and the little niche, at a similar height, just before the end corner, containing a statue of the church's patron Mary with the infant Jesus. You soon reach the modern sculpture of **Cardinal Basil Hume** that stands in the Memorial Garden **(Qu 9)**.

Having admired the Basil Hume statue and studied its surroundings, cross with care to the other side of Bewick Street. On the wall of Bewick House there is a plaque dedicated to Thomas Bewick, the wood engraver and naturalist who lived near here for thirty-one years, close to his workshop which was behind the Church of St Nicholas, and before his move to Gateshead in 1812. In the pavement you will find a large brass engraving made in 2003 to celebrate the two hundred and fiftieth anniversary of his birth **(Qu 10)**.

This fine building itself was erected in 1884 for the Tyne Improvement Commission that oversaw the development of the Tyne until the Commission was replaced by the Port of Tyne Authority in 1968. The insignias of local corporations belonging to the Commission are still visible on the façade. The building now contains apartments with a bar on the ground floor.

Walk a couple of paces back up Bewick Street, turn right into Thomas Bewick Square, passing the 'reborn' Town Wall pub, and then turn right again to rejoin Pink Lane. The lane was originally a communication alleyway behind the town wall. It is now hosts a mixture of bars and small businesses. A few metres on the right beyond the metal railings you will find evidence of the site of Gunner Tower, part of the old Town Wall. A plaque refers to its conversion for use at one time by the Company of Slaters and Tylers. This 'Company' dates from about 1450 and is another constituent member of the Freemen of Newcastle.

On the left you pass the old Post Office before arriving back at Neville Street and the opportunity to admire one of the three clocks on the portico of the Central Station. The clock was restored in 1993 together with one on each end of the portico. Turn left and just beyond the pedestrian lights see how much of Grainger Town that you can recognise in the form of the artwork, *The Grainger Town Sculptural Map* (Hanson and Watkinson, 2003). Cross the road to return to the Central Station and the end of the walk.

Quiz questions

1. Who unveiled a plaque in the Central Station in 2000 and which anniversary did the plaque commemorate?
2. How much is the admission charge for children under four to the Life Science Centre?
3. Who was Rachel Burns?
4. What is the name of the vessel you see on first entering the Discovery Museum?
5. What is the date on St Matthew's Church Hall?
6. Which music society did William Rea create?
7. When did Mo Mowlem live in Summerhill Grove?
8. Why do you think 'Mersa Matruh 42' appears in the window?
9. Name the two saints whose names and dates of death are engraved in stone in the far corner of the Basil Hume Memorial Garden
10. Which animal is engraved in the pavement outside Bewick House?

9. Newcastle Quayside East: Holy Jesus Hospital and Sandgate

Start:	**St Nicholas' Cathedral**
Finish:	**Guildhall**
Distance:	**2.75 miles**
Route:	**St Nicholas' Cathedral, Holy Jesus Hospital, All Saints' Church, Sandgate, St Ann's Church, East Quayside, Central Quayside, Guildhall**
Accessibility:	**On paved paths with some steep sections. Steps in one section with alternative route**
Refreshments:	**Along the Quayside**

The walk starts from St Nicholas' Cathedral. From the Cathedral, walk past the Queen Victoria Monument, along Mosley Street, over the junction with Grey Street and Dean Street to the Pilgrim Street roundabout (Linekers Bar and Metro Radio), previously known as the Swan House roundabout.

Turn right and walk towards the Tyne Bridge. Ahead to the left you will see the imposing tower and spire of All Saints' Church. Just before the railway bridge turn right to follow the sign to the Holy Jesus Hospital and at the bottom of the ramp turn right to go through the

Shipping links

underpass. Then bear right to walk round and pass the entrance to Cuthbert House. Continue ahead through a further short section of underpass. Turn right to the former **Holy Jesus Hospital**, with its arched arcade and redundant water fountain **(Qu 1)**.

Sadly it is not located in a pleasant environment and its current occupants, the National Trust, describes it as 'a remarkable historical oasis amongst a desert of concrete and cement'. When the building is closed, the outside of the Tower can be seen by walking in an anti-clockwise direction to the courtyard at the rear of the building.

Holy Jesus Hospital

This building occupies a site that has seen several uses during the last seven hundred years or so. An Augustinian Friary was built here in the early 1300s occupying an extensive area with church, cloister, guest house, garden and other associated buildings. It served as such until the Dissolution of the Monasteries led to its demise in 1539. The buildings then came to be used on behalf of the Monarch by The Council of the North on the rare occasions it met in Newcastle rather than in York. It became known as the 'King's Manor' hence the use of the name Manors for this part of the town. In the 1550s a Tower was built, probably to store armaments to aid the defence of the town, with the friary's north wall forming part of the Tower wall. However, in the early 1600s the monastery buildings themselves were demolished leaving only the Tower.

It was on the site of the former friary that the Holy Jesus Hospital was built in the late 17th century as an almshouse or dwelling for poor Freemen of the town, their widows and unmarried children. For this reason it was known locally as the Freeman's Hospital, an interesting forerunner in name only to Newcastle's state-of-the-art Freeman Hospital. The 'hospital' which consisted of some 42 individual dwellings and some common areas remained in use until 1937 when new accommodation was built in the Spital Tongues area. It is noted for being one of the very few surviving brick buildings of Newcastle from the late 17th century.

In 1800 a further building was constructed adjacent to the Holy Jesus Hospital in the form of the Soup Kitchen. This served to make and dispense soup for the 'deserving poor', at a charge, and only in cold weather during the first three months of the year. This operated until 1891 and thereafter the Soup Kitchen buildings were used as a prison laundry and then as a chemical factory until 1961.

The Holy Jesus Hospital premises were neglected following the move to Spital Tongues and the whole complex only just survived demolition at the time of the construction of the central motorway in the 1960s. However, it was saved, the building was renovated and it re-opened in 1971 to exhibit much about the history of Newcastle and its surrounds as the John George Joicey Museum. Unfortunately the major road and building developments that you can witness today hampered access and the Museum closed in 1993 with its content being transferred to the Discovery Museum.

The building is owned by Newcastle City Council and since the year 2000 it has been managed by the National Trust which has based its Inner City Project here and sub-let other rooms for use as offices. In 2011 The Trust restored the name plaque which can be seen in its original form high above the entrance It is open at varying times and details can be obtained in advance by telephone (0191-2557610) or on the National Trust website (www.nationaltrust.org.uk).

Now retrace your steps past Cuthbert House but instead of returning through the underpass to Mosley Street turn left in the direction of Aidan House and pass under the railway arch. At the end of the railings turn left and cross the road to follow the pavement to the left of Bede House. Follow the surfaced path with the church on your left to reach a board with information about the church and the humble origins of the poet and physician Mark Akenside **(Qu 2)**.

Continue ahead to admire the front portico of **All Saints' Church** now known as St Willibroad with all Saints. An arched gateway leads into the old church cemetery where many of the faded gravestones bear details of the varied occupations of the 19th-century parishioners such as, tinplate worker, innkeeper, shipwright and master mariner.

Retrace your steps a few metres and then turn left to exit the church grounds and walk down the road. Turn left into the narrow Dog Bank immediately below the church grounds. This ancient road, which once possessed houses inhabited by silver dealers and is now lined

All Saints' Church

All Saints (sometimes called All Hallows) was one of the four ancient parishes of Newcastle. A medieval church, dating from the late 13th century, originally occupied the site. However, by the 1770s the church was in a dangerous state and it was eventually decided that it should be demolished and replaced with a new building. The new church, designed by David Stephenson, was completed in 1796.

The church is possibly best viewed from the Quayside, from where its dominant position can be appreciated. Broad steps lead up to the impressive portico of this most unusual building. Behind its square tower surmounted by a narrower steeple, the main space for the congregation is oval; it has been likened to the Pantheon in Rome.

All Saints' portico

On entering the interior you might initially be slightly disoriented because you come in under a gallery with no obvious central focal point. Overall, the interior is splendid with its 18th-century mahogany woodwork and other notable features, including painted boards with the Lord's Prayer, the Creed and the Ten Commandments, and two fonts.

In 1961 the church was deconsecrated and later, in 1983/84, was adapted for use as an auditorium for recitals and other musical events. Later it was leased by the City of Newcastle to a branch of the Old Catholic Church and is now used for services as The Church of St Willibrord with All Saints.

St Willibrord (658-739), born in York, was a pioneering English missionary to what is now the Netherlands and Luxembourg and later to Denmark. He founded his largest monastery in Echternach, in Luxembourg. Once every year in Echternach he is celebrated in a sacred dance, in which the local bishop and townsfolk take part.

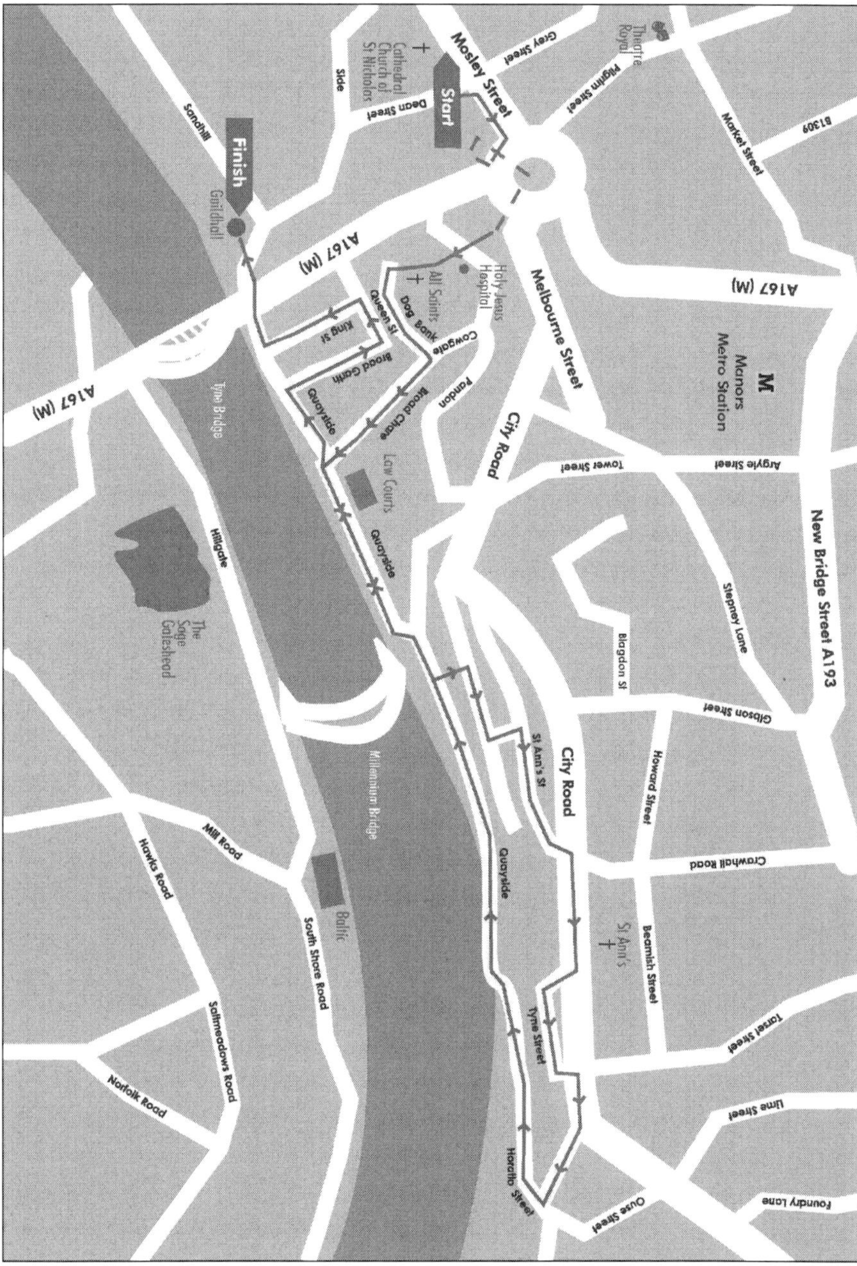
Start
Finish
Mosley Street
Grey Street
Theatre Royal
Pilgrim Street
Market Street
B1309
Cathedral Church of St Nicholas
Side
Dean Street
Sandhill
Guildhall
A167 (M)
Holy Jesus Hospital
All Saints
Melbourne Street
A167 (M)
M
Manors Metro Station
Queen St
King St
Dog Bank
Cowgate
Broad Garth
Pandon
Broad Chare
Quayside
Tyne Bridge
A167 (M)
City Road
Tower Street
Argyle Street
Law Courts
New Bridge Street A193
Quayside
Hillgate
The Sage Gateshead
Stepney Lane
Blagdon St
Gibson Street
St Ann's St
City Road
Howard Street
Millennium Bridge
Mill Road
Hawks Road
Crawhall Road
Quayside
Baltic
St Ann's
Beamish Street
South Shore Road
Tyne Street
Saltmeadows Road
Tarset Street
Norfolk Road
Lime Street
Horatio Street
Ouse Street
Foundry Lane

with modern dwellings, is cobbled and the pavement is uneven in parts. (It can be avoided by returning to Bede House, turning right and following the road with the railway arches on your left to re-join the route at Trinity Gardens, see below).

At the bottom of the bank you pass a small grassy bank that is reserved for a sculpture in memory of Admiral Lord Collingwood (see Trinity House). Now turn left and walk a few metres to the open space of Trinity Gardens. Ahead is the huge glacial boulder, *Give and Take*, carved in geometric form (Peter Randall-Page, 2005). This stands over the now submerged course of the Pandon Burn as it makes its way to the Tyne. To your left, looking up beyond the steps, you will see the remains of the Corner Turret part of the Town Wall.

Now retrace your steps to the end of Dog Bank and continue down Broad Chare. Immediately on your right, you will realise that you are getting close to the Law Courts when you pass Broad Chare Chambers with its impressive list of barristers. Next to this is **Trinity House (Qu 3)**.

Continuing ahead, you will notice the loading bays of the former warehouses in which are now housed Caffe Vivo, the **Live Theatre** and The Broad Chare pub and dining room.

After passing Live Theatre, you soon reach the end of Broad Chare, with the Law Courts on the left-hand corner of the street, and the Quayside, with much that we will admire later, a short distance ahead. Turn left to pass in front of the Law Courts, an early contribution in 1990 to the regeneration of the Quayside. Continue ahead to pass The

Trinity House

This is the historic property of the Guild or Fraternity of the Blessed Trinity, more generally referred to as the Corporation of the Newcastle upon Tyne Trinity House (not to be confused with those of Hull and London). The Guild acquired the site in 1505 when it set about creating the buildings and expanding its land holdings. Its function was to ensure the welfare of seafarers. In practical terms, under some seven Royal Charters, Newcastle upon Tyne Trinity House exercised power to control navigation in and around the River Tyne. It was responsible for the installation and maintenance of navigation aids such as buoys and beacons and lighthouses to guide ships into the Tyne and the licensing of masters, mates and river pilots. In order to undertake these tasks, money was derived from its power to levy ships entering the river. However, with the passing of time, these functions were gradually taken over by other authorities and the House is now mainly concerned with the preservation of its traditions and its buildings, although it still carries out some education and training programmes.

There is little to see from outside, apart from the coat of arms with its motto *Deus dabit Vela* (God will give us sails) and the reference to the building of 'This Trinity Hall'. When the gates are open it is worth making a discreet visit into the courtyard which is surrounded by the constituent parts of the House. These include the banqueting hall, the board room, the master's room and the chapel. Some of the former almshouses now remain as offices. In later life Admiral Lord Collingwood (1748-1810) became an Honorary Freeman of the Newcastle upon Tyne Trinity House and the House plans to erect a sculpture, *The Collingwood Wave* at the corner of Dog bank and Broad Chare to commemorate the bicentenary of his death. This is intended to be installed when funds are available and you can see a scale model of the sculpture in the yard of Trinity House. Trinity House is normally closed to visitors but small group tours can be arranged.

For further information see: www.trinityhousenewcastle.org.uk

Live Theatre

Live Theatre opened in its present location on the Quayside in 1982. However, it began as a touring company in the 1970s bringing regional-flavoured productions to many people who had not normally considered this form of entertainment. Since its early days it has proved to be a launching pad for both actors and writers. Thus a young Tim Healy performed in *The Pigeon Man* by Tom Hadaway in a miners' social club in Shiremoor in 1974, while in 1986 a teenage Robson Green appeared in Hadaway's *The Long Line*.

From its modest beginnings it has blossomed into a highly successful venture. Today it offers dedicated writers' rooms and it can justifiably claim to be 'one of the country's leading new writing theatres'. It also plays an important part in drama education for young people.

Productions with a local flavour that have received wide acclaim include, *Close the Coalhouse Door* by Alan Plater, and more recently, *The Pitman Painters* by Lee Hall and *A Northern Odyssey* by Shelagh Stephenson. Nor does the theatre shy away from topical issues as, for example, in the 2010 play *Motherland*, by Steve Gilroy, about the deaths of UK soldiers in Iraq and Afghanistan. With its 200 seats, some of which are in cabaret style, it provides a friendly and informal venue offering something for everyone, including music and stand-up comedy.

After a major two-year £5.5m refurbishment and expansion programme, the theatre complex reopened in September 2007. It occupies an historic site incorporating several Grade II listed buildings including warehouses and almshouses. This venue is a real gem. The theatre bar is available two hours prior to performances and drinks may be taken into the auditorium. Caffe Vivo is open throughout the day and its pre-show dinners are very popular. In May 2011, The Broad Chare, a gastro pub, opened adjacent to the theatre in a 'creative partnership', to provide a further pleasant amenity.

For further information: tel 0191-2321232; www.live.org.uk

Waterline pub, immediately beyond which, on the left, is Milk Market. This whole area is **Sandgate**, an area which has seen very significant changes in the relatively recent history of Newcastle. It was here that men who worked on the river and their families once lived. Among them were the **Keelmen**.

At the traffic lights turn right, cross the road and then turn left to arrive at the entrance to a small walled area, bearing the name 'Sandgate'. If you look up to your left, beyond the trees you should also be able to the white clock tower of the **Keelmen's Hospital (Qu 4)**.

Here as we pause at the entrance to the 'new Sandgate' we begin to encounter a number of artworks funded by the Tyne and Wear Development Corporation, as part of the regeneration of the Quayside

Corner Turret

Sandgate

At one time, as the name suggests, this was where one of the medieval town gates gave access to the important riverside area of the town. The area had been built on land reclaimed from the river. It was once one of the most crowded and unhealthy parts of the town.with dirty narrow streets enlivened by noisy ale-houses. It was noted for its Milk Market, a very busy daily food market in the 18th and 19th centuries. During the late 19th-early 20th centuries there was also a used clothes market which probably owed the name, Paddy's Market, to the fact that a very large Irish population came to live and work here.

The 1900s saw a gradual transformation of the area as slum housing was demolished, population moved and trade on the river declined. However, what is now known as the East Quayside was dramatically altered following the plan proposed in 1991 by the internationally-known and locally-born architect, Sir Terry Farrell to regenerate the area. As you proceed, you will see that work to transform the Quayside still continues.

Keelmen

It was here that the keelmen and their families formed a closely-knit community. This group of men famed for their hard living and drinking life styles are mentioned as early as the beginning of the 16th century. With their flat-bottomed boats or keels they were the life blood of commerce on the river transporting coal to the larger vessels or colliers unable to berth at the riverside. Their physical prowess was matched by their industrial muscle which lead to many disputes and strikes. They probably enjoyed racing each other on the river but they did not form part of the world class group of professional oarsmen such as Clasper, Chambers and Renforth. It's likely, however, that they were happy to gamble on the outcome of the popular boat races on the Tyne in the 19th century. The construction of loading bays known as staiths, the replacement of the stone bridge by the Swing Bridge and the advent of the railways all combined to bring their role to an end in the 1880s.

The keelmen are recalled in a popular Tyneside song, *The Keel Row* which was apparently first published in the late1760s. Its origins are rather unclear but it has something of a Scottish reel about it perhaps reflecting that many in this community were of Scottish blood.

As I cam thro' Sandgate, thro' Sandgate, thro' Sandgate,
As I cam thro' Sandgate, I heard a lassie sing,
Weel may the keel row, the keel row, the keel row,
Weel may the keel row, that my laddie's in.

(see www.art-on-the-riverside.co.uk). The Sandgate Steps are flanked by two lighthouse-looking artworks, *Decorative Glasswork* (Cate Watkinson, 1996) and dominated by the bronze torso and head of the Siren, part of *River God & Siren* (Andre Wallace, 1996). Further down and nearer to the river is the River God who appears to be blowing a kiss towards the seductive sea nymph. It is said that he would have been emitting flames had health and safety considerations not intervened!

Enter the walled area and bear right to follow the ramped path and after some 40 metres just before the path turns to the right, stop to admire, on your left, the symbolic relief *Keel Boatmen* (Neil Talbot, 1996) and the engraved lines of the *Keel Row Song* (Graciela

Keelmen's Hospital

The keelmen created a charitable trust in 1699 and this led to the erection of the Keelmen's Hospital in 1701. This is another of the few early brick built buildings in Newcastle that have survived to this day (see also Holy Jesus Hospital and Alderman Fenwick's House). This was not a hospital in the modern sense of the word but more like an almshouse with some sixty dwelling places for sick and aged keelmen and their families. Beneath the distinctive clock tower with its sundial are two inscriptions. One refers to the fact that the keelmen built it 'by their own charge' while the other states that in 1786 Alderman John Simpson was 'an example of benevolent'. He donated the interest at 5% on £100 to be distributed annually among the ten oldest resident keelmen. The residence closed in 1937 and much later it was converted into student a accommodation for Newcastle Polytechnic (later Northumbria University). It is owned by the City Council and is currently vacant.

Ainsworth, 1996). Now follow the ramp between the decorative iron railings with their nautical motifs (Alan Dawson, 1996) to exit from the Sandgate Steps. Turn left. and continue past the Malmaison Hotel to Keelman Square where you will find two further artworks: *Column* and *Steps and Rudder* (Andrew Burton, 1996).

(At this point you have covered a mile or so and if you wish to omit the next 0.75 miles, then you can simply turn right and pass through the artwork *Swirle Pavilion* to reach the riverside path. Now turn right and continue the walk as described below from the *Swirle Pavilion* to the Guildhall).

Continue ahead a short way and then turn left up The Swirle, named after another of the streams that now flow underground into the Tyne. Turn right at the junction with a minor road and then right again when you come to a main road (City Road). Continue ahead to arrive opposite the elegant-looking Church of St Ann (1764-8 by William Newton). It was built on the site of a medieval chapel with stone from the demolished quayside section of the Town Wall. Many of the victims of Newcastle's 19th-century cholera epidemic were buried in the churchyard here.

Opposite the church, turn right into Tyne Street. This is a very old street, once famed for its taverns and lined with back-to-back terrace houses, all in stark contrast now to its smart row of apartments. Almost immediately, as the street bears left, stop to admire the fine view of the river and the bridges **(Qu 5)**.

Walk down to the end of the housing, turn left, then right along the narrow paved area to rejoin City Road. Turn right and on your left you will see the former premises of the Tyne -Tees Shipping Steam Co Ltd., now the Hotel du Vin and Bistro.

Proceed ahead for a few metres, crossing with care, via the traffic island, to the monument dedicated to William Lisle Blenkinsopp Coulson (1841-1911). Make sure you read the interesting inscriptions on both sides of the plinth **(Qu 6)**.

Turn right to go down Horatio Street (at one time called Nelson Street). On the right, is the Sailors' Bethel opened in 1877 as a chapel for seamen. 'Bethel-el' is Hebrew for 'House of God' and the Christian inscription IHS (the first three letters of the name Jesus in Greek) above the doorway reveals its original religious significance. It was de-consecrated in 1949 and after various uses it is now office accommodation. Its history is recorded on an adjacent plaque.

Follow the pavement to meet the lower road. Cross the road and go between the housing to reach the riverside. Turn right and walk past Mariners Wharf towards the bridges with the

Gateshead Quayside, Baltic and Sage buildings ahead on your left. Here moored along the quay that was once busy with merchant ships you will find boats that could take you on a sightseeing journey on the River Tyne (see www.riverescapes.co.uk or Tel 01670785777;).

Look out for more riverside sculptures. The tall conical *Blacksmiths Needle* (Members of the British Association of Blacksmith Artists, 1996) aptly bears the phrase, 'Gleams through the trees the red light of the forge'. It is divided into sections, each one of which contains objects relating to the senses. You may like to see which ones you can identify!

Just a few metres further, in the square in front of the impressive St Ann's Wharf building, you may notice a large round stone shaded to represent a half moon. This stands as a reminder of the Half Moon Inn that once stood here. A few steps further and you arrive at the golden globe topped *Swirle Pavilion* (Raf Fulcher,1998). It is said to be both a sculpture and a building and it lists the names of ports associated with the Tyne's earlier shipping trade **(Qu 7)**.

You pass the popular Pitcher and Piano with its glass panelling enabling customers to enjoy good views. Behind, stands the Malmaison Hotel in what was formerly a warehouse of the Cooperative Wholesale Society (built 1899-1900), as evidenced by the original name below that of the hotel. It is the only frontage surviving the redevelopment of this stretch of the quayside and being constructed of reinforced concrete it is considered to be of some architectural importance. Between the Pitcher and Piano and the Gateshead Millennium Bridge you will find an information board about the bridge and the lengthy North Sea Cycle Route **(Qu 8)**.

About 150 metres ahead lies **Wesley Square** with its memorial fountain. John Wesley, preacher- founder of Methodism, is said to have preached his first sermon in

St Ann's

Tyne view

A change of use

Newcastle near here in 1742 **(Qu 9)**.

This area is particular busy on a Sunday because of the **Quayside Sunday Market** that extends more or less from here to the Tyne Bridge.

On the other side of the river, opposite the Law Courts, notice amid the architectural and cultural splendour of the Gateshead Quayside, the plainer structure of the shore-based H.M.S. Calliope of the Royal Naval Reserve. Use the second set of traffic lights to cross over to the other side of the road to Great Coffee, then turn left

You are going to pass several Quayside buildings relating to Newcastle's earlier importance as a trading port. In October 1854 a dreadful fire, the result of an explosion on the Gateshead side of the river, destroyed many buildings and cost many lives on both sides of the Tyne. The only building that survived on this side of the river was the Custom House (see below). The ruined alleys or chares, which had been previously overcrowded, had of necessity to be cleared. John Dobson, whose son, perished in the fire, was then mainly responsible for replacing the dwellings with Newcastle's first genuine office buildings in1858-63.

A few metres beyond Enterprise Chambers at Coronation Buildings, once a shipping office, is Trinity Chare with a NE1 pocket garden pending further construction work. Next to this is the Custom House of 1776. It was once responsible for collecting taxes on behalf of the King and it proudly bears the Royal Coat of Arms of the House of Hanover. The Theatre Royal is said to be the only other local building showing this particular crest. The building maintains a legal role now as a base for many barristers. A plaque recalls some details of its history.

Proceed ahead for some 40 metres and next to Goldwater Solicitors you arrive at an archway and Fenwick's Entry at Broad Garth. Here, dedicated to **Thomas Spence**, you will find one of Newcastle's more recent heritage plaques **(Qu 10)**.

Wesley Square

The area bears the name of Wesley due to its connection with John Wesley who visited and preached in the once run-down area of Sandgate. The Wesley Memorial Fountain was originally erected in Milk Market (see above) in 1891 to mark the centenary of his death but it was subsequently repositioned on its current site as part of the regeneration of the Quayside

Here, apart from one of the few modern public conveniences in the city, you will find several things of interest. First of all you will recognise another *Decorative Glasswork* by Cate Watkinson to match the two we encountered at the nearby Sandgate Steps (see above). Secondly, *River Tyne* (Neil Talbot 1996), depicting the course of the river, is etched on a wall that, according to the plaque, stands on the line of the medieval town wall. It is interesting to try to identify the landmark buildings that are depicted along the length of the Tyne, such as Tynemouth Priory and Hexham Abbey. You may notice the artist's name engraved in the boat at the mouth of the river.

Quayside Sunday Market

Over centuries, the Newcastle Quayside has been the scene of several different markets, the only one of which that now survives being the Quayside Sunday Market. This takes place every Sunday morning until 2.30 pm when up to two hundred stalls, offering a very wide variety of goods and produce, attempt to entice customers from among those who come to seek bargains or just to enjoy the vibrant atmosphere. Since 1976 the market has been regulated by the City Council.

Thomas Spence (1750-1814)

Of very humble origins, this self-taught campaigner against oppression and exploitation has been described as 'the leading English revolutionary of his day'. His radical speeches and political pamphlets were to lead him into a lot of trouble. His lecture in 1775 to the Literary and Philosophical Society, later published and sold by him on 'Property in Land Every One's Rights', was apparently too much for the Lit and Phil members to bear and consequently he was expelled from the Society. Campaigning in London, he went on to enrage higher authorities with his radical ideas, resulting in charges of seditious libel and high treason for which he suffered various periods of imprisonment.

For further information see: www.Thomasspence.co.uk

Walk up the cobbled chare for some 100 metres to a housing development in Peppercorn Court, a pleasant example of regeneration for domestic accommodation. Turn left to exit from this development onto Queen Street. Looking up to the right you have a splendid view of the dominating position of All Saints' Church, while to the left in Gateshead you can see the former Church of St Mary's.

Turn left down King Street. Towards the end of the street is Sabatini's which, when viewed from the Quayside,can be seen to occupy what must be one of the narrowest properties in Newcastle! At the end of the street on the wall of the property you will find another indication of maritime connections, in the form of a list of the services provided by the original occupants of the building, the Tyne-Tees Shipping Company. Some time ago the **Northumberland and Newcastle Society** campaigned to have this sign repaired when we were in danger of losing it.

Northumberland and Newcastle Society

The Society, which was established 1924, aims to protect and enhance the environmental and cultural heritage of the County and City.

To achieve these aims it operates through its Tyneside and County Committees which review all planning applications in Newcastle, North Tyneside and Northumberland. It engages in consultation on many historic buildings and seeks to promote good design, sustainability and sympathetic development.

Notable past achievements include: heading the appeal to restore the Lantern Tower of St Nicholas' Cathedral; successfully improving the design of prominent electrification gantries on all listed bridges in Northumberland and Durham; maintaining pressure to save Newcastle's All Saints' Church, Blackfriars Monastery, Armstrong Bridge, Alderman Fenwick's House, Jesmond Cemetery's John Dobson gates, the east side of Eldon Square, and the iconic art deco Wills Building on the Coast Road.

Two on-going activities are running a 'Cut the Clutter' campaign against superfluous road signage and monitoring and attending Public Enquiries into Windfarm and Opencast planning applications.

The Society is recognised as a major force in the area and is regularly consulted by local authorities on planning and environmental matters.

For further information: www.nandnsociety.org.uk; Tel 01912816266

Turn right to continue along the Quayside to pass The Slug and Lettuce and the Premier Inn located in the early 1860s Exchange Buildings, once described as 'palatial mercantile offices' (Middlebrook, 1950). On the wall of the Premier Inn you will see a plaque referring to the Sailing Ship Owners who were once based here. Walk ahead under the Tyne Bridge. The gracefully curved building on your left is the **Guildhall** and the end of the walk. The Quayside buses that will return you to the Haymarket, the Central Station or Gateshead, stop a few metres ahead.

Guildhall

There are records of important buildings on this site since the beginning of the 15th century. However, as Newcastle grew more prosperous largely due to the increasing demand for its coal, so there was a need to reflect this with an appropriate building to house the council offices, a court, an exchange and a weigh house. In the mid-1660s it fell to Robert Trollope to build what we now know as the Guildhall. Late 17th-century illustrations show a building, with a tower and adorned with turrets, of which any town would be proud. The exterior was substantially remodelled in the late 18th century and early 19th by architects such as David Stephenson, William Newton and John Dobson. This was the centre of local government until 1858 when the council offices were moved to the new Town Hall opposite St Nicholas' Cathedral. Interestingly enough, part of the building is now occupied by the Association of North East Councils.

Much of Trollope's influence still remains in the interior which contains several magnificently decorated rooms which are still used on ceremonial occasions. In March 2010 The Hall of the Stewards of the Freemen witnessed the first admission of women family members to the rank of 'Freemen'. Unfortunately the Guildhall is not open to the public except with the officially guided City Tours programme and special events.

Quiz questions

1. **How many brick arches are there at the front of the Holy Jesus Hospital?**
2. **What was the original name of the street where Mark Akenside was born?**
3. **What are the two symbols shown at the front of Trinity House which depict its connection with the sea?**
4. **What time is shown on the clock of the Keelmen's Hospital?**
5. **How many bridges can you see from the top of Tyne Street?**
6. **Which weak and defenceless groups did Blenkinsop Coulson try to help?**
7. **How many ports are listed in the Swirle Pavilion?**
8. **What is the length of the North Sea Cycle Route?**
9. **In what month of 1742 did John Wesley preach his first sermon in Newcastle?**
10. **What building did Thomas Spence have built in Broad Chare?**

10. Newcastle Quayside West: Sandhill, Cathedral and Castle

Start/finish: **Guildhall**
Distance: **1.75 miles**
Route: **Guildhall, Quayside, Town Wall, Forth Street, Westgate Road, Collingwood Street, St Nicholas' Cathedral, Castle, Guildhall**
Accessibility: **In order to appreciate some of the old paths to and from the Quayside, the route includes several ascents and descents via steep steps which are not suitable for wheelchairs. However, the features listed under 'Route' above can be accessed from other points including Newcastle Central Station**
Refreshments: **Cafés and pubs throughout the walk**

We commence this walk from the historic Guildhall. The frontage of the Guildhall is on **Sandhill** and for a short distance we will be walking parallel to it.

The starting point is on the riverside path. The Lort Burn, which runs underneath Dean Street, enters the river here.

With the river on your left, proceed along the path to come to two plaques commemorating visits by the Cutty Sark at the time of the Tall Ships races. A plaque on Charlie's restaurant, located to the left of the protruding veranda, indicates that the ancient

Guildhall

Sandhill

The Tyne used to overflow this area and when the tide was out there remained a hill of sand, hence the name. The name stuck even after the river's defences were built. Its location on the river made it a hub for incoming and outgoing traffic. Sandhill was an important centre, with markets where you could buy a variety of goods, especially fish, and where proclamations were made and where the townsfolk gathered for recreation and entertainments not least bull-baiting which took place here until 1768.

By the late 17th century, together with the nearby Side and The Close, Sandhill had shops for merchants and other trades and fine merchants houses; several of these superb properties still exist and you will pass some of them later on this walk. Bessie Surtees House is a fine example. Sandhill's location on the waterfront made it a very convenient place for anyone with shipping interests. However, it was perhaps the existence of the Guildhall, the centre for local government and the administration of justice, which meant that Sandhill was recognised as being the heart of the town. This was one reason why, in 1740, the Guildhall was the focus by rioting keelmen, protesting about their dire conditions. They ransacked the building, destroyed many records and made off with the corporation's money. In 1742, in complete contrast, John Wesley, who had great empathy with folk such as the keelmen, preached a sermon from the steps of the Guildhall.

In the second half of the 19th century Sandhill and other parts of the Quayside declined as newer businesses located away from the riverside, leaving warehouses and pockets of slums. The slums have gone and the current redevelopment programme is changing the face of this former town centre area. Happily, some of its iconic buildings remain.

St Thomas' Chapel, which was demolished and replaced by the Church of St Thomas the Martyr in Barras Bridge in the 1800s, was located near here.

Carry on, going under the Swing Bridge. On your right you pass the Fish Market (1880), now a nightclub, with sculptures on the roof of two fishwives and Neptune as reminders of its past usage. It replaced a fish market by Dobson (1826). You pass an information board, with details of the Tyne's older bridges, and a Royal Bank of Scotland milepost reminding us that we are on a section of the long distance Hadrian's Way path. Go under the High Level Bridge. Over to your right you see the black and white building known as **The Cooperage**.

Immediately on the right is The Quayside pub, which has a plaque which gives information about its history **(Qu 1)**, **(Qu 2)**.

The Cooperage

The building dates from the 15th century, with later additions. It acquired its name in the 19th century when a cooper moved his business there. For a number of years it was a pub which closed in 2009. Happily, under new owners, this Grade 1 listed building has reopened on Thursday through to Saturday. A full relaunch is planned.

The Cooperage

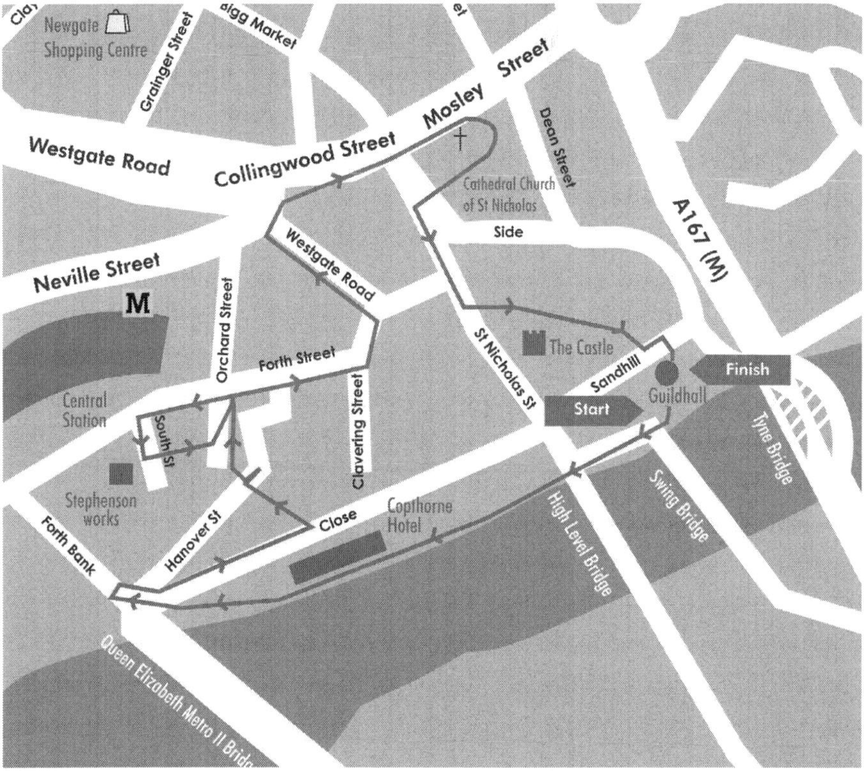

You come to the Copthorne Hotel (Arup Associates, 1993), one of the earliest of the modern redevelopments in this part of the Quayside. A former Mansion House (1691) which was destroyed in 1895, occupied part of this site. A nearby information board tells the story of the 'Cleaning up the Tyne'. The success of the cleaning scheme is shown by the presence of anglers around here. When you reach the blue Queen Elizabeth II (Metro) Bridge turn right and follow the line of the bridge, on the paved path, to exit onto a road. Bear left and after a few metres cross over to Skinnerburn Road. The Skinner Burn, another of Newcastle's culverted burns joins the river here.

Walk up the road for a few metres and cross the road via the pedestrian refuge. The oriental style building above you is The Waterside Palace Restaurant. Turn right and follow the pavement. Cross Hanover

West Quayside

Street and continue ahead. There are new developments on your left and the Copthorne Hotel on your right. Stop opposite the blue hotel sign on the hotel wall. You have now arrived at the foot of the section of the Town Wall known as the 'Breakneck Stairs'. Although this section of the Wall has been demolished, from the steep slope on your left you can get an idea as to why it was so called. This is where the Wall turned left to run parallel with the river.

Turn left and go up the steps, keeping to the left until you arrive at the narrow Hanover Street. Here you can see the granite insets in the road surface to accommodate the wheels of horse-drawn vehicles. Turn right and walk 30 metres to two information panels that give interesting facts about the area **(Qu 3)**.

Walk back and cross over to Whitefriars Place, an apposite name because the Carmelite or White Friars had their friary here. Go up the steps and follow the path to arrive at what is one of the most impressive existing sections of the Town Wall. Proceed ahead, alongside the wall on your right. At the end of the wall, on the other side, there is an information panel with details about the wall and the surrounding area **(Qu 4)**.

Turn left and walk past The Telegraph pub to **Central Square.**

Carry on. You might be accompanied by the noise of trains and public address announcements as you are now walking behind the busy Central Station. Until

Impressive section of the Town Wall

Central Square

The original building, constructed as a state of the art sorting office for the Post Office in 1934, became too small for its purpose and the Post Office transferred to Team Valley in Gateshead in the 1990s. It was converted by Carey Jones (1998-2000) and was the first new office development south of the Central Station

Parabola Estates, the owner, has not only provided prestigious office space but incorporated art works into the development. An addition to the complex is the Central Square South building, built in a complementary style

Outside, the eye-catching sculpture *DNA DL90* (Abigail Fallis, 2009), incorporates the ubiquitous shopping trolley, representing today's consumers, into a double-helix shape. It was opened by Sir James Crick (of DNA fame). This work is the first in a proposed series to replace the sculpture *Vulcan* by Sir Eduardo Paolozzi (1924-2005) which originally stood here.

The seven-metre tall bronze statue, *Vulcan* (2000) is a representation of Vulcan, the blacksmith of the gods, and was a reminder of this area's heavy engineering history. Sir Edward produced other versions of Vulcan, including a five metre welded steel sculpture (1999) which is displayed in the national Dean Gallery in Edinburgh in a former orphanage which was converted by the eminent architect Sir Terry Farrell.

recently much of the properties here were disused and dilapidated but in 2008 the City Council approved a plan for the revival of this area. A nine acre site is now designated as the Stephenson Quarter, because of its connection with **George Stephenson** and his son **Robert Stephenson**, and you will probably encounter lots of evidence of redevelopment activity here.

You come to South Street. Pause here and look a little ahead where, on the right, you can see the original station building, capped with a water tank. Now turn left and proceed along South Street.

South Street factory site

On your right a plaque on the wall indicates that the building, now partially restored, is the remaining part of the Forth Street Works set up by Robert Stephenson in partnership with his father and others and which has been repaired and restored by the **Robert Stephenson Trust.** It is now under the control of Silverlink, the developer of the Stephenson Quarter. There is an entrance on the other side of the building (which we will not be visiting) where the building is identified as The Robert Stephenson Centre which houses occasional events and exhibitions.

George Stephenson (1781-1848)

George Stephenson was an engineer and inventor who was born at Wylam in Northumberland in a small cottage located on the Wylam Waggonway, a wooden track on which coal was carried from the nearby mine to the River Tyne for subsequent transport. His father worked as a fireman, at Wylam Colliery. From these humble beginnings, with no money for schooling, George followed his father into working with stationary engines in local collieries. Realising the value of education he attended classes to learn to read and write. His fascination with machines, particularly colliery engines, led him to teach himself in his spare time how these engines worked (by taking them apart and reassembling them!). His knowledge soon led to promotion and in 1812 he was made enginewright, i.e. responsible for the maintenance of all of the machinery, at Killingworth Colliery.

There, he engaged in a programme of inventing. In 1814 he built his first railway locomotive *Blucher* named after the Prussian General Blucher whose fast march to Waterloo enabled his troops to help in Napoleon's defeat. Thereafter he built ever improved versions and in 1815 found time to invent a miner's safety lamp.

His reputation grew and in 1823 he set up in partnership, with his only son Robert and others, as Robert Stephenson and Company, which was the first locomotive works in the world. *Locomotion* was the first locomotion engine they produced. Subsequently he was employed as engineer by a number of railway companies, including the Stockton and Darlington which opened the first public railway, the Stockton and Darlington line, in 1825. Stephenson himself guided the *Locomotion*, which completed the nine-mile distance in just under two hours. Another success came when another of the Stephensons'

engines, the *Rocket*, won a trial held by the directors of the proposed Liverpool & Manchester Railway. George Stephenson also designed many of the bridges needed for the early railway lines. In 1847 he became the first president of the Institution of Mechanical Engineers.

Stephenson is commemorated in a monument near the Central Station, Newcastle. It has been suggested that the word 'Geordie' arose because local miners preferred using the 'Geordie', the safety lamp invented by Stephenson, to the 'Davy' invented by Sir Humphrey Davy. However, that is only one of several ideas about the word's derivation. He will be best remembered for his work with railways.

Robert Stephenson (1803-1859)

Robert was the only son of George Stephenson and his wife Fanny. George was largely self-educated and, probably because of this, made sure that his son received a formal education. After attendance at Dr Bruce's Academy in Newcastle, Robert was apprenticed to the manager of Killingworth Colliery and then spent some time at Edinburgh University. Thereafter he worked with his father on railway projects and set up, with his father and others, Robert Stephenson and Company. Many of the successful projects credited to George Stephenson were, in fact, worked on jointly by father and son. From 1824 to 1827 Robert worked as an engineer in Columbian gold mines.

In 1833 he became Chief Engineer for the London and Birmingham Railway and overcame several civil engineering problems before the line was opened in 1838. In that year he worked on railway projects in Italy. For the next twenty years he was called on as adviser on railway development in Europe and Egypt. During the same period he designed many bridges, including the High Level Bridge between Gateshead and Newcastle (1849) and the Royal Border Bridge over the Tweed (1850) and, in the same year with William Fairbairn, the box girder Britannia Bridge over the Menai Strait.

He succeeded his father as President of the Institution of Mechanical Engineers, serving from 1849 to 1853 and was President of the Institute of Civil Engineers from 1855 to 1857. From 1847 until his death in1859 he was Conservative Member of Parliament for Whitby.

Robert Stephenson was buried in Westminster Abbey. At that time he was referred to as 'the greatest engineer of the present century'. He is commemorated in a statue outside Euston Station in London. In Newcastle his memory is being revived by the efforts of the Robert Stephenson Trust.

Robert Stephenson Trust

The Trust was formed in 1988 and aims 'to make Robert Stephenson famous again'. Initially it focused on saving from dereliction the last remaining part of the industrial complex where Robert Stephenson and Company operated. The Trust raised around £500,000 and succeeded in rescuing the premises at 20 South Street which it designated as 'Stephenson's Works'.

Until February 2009 the Trust operated from these premises but after disputes over rent with the new owner Silverlink it moved out, expressing disappointment that it was no longer possible for it to open the building to the public on two days per week. Stephenson's Works is open for exhibition on an occasional basis by the new owners.

The Trust continues its educational and promotional activities from Neville Hall, headquarters of The North of England Institute of Mining & Mechanical Engineers.

Over to your left, in the space between the buildings, you will see *Reach for the Stars* one of the last works of Kenneth Armitage (1916-2002) who sadly died shortly after its completion. Walk past the sculpture. Turn left, walk to the end of the road and then turn right. Continue ahead **(Qu 5)**.

You reach Clavering Place. We are going to turn left to go under the railway but before doing so if you look to your right you can see two late 18th-century brick houses **(Qu 6)**.

Further to the right of these two houses are the remnants of Hanover Square. The square, dating from the 1720s, was to be the first square in Newcastle, in what was a fashionable part of the town. However, it was never finished and most of it has been demolished.

Our walk continues by proceeding through the tunnel to arrive near the end of Westgate Road. Immediately opposite is Cooper's Studio, a Grade II listed building, originally Cooper's Auction Yard built in 1897 as a horse, carriage and cycle auction room and now converted into offices by Ryder (2009). During its restoration Roman remains were discovered and these have been retained in situ.

Turn left and walk along Westgate Road. At the time of writing a new 98-bedroom budget hotel is being constructed for the Sleeperz company. Sleepeze, which opened its first hotel in Cardiff in 2008, aims to build on Network Rail sites near important railway stations. The Newcastle hotel is the second to be constructed for this newly-established hotel chain. Several of the properties here look down-at-heel although there are plans for further redevelopment. On your left you come to **Bolbec Hall** (Frank W. Rich, 1907) which is currently for sale. Rather than the somewhat flamboyant style adopted in his earlier designs in Newcastle, he is seen here 'in a more reflective and antiquarian mood' (Lovie, 2001), although the overall effect is more ornate than the simple Greek revival design of the adjacent **Literary and Philosophical Society** (John Green,1825) **(Qu 7)**.

The Society, affectionately known as the Lit and Phil, built Bolbec Hall with the hope of gaining income from lettings to help to finance the Society's activities. Next we come to Neville Hall (A.M. Dunn, 1870) which is the headquarters of the **Institute of Mining and Mechanical Engineers**. It is a solid-looking Victorian edifice, another contrast with the simplicity of the Lit and Phil building.

From outside the Lit and Phil if you look over to your left you will see the fine **Stephenson Monument**.

Cross Westgate Road at the pedestrian lights outside the Lit and Phil entrance and

Neville Hall

Bolbec Hall

The Lit and Phil built this adjacent building which opened in 1909 as an investment to produce rental income. Many tenants including Oxfam and most notably the City Coroner's Court benefited from its spacious accommodation and its convenient location near to the Central Station. However, in 2010 faced with increasing cost of maintaining the premises while preserving its own activities, the Lit and Phil put Bolbec Hall up for sale. Fears have been expressed as to its future use but at the time of writing the outcome was still unclear.

Literary and Philosophical Society

The Lit and Phil was founded in 1793 by a group of men eager to discuss and to share concepts and issues of interest. They were encouraged to form a 'learned society' by the Reverend William Turner, a dynamic young minister of the Unitarian Church in Hanover Square. In 1825, after meeting in various venues across the town, they were able to open their present premises in Westgate Road. The land, which stands on the line of Hadrian's Wall, had been the site of the town house of the Nevilles (Earls of Westmoreland) who also owned the Barony of Bolbec. This provides the basis for the names given to the two adjacent properties to the Lit and Phil as well as to nearby Neville Street and Westmoreland Road.

Early membership, that included William Armstrong (later Lord Armstrong), Joseph Swan (later Sir Joseph Swan), George and Robert Stephenson among others, reads like a roll of honour of the leading citizens of Newcastle. Lectures drew great numbers and, for example, in 1879, 700 people attend a demonstrated by Joseph Swan of his incandescent carbon electric light. In addition to conducting and encouraging research, the Society was influential in setting up other local bodies, such as the Society of Antiquaries, the Institute of Mining and the College of Physical Sciences which was to form part of the origins of Newcastle University.

Today the Society continues its educational work through a regular programme of lectures, concerts and recitals open to the public free of charge and which take place in the lecture hall downstairs.. However, pride of place goes to its library upstairs that contains some 160,000 books on a wide variety of subjects together with over 6,500 CDs and 10,000 LPs to suit most tastes. The library is housed in a splendid reading room which maintains a pleasant and homely atmosphere. Here there is an opportunity to read or study surrounded by the portraits and sculptured busts of the great and the good who have also graced this building in times gone by. There is usually a notice at the front door which states, 'Please come in and have a look around'. It is well worth while accepting this invitation.

For opening hours and further details see:www.litandphil.org.uk

Institute of Mining and Mechanical Engineers

In the 1850s a group of men involved in the coal industry, motivated by their concern at the human cost of mining explosions, established a Society for the Prevention of Accidents, later to be known as the Institute of Mining and Mechanical Engineers. Its first President was Nicholas Wood, a principal 'viewer' or colliery manager and an associate of George Stephenson. Meetings were originally held in the premises of the Lit and Phil but in 1872 the Institute moved into the newly completed adjoining building, Neville Hall.

Four years later the Institute was incorporated by Royal Charter.

Today the Institute of Mining, as it is generally referred to, continues its educational work in the field of mining and related engineering largely through the maintenance and use of its extensive library in the splendid Nicholas Wood Memorial Hall. The Hall, named after Nicholas Wood, the Institute's first president, is a beautiful example of 19th-century architecture and its light and airy atmosphere provides a dramatic contrast with the underground conditions associated with the industry. The library holds a unique collection of more than 30,000 volumes on mining, metallurgy, railways and geology, with archive material on most of the north-east coal mines. A lecture theatre with its semi-circular tiered seating that was added in 1902 is the still the venue for a regular series of lectures. These cover a wide range of topics on mining and energy related topics and are open to the public as well as to the four hundred or so members. These two attractive rooms together with a smaller boardroom are available for private hire. In 1972 the Freemasons acquired a section of the building as the base for the Provincial Grand Lodge of Northumberland and Newcastle city lodges.

For further details of the activities of the Institute see: www.mininginstitute.org.uk

Stephenson Monument

This monument to George Stephenson is the work of John Graham Lough (1798-1876) described as 'Northumbria's most outstanding sculptor of the nineteenth century' (Hall, 2005).

It was financed by public subscription. The public certainly turned out in large numbers, estimated to be in excess of 100,000, to witness the unveiling of the statute in 1862. The ceremony was accompanied by a large procession of workers and the town was evidently enlivened by numerous celebratory events

Lough had shown a model of the statue at the Literary and Philosophical Society before it was cast in bronze in London. It was fitting therefore that the monument should be erected opposite both the Lit & Phil where George Stephenson himself had demonstrated his safety lamp and the Institute of Mining and Mechanical Engineers where his son Robert had been in discussion about the nature of a memorial to his father. At the same time he was honoured close to both the railway station and the site of Robert Stephenson's factory in South Street.

Stephenson is shown holding a scroll, presumably of plans, and the four figures reclining below him represent various aspects of his work; a blacksmith with a hammer and anvil, a plate layer with a section of rail, a miner with a safety lamp, and an engineer with a model locomotive. The monument attracted some criticism for the classical attire of the five figures but this is very much in the style of the sculptor. It is said to show the enhanced status of Stephenson who rose from very humble beginnings to be acclaimed (perhaps controversially) as the 'Father of the Railway'.

Lough himself enjoyed the patronage of wealthy aristocrats and landowners among them Sir Matthew Ridley for whom he carried out several commissions at Blagdon Hall, the Ridley ancestral home.

arrive at Collingwood Street. The street was built in 1810 to provide an east-west link with Mosley Street (a short distance ahead) and Westgate Road. In the late 19th century, Collingwood Street (with Mosley Street) became Newcastle's business centre and its original properties were replaced with elegant buildings for financial institutions and offices. Many of these are now pubs and restaurants.

On the corner on which you are standing is The Sun Insurance Building (Oliver, Leeson and Wood, 1904); notice the company's distinctive logo on the top arch. Some 50 metres further on, the fine building now occupied by the Allied Irish Bank, was by R.J. Johnson (1891) for another banking house. On the next corner Collingwood House, originally for the Bank of Chicago (Mauchlen, Weightman and Elphick 1974) provides a startling contrast with the nearby19th-century buildings.

Collingwood Street was named after **Admiral Lord Collingwood**.

Admiral Lord Collingwood (1748-1810)

Cuthbert Collingwood was born in the Side in Newcastle, the son of a (not very successful) trader. His home was very near the river and ships and sailors would have been regular sights for the young boy. In 1759, at a time when England's navy really seemed to rule the waves with ships' crews regularly sharing prize monies, it was 'Small wonder, perhaps, that the 11 year old Cuthbert Collingwood was drawn to the sea and its potential for heroes and glory' as Max Adams points out in *Collingwood, Northumberland's Heart of Oak*. In 1761, aged twelve, Cuthbert entered the navy.

During his fourteen years as a midshipman and master's mate he developed into an experienced and highly capable seaman. In 1775, following his valiant efforts at the Battle of Bunkers Hill near Boston USA, he gained his promotion to lieutenant. Thereafter his reliability, together with his braveness and coolness in battle and man management skills, led to his reaching the rank of flag captain in 1793 and Rear Admiral in 1798. Since 1793 he and Nelson had been fighting the French and it was at the Battle of Trafalgar in 1815 that Collingwood's major contributions before and after Nelson's death, when he took control of the British fleet, led to his being created Baron Collingwood.

In 1791 he had married Sarah Blackett, daughter of the Mayor of Newcastle. They lived in Morpeth and had two daughters. Collingwood's naval duties meant that he was able to visit home only rarely but he remained a devoted family man.

There is a Collingwood Memorial in St Nicholas' Cathedral and a splendid monument to him near the mouth of the Tyne. The two hundredth anniversary of his death in 2010 was celebrated in a series of events.

At the traffic lights cross over to **The Cathedral Church of St Nicholas**.

Leave the cathedral by the main entrance and walk clockwise round the exterior of the building. Walk through the small **St Nicholas' Square** incorporating the statue of Queen Victoria (Alfred Gilbert, unveiled1903) which you pass on your left **(Qu 8)**.

Opposite the small graveyard on your right, notice the sculpture nicknamed the **Vampire Rabbit** above a doorway on your left.

On the building in front of you there is a bust of Thomas Bewick and a plaque about him.

Continue round the building to the road. Turn left into St Nicholas Street, constructed in the 1850s to provide access link to the newly-constructed High Level Bridge. Walk ahead. Over the road on your right, is the former General Post Office (James Williams,1876) which,

The Cathedral Church of St Nicholas

Originally one of the town's four parish churches, work on the present building was commenced on the site of an earlier church, possibly a wooden construction, at the end of the 12th century. As a result of subsequent repairs and additions, what we see today is mostly a 14th-century building surmounted by its magnificent 15th-century lantern tower. From the outside we see an elegant building, sadly somewhat hemmed in by later development which belies the spaciousness found inside.

In the 16th century an abortive attempt was made to create a bishopric in what was to be the City of Newcastle incorporating Gateshead. Some 300 years later, in 1882, a new Diocese of Newcastle was established, with St Nicholas', which was one of the largest parish churches in England, becoming the new cathedral. The new diocese stretches from the north bank of the Tyne to the Scottish border to the north and to the Cumbrian border to the west. The creation of the new diocese did not meet with universal approval. Joseph Cowen, for example, made a vitriolic attack against the proposal during the passage of the enabling bill through parliament. However, the scheme's proposers succeeded and Canon Ernest Rowland Wilberforce, grandson of William Wilberforce the anti-slavery campaigner, was consecrated as the first bishop of the new diocese.

It is not surprising that the change to cathedral status brought about major additions to the building's interior furnishing. Bishop Wilberforce engaged Robert J. Johnson to design and supervise the installation of wood and stone fittings - which were to be in a style in line with English cathedral tradition. In addition to these, there are many other interesting features both from before and after the late 19th-century alterations.

There is much to see inside including some outstanding stained glass, miserichords and memorials. A guidebook and several children's 'trails' leaflets (all reasonably priced) are available to help with your visit. Some of the personalities discussed in *Discovering NewcastleGateshead* are remembered in various ways in the Cathedral. These include, to the right of the Mosley Street entrance, The Collingwood Memorial commemorating Admiral Lord Collingwood.

Higher up on the left hand (north) side in St George's Chapel, four stained glass windows (A. K. Nicholson, 1935) each in memory of a famous north easterner: Andrew Laing (industrialist after whom the Laing Art Galley was named), Sir Charles Parsons (of turbine fame), Lord Stamfordham (statesmen and secretary to Queen Victoria and King George V) and

St Nicholas' Cathedral

Viscount Grey of Falloden (Foreign Secretary 1905-1916 and notable ornithologist). The windows are full of appropriate illustrations; notice St Christopher holding the Turbinia in the Parsons window.

Near the top of the north side, the Danish Memorial (R.Sims, 1982) commemorating the Danish Merchant Fleet who were headquartered in nearby St Nicholas' Building during World War II and the Danish seamen who lost their lives in that conflict.

At the top of the south side on the east wall, a modern-style stained glass window (L. Evetts, 1962) with the inscription 'Thanks be to God for the preservation of this cathedral in time of war 1939-1945'.

At the top of the south side, just below the Evetts window, the memorial to John Collingwood Bruce, the eminent antiquarian and acknowledged authority on the Roman Wall.

St Nicholas has had a choir since at least the 16th century. In 2008, following a not uncommon practice, the boys' and men's choirs were augmented with a girls' choir to help to maintain this historic tradition.

Apart from its clergy and administrative staff the Cathedral has a team of volunteers to help out with the many and varied activities which take place throughout the year. This includes manning the Cathedral café, which is open Mon-Fri from 10.00 to 3.00. The cohort of volunteers also includes cathedral guides who are on hand to give assistance, if needed, to its many visitors.

For further information see: www.stnicholascathedral.co.uk

after being unoccupied for a number of years was converted by Alan J. Smith (2000) as the Red Box Building for mixed use. Next to this is St Nicholas Building (William Parnell, 1863), also converted by Alan J. Smith (1997). During World War II Newcastle was the official home town for 3,000 Danish seamen serving in the British Merchant Navy. Their unions and clubs were housed in St Nicholas Building and they are remembered in St Nicholas' Cathedral.

Keep straight ahead. You are now approaching the **Black Gate** and the **Castle**. Both buildings are managed by **The Society of Antiquaries of Newcastle upon Tyne** on behalf of the City Council. The area occupied by the Castle and grounds is known as the Castle Garth.

You arrive at an information board giving details about the Black Gate. Turn left and go through the arch beneath the building. Now follow the wooden walkway over the remnants of the original castle defensive ditch and carry on

A noted local artist

St Nicholas' Square

This is one of the pocket parks, initiated by Newcastle NE1 to improve Newcastle's City Centre. Much of the ground space is covered with the representation of a starburst in the form of a star with extended rays. This is a development from a compass rose and is in recognition of Newcastle's maritime history. At the same time it has religious significance in that Christ was described by Bede as 'the bright morning star'. Because this park is within the Cathedral's domain, approval for its construction had to be obtained from the Cathedral Fabrics Committee for England.

Vampire Rabbit

This is above the back entrance of No 27 Dean Street, part of the Cathedral Buildings office block built for the Church Commissioners by Oliver, Leeson and Wood in 1901. Is it a rabbit or is it a hare? Christopher Golding in *Tyneside's Finest a miscellany* (Grundy et al, 2006) comments on 'the inappropriately baroque grandeur of such a doorway in a back alley' and speculates on possible explanations for its presence. His suggestions include that it was simply a joke by the architects, based on the Easter bunny tradition, a connection with Thomas Bewick whose workshop was in this alley and who carved many hares, and a possible link with the Cathedral's patron saint, St Nicholas, and his association with woodland animals such as hares. It has also been suggested that it is a reminder of earlier days, when the rabbit, or its predecessor, was located around here to deter body-snatchers.

Black Gate

This was the main entrance to the castle. It was built out from the earlier north gate by King Henry III in 1248, in order to provide a stronger entry point. To achieve this, the lower part had an arched passage and vaulted guard chambers together with a portcullis and drawbridge. Over the centuries it underwent various alterations, including the addition of two storeys in the 17th century. At this time the building was let out to tenants, from one of whom, Patrick Black, it got its name.

In the middle of the 19th century, the dingy houses which had surrounded the Black Gate were demolished to make way for the new St Nicholas Street. In 1883 it was restored by R. J. Johnson and it now stands in its uncluttered position, where it can be enjoyed by local citizens and visitors.

Through the Black Gate

Castle

Newcastle got its name from the 'new castle' built in 1080 by Robert Curthose, the eldest son of William the Conqueror. It was a fortified enclosure surrounded by an earth rampart, set on a mound commanding the crossing point of the river below. The site had previously been occupied by the Roman fort of Pons Aelius as well as a cemetery of the Anglo-Saxon settlement of Monkchester. During the late 12th and early 13th centuries King Henry II (1154-1189) and King John (1199-1216) rebuilt and considerably strengthened the original castle. The improvements included a strong stone keep with an enclosing wall, in which there were three small gates, and a stone hall which was on the site where the Vermont Hotel now stands There was a gatehouse at the north end which was replaced by a stronger outer gateway in the mid-13th century.

With the construction of the Town Wall, the castle wall was in effect redundant and gradually decayed. The keep also fell into disuse and by the 17th century was completely derelict. The whole of the castle area, the Castle Garth, became covered in dwellings and shops. In 1812, the corporation of Newcastle bought the castle from the Crown and commenced a restoration programme, including raising the roof and adding battlements and a flag tower. What had become slum properties within Castle Garth were gradually removed, starting in the 1840s with the coming of the railway. In 1847 further restoration was carried out by John Dobson for the Newcastle Society of Antiquaries who had leased the castle from the corporation.

Today the sturdy castle keep, one of the best preserved Norman keeps in England, stands as a proud reminder of Newcastle's medieval beginnings.

Inside there is much for the visitor to appreciate including a fine Norman chapel as well as the thickness of the walls which adds to the feeling of impregnability in this well-preserved ancient building.

The Society of Antiquaries of Newcastle upon Tyne

The Society, founded in 1813, is the oldest provincial antiquarian society in England. Its aim is to 'encourage a deeper understanding of the history and archaeology of North-East England' and in fulfilment of this holds a variety of meetings and has a programme of publications including its refereed journal *Archaeologia Aeliana.* From its earliest days the Society has built up collections of books and artefacts and continues to do so. The Society's library and many of its collections are housed in the Great North Museum, where the Society also has an office. Its collection of Northumbrian and similar pipes is held in the Chantry Museum in Morpeth.

In addition to its other activities, the Society administers the Castle Keep and Black Gate on behalf of the City. At the time of writing plans are being discussed for new uses of the Black Gate as part of the Heart of the City project.

For further information see: www.newcastle-antiquaries.org.uk

under the railway arch to come to an open area, part of Castle Garth.

The Castle Keep is on your right. The Bridge Hotel is opposite. On the left is the Vermont Hotel, formerly the offices of the Northumberland County Council, and the Moot Hall, formerly a county court and prison. In 1400 Newcastle town was separated from the County of Northumberland, except for the Castle Garth which remained part of Northumberland. This situation continued until 1974 when the area reverted to Newcastle **(Qu 9)**.

Walk ahead and go down the steps. After a few metres, on the right, is a small remnant of the castle wall. At the bottom of the stairs turn left and walk ahead passing Bessie Surtees' House on the way back to the Guildhall and the end of the walk **(Qu 10)**.

Quiz questions

1. **What was the original use of the building now occupied by The Quayside pub?**
2. **What is the name of the road that runs parallel to the river here?**
3. **What type of street surface is used in Hanover Street?**
4. **How did Orchard Street get its name?**
5. **What is the name of the Casino which you pass?**
6. **What is the name of the nearer house?**
7. **What event is commemorated in a plaque outside the Lit and Phil building?**
8. **What is Queen Victoria holding in her left hand?**
9. **What is the significance of the shields on the railings outside the Vermont Hotel and the Moot Hall?**
10. **What is the name of the stairs by which you descend from Castle Garth?**

11. Ouseburn Regeneration

Start:	Haymarket Metro Station
Finish:	Monument Metro Station
Distance:	5.5 miles (with a cut-off point after 3.5 miles)
Route:	Haymarket Metro Station, Northumbria University City campuses, Biscuit Factory, former Newcastle Stadium, Ouseburn Village Green, Hoult's Yard, Quayside East, Ouseburn, New Bridge Street, Monument Metro Station
Accessibility:	Mostly on pavements and surfaced paths
Refreshments:	Cafés and/or pubs in Haymarket area, the Biscuit Factory, Ouseburn Village and Hoults Yard

Ouseburn Regeneration

The River Ouseburn runs for 14 kilometres from its source near Callerton in Northumberland to its confluence with the River Tyne at Newcastle. For the last one-third of its journey it runs through the Newcastle suburb of Gosforth and then Jesmond Dene before emerging after a culvert for its final kilometre through the Lower Ouseburn Valley. Locally, the name 'Ouseburn' is sometimes taken to be the small area around Lime Street and The Cluny and Ouseburn Farm (all of which are seen on the walk). However, the Ouseburn Regeneration Area is much wider. It lies between two places subject to Newcastle City Area Action Plans: on the east, the East Walker Riverside, on the west Newcastle City Centre. The regeneration project also embraces parts of Shieldfield, Byker and St Ann's.

Historically, the lower Ouseburn Valley and surroundings were at the forefront of the industrial revolution on Tyneside. Glass making was established by the early 18th century and a variety of manufacturing activities followed, including foundries, linen and corn mills, lead works, potteries, tanneries and a miscellany of chemical works producing, for example, soap, sulphuric acid and paint. All of this was accompanied by a large increase in the local population.

A combination of many factors including lack of demand, transfer of manufacturing to larger units - sometimes with improved methods of production, workers' protection legislation and foreign competition led to a decline in Ouseburn's industrial output. Many residential terraces were demolished and people were rehoused elsewhere. Hence, the description of the area in the mid-20th century as a 'derelict backwater' was particularly apposite.

There have been a number of regeneration projects over the last few decades, including the construction of residential and commercial properties, and there are several examples of thoughtful refurbishment of redundant industrial sites. New businesses have been established and there has been a mini-boom in art galleries and other cultural activities.

Regeneration is ongoing and, as well as completed works, you can expect to see redevelopments taking place and cleared spaces waiting for the builders' equipment to move in.

To find out more visit www.ouseburnnewcastle.org

From the entrance to the Metro Station in Northumberland Street walk towards the church for a few metres then turn right into St Mary's Place. A plaque tells you that the terrace of houses on your right was built by John Dobson to complement St Thomas' Church which he had recently designed. Walk ahead crossing the dual carriageway (John Dobson Street).

At the next junction (College Street) go straight across, then turn right and proceed ahead along College Street. On the left, the attractive red brick building is College House (1883), now owned by Northumbria University. High in the wall, in a niche, is a statute of Dame Eleanor Allan. She was the daughter of a city goldsmith and widow of a wealthy tobacco merchant who, in 1705, founded the school which bears her name. From its beginnings in the west end, it moved to this building but is now located in much larger purpose-built premises in Fenham.

At the crossroads, pause and look over to the right to a building with a statue on the top. This is Burt Hall (1895) former home of the Northumberland Miners' Association and commemorating Thomas Burt. The statue represents a miner going home and is based on the painting *Going Home* by Ralph Hedley in the Laing Art Gallery. The red brick building opposite is Northumbria University's Sutherland Building (1887), formerly part of Durham University College of Medicine.

Now turn left and walk along the pedestrianized Northumberland Road. On your left you pass St James' United Reformed Church (1884). Over to your right is another University building, originally Trinity Presbyterian Church (1895). A little further, on your left, is Brady and Martin Court, a housing development which incorporates the attractive bow-fronted frontage of the property originally occupied by Brady and Martin, wholesale chemical manufacturers. We are going to cross the road here but you might like to note that a short distance ahead is Sport Central, Northumbria University's state-of-the art sport's complex. Newcastle Eagles basketball team is also centred here.

Cross the road towards the sculpture *Book Stack* (Fred Watson, 1992) **(Qu 1)**.

Take the path to the left of the revolving glass doors and follow the wide path with bold sculptures (Nico Widerberg, 2009) in the middle. This path, together with the pedestrian bridge over the motorway, was constructed to create a link between the existing Northumbria University City Centre Campus and the new City Campus East, which was completed in 2007. Go over the bridge and carry on to meet a service road. The area on your right, now occupied by the futuristic buildings of the new campus, was the location of Manors Goods Station, a railway station built in 1907 and destroyed by enemy bombing in 1941.The goods stored there, including butter, lard and sugar according to one commentator, provided plentiful fuel for the ensuing fire which burnt for two days and was fought by firemen from all over Northumberland and Durham.

Cross over the service road, turn right and walk ahead. At the junction, cross the road and turn left to walk past Christ Church (1861) which has been described as 'one of the very best examples of Victorian Gothic buildings' (Prins and Massingberd-Mundy, in Pickering ed,1982) **(Qu 2)**.

Over the road on the left is a remnant of the Shield Field where Charles I is said to have played golf during his imprisonment by the Scots in Newcastle following the end of the Civil War in 1646.

Carry on past the adjacent primary school and the Queens Arms, which has a plaque with details of its history. Continue in the same direction along Copland Terrace.

On the left, just before a junction, you pass the Martin-Luther-Kirche, which serves the local German-speaking Lutheran congregation. Bear left and descend towards a junction. On the left is **The Holy Biscuit**. On your right, the construction of 396 University of Northumbria

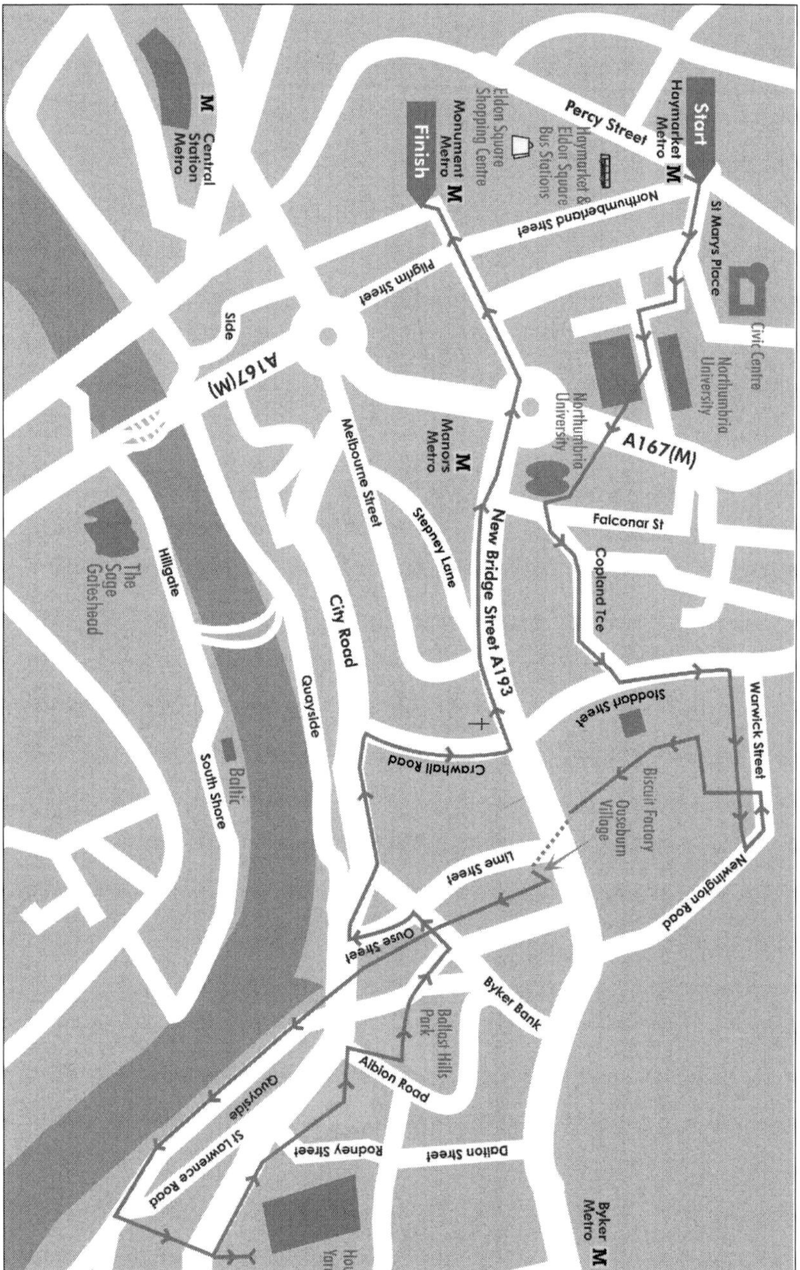
Start
Finish
Haymarket Metro
Percy Street
Haymarket & Eldon Square Bus Stations
Eldon Square Shopping Centre
Monument Metro
Central Station Metro
Northumberland Street
St Marys Place
Civic Centre
Northumbria University
Northumbria University
Pilgrim Street
Side
A167(M)
A167(M)
Manors Metro
Melbourne Street
Stepney Lane
New Bridge Street A193
Falconar St
Copland Tce
Hillgate
The Sage Gateshead
City Road
Quayside
Warwick Street
Stoddart Street
Crawhall Road
South Shore
Baltic
Biscuit Factory
Ouseburn Village
Lime Street
Newington Road
Ouse Street
Byker Bank
Ballast Hills Park
Albion Road
Quayside
St Lawrence Road
Rodney Street
Dalton Street
Byker Metro

A learning environment

student residences provides an example of the regeneration of the area. You come to the junction. Cross the busy road to the **The Biscuit Factory**, claimed to be Britain's biggest commercial art store, with two floors of exhibition spaces and two floors of artists' studios, a café and an adjacent restaurant **(Qu 3)**.

An offshoot of the Biscuit Factory is **The Biscuit Tin Studios** which we pass a little later.

Turn left (or turn right if exiting from the Biscuit Factory) and continue ahead as far as the pedestrian traffic lights, then turn right onto the pedestrian/cycle path in the direction indicated to 'Ouseburn Community Centre'. Carry on, keeping on the main path. Over to your left note The Biscuit Tin Studios (see above). You reach a blue sign 'Jesmond Dene 1¼, Longbenton 3¼'. Turn left and after a few metres exit onto Newington Road. Turn left, then left again and walk to an information board. This tells the story of the 1907-1911 construction of the Ouseburn Culvert, through which the river runs for 700 metres. During World War II part of the culvert had a concrete platform floor installed to provide an air-raid shelter for local people. **(Qu 4)**, **(Qu 5)**.

Walk a short distance to reach a path on the left which is accessed through a metal barrier. The green metal bottle, on the rail, inscribed 'Ouseburn Riverside Walkway', is one of many which are placed on this route. Walk along the path. The sculpture over to your right incorporates a representation of the meandering Ouseburn, with the names of the places through which it passes recorded on the ground-level plinth.

At the junction of paths, turn right and proceed for 20 metres then take the narrow path on the left. After about 75 metres the path joins another path. Bear left and continue alongside the sports field on your left. This is the site of the running track of the former, short-lived **Newcastle City Stadium.**

You descend to a junction of paths. Turn right and walk ahead. On your right there is a small training area for horse riders from nearby stables. The surface is made from used

Newcastle City Stadium

This was alternatively known as the Ouseburn Stadium. The City Council, which constructed the track on derelict ground in the 1950s, had ambitious plans for its development, including a banked cycling track, but these fell through and only limited facilities were provided. However, athletics meetings were held until the early 1970s. Thereafter it fell into disuse, not least because of the continuing expansion of Gateshead Stadium in which a tartan synthetic track was laid in 1974. Local champion athlete Brendan Foster, broke the world 3000 metre record on the Gateshead track in the same year.

The Biscuit Factory

This prestigious art gallery owes its name to the fact that the building was recorded as being 'The Tyne Biscuit Factory' as early as 1870 before being referred to as the 'Newcastle upon Tyne Biscuit Manufacturer' in 1900. Over the following years it seems to have changed its use several times, being a warehouse, a furniture store, a wallpaper and paint depot, a retail outlet for carpets and kitchen furniture and a furniture factory before being purchased by the current owner in 1984. However, it was not until 2001 that the property was extensively renovated in order to create its present first-class exhibition facilities before opening in November 2002 as The Biscuit Factory Art Gallery.

Two spacious floors provide a light and airy ambience in which to display the wide variety of the gallery's contents, which include paintings, sculptures, photographs, ceramics, jewellery, drawings, glass work and prints. The gallery takes particular pride in being able to 'celebrate and showcase local artists' as well as leading national and international talent. It hosts special events, talks, previews and charity evenings and it also provides an exciting venue for private hire for such as wedding receptions and corporate meetings. The Biscuit Factory describes itself as 'a fun and relaxed place to buy original and contemporary art' and the tastefully laid out interior with its comfortable access for public viewing certainly encourages any prospective clients. Apart from viewing the extensive collection of original art, there is the opportunity to enjoy refreshments at the adjoining restaurant or, inside, the top floor Factory Kitchen café. The latter offers excellent views beyond the Metro and road bridges to colourful sections of the distinctive Byker Wall housing complex (see below). On a fine day you can enjoy sitting outdoors on the café's terrace where the views may suggest the need for further regeneration. The gallery is open seven days a week and admission is free.

For further information see: www.thebiscuitfactory.com; Tel 0191-2611103

The Holy Biscuit

May 2010 saw the beginning of an innovative partnership between The Biscuit Factory and the Methodist Church with the inauguration of The Holy Biscuit art facility. Shieldfield Methodist Church which had opened in 1973 had suffered from population movements and dwindling congregations leading to services ceasing in the 1990s. Discussions between Ramy Zack, owner of The Biscuit Factory and the Rev Rob Hawkins, Methodist Minister and a Newcastle University Chaplain, resulted in the conversion of the building into a centre for exhibitions and educational arts projects. While Ramy Zack has generously funded the redevelopment, seen as a further step in extending the artistic link with the Ouseburn Valley, the Holy Biscuit centre remains under Methodist ownership as a non-commercial Christian artistic organisation. It is expected to promote cultural learning and training programmes involving universities, schools and community groups.

For further information see, www.theholybiscuitfactory.org;Tel 0191-2321693

The Biscuit Tin Studios

This is a further example of the expansion of the Shieldfield/Ouseburn arts quarter as a consequence of the refurbishment of former industrial premises. In this case a former print works in Warwick Street has been converted into some forty studios which The Biscuit Factory lets out to a wide range of art practitioners.

For further information see: www.ouseburnopenstudios.org

tyres, which not only serves to soften the landing if you fall off but also provides a good example of recycling - most appropriate for an area of regeneration!

Shortly you arrive at a road. Turn left, go under the arches and carry on down the road to arrive at a junction with Stepney Bank. Turn left and proceed ahead. On your right is the entrance to Stepney Bank Stables (see below). You arrive at the headquarters of the Ouseburn Trust and, on your right, the small Ouseburn Village Green. The area here is designated Ouseburn Village.

The walk will take you past the Cluny, at 36 Lime Street on your right, to cross a bridge. However, before continuing you will probably wish to take time to explore the many attractions in this section of the Ouseburn Regeneration programme. You may prefer to wander on your own or you can see the main attractions if you take the following short **Tour of Ouseburn Village** which starts from the Ouseburn Trust centre and passes the **Ship Inn, Ouseburn Farm, The Cluny, 36 Lime Street, Seven Stories and Stepney Bank Stables**.

To continue the walk, go down the path to the left of The Cluny. Just before the bridge there is a path on the left. It's worth going along for a short distance. Here you have a good view of the farm and an information board with details of the former lead industry located here. There is a series of plates on the ground illustrating some of the business activities which were situated here in its industrial heyday. One of these shows a wherry, the type of small vessel used to transfer cargo from the larger ships to the firms for which they were destined. You also have a good view of the concrete Metro viaduct (1979) and the railway bridge (1839) designed by John and Benjamin Green, the noted local Victorian architects. Its original laminated timber arches were replaced with wrought iron in 1869 and it was widened in 1887.

Now cross the bridge and turn

Meandering Ouseburn

Underneath the arches

Ouseburn Village

Tour of Ouseburn Village

Start at the Ouseburn Trust building. This is the administrative centre of the Trust. It has displays of local events and attractions. Materials about the Ouseburn Valley are available. For further information: Tel 0191 2616596.
Walk a few metres to the Ship Inn.

Ship Inn

Tucked in below Byker Bridge (1878), the Ship Inn dates from the 19th century. Its name is a reminder of the former importance of river craft to the development of industry in the Ouseburn Valley. It was rebuilt in 1905 and remains a popular pub.
From the Ship Inn proceed to Ouseburn Farm.

Ouseburn Farm

This is a fascinating place for children (and adults!). It is an education and training centre with emphasis on sustainability, which Prince Charles found commendable when he visited in September 2010. There is plenty of information inside and in the outside enclosures you will see chickens, ducks and geese as well as goats, sheep and pigs.
For further information see: www.ouseburnfarm.org.uk: Tel 0191 2323698
Walk, below the remains of a former chimney, to the Cluny.

The Cluny

The building now occupied by The Cluny was originally a flax mill by Dobson (1848) and then a flour mill, which subsequently became a bonded warehouse where Cluny whisky was stored, hence the name. It is a pub and 'a top live music venue'. For further information: Tel 0191 2304474
The Cluny is located in 36 Lime Street.

36 Lime Street

The building not only houses The Cluny but the name '36 Lime Street' is given to the cooperative organisation which operates from here. The guiding principle of the organisation is 'to provide secure, affordable studio places for creative artists and in doing so to contribute towards the regeneration of the site'. In addition to the ongoing studio activity of the forty artists who work here, special events and exhibitions are held periodically. It is open to the public on Fridays and weekends. For further information: Tel 0191 2615666
A few metres further along on your left is the entrance to Seven Stories.

Seven Stories

Seven Stories is the first museum in the UK wholly dedicated to the art of British children's books. It is a centre for children's literature where 'the heritage of British children's books is explored and celebrated'. It holds special events and exhibitions including visits by popular children's authors. Seven Stories is located on the seven stories of a converted 19th-century flour mill, just one example of a tasteful restoration of former industrial architecture. There an admission charge but entry to the book shop and the café is free after you register at the reception desk. For further information see: www.sevenstories.org.uk; Tel 0845 271077

The building on the other side of the road is the indoor riding arena of Stepney Bank Stables.

Stepney Bank Stables

The stables are run by an award-winning charity. Riding and riding lessons are available for able-bodied young people and training for the British Horse Society qualifications are undertaken. Since the construction of a new indoor arena in 2002, the organisation has been able to increase its valuable work with young people from disadvantaged backgrounds or with mobility problems. Further up Stepney Bank, on the right, are the original stables which are still used for stabling horses.
For further information see: www.stepneybank.co.uk; Tel 0191 2615544

You need to retrace your steps to The Cluny to continue the walk.

immediately right to join a riverside path. As you walk along the path there is a good view of the seven stories of Seven Stories; a quaint little boat, the *Sea Song Sang*, is moored there – the product of a project with children, by local artist and boat-builder Andy Comley. You might also notice some more green metal bottles on the railings, a reminder that glass bottles were made around here for 300 years or so until the 1930s. Shortly you pass an area where small pleasure craft are moored. Go underneath a bridge.

On the other side of the river, in the distance you can see the chimney of the former Maynards Toffee Works. Maynards was established in 1906 taking over the site of the defunct Cattle Sanatorium (1870) where, in the days before refrigeration, live cattle and sheep imports were examined to assess their state of health before being incorporated into the nineteenth-century food chain.

Carry on along the riverside path. On your left you pass the remains of furnaces of the Liddle-Henzell Glass Works, together with two plaques giving historical details. You go under Glasshouse Bridge (1878) to arrive at a green metal waymarker for the 'Ouseburn Riverside Walkway' which has references to local industry, including Maling and Henzell. Also, on your right, is the Ouseburn Barrage which was completed in 2009. Bearing in mind that the River Tyne is tidal, the construction of a lock means that the Ouseburn can be kept at high water level. Hence, it continues to be navigable for small craft and prospective residential and business properties will have an outlook of flowing water rather than twice-daily mud flats.

Walk past the Tyne pub on your left. Turn left.

(Over the road there is a bus stop. This is a convenient cut-off point if lack of time (or tiredness) means that you need to finish here. From the bus stop you can take a yellow bus to the Guildhall or the Haymarket Bus Station.)

To continue the walk, proceed ahead along the pavement on the left-hand side of the road. You pass the Byker Ouseburn Regeneration Centre building on your right. On the opposite bank of the river, the tall tower which you can see is for kittiwakes to roost; hopefully, gathering here instead of on buildings. The riverside here is a popular place for anglers, a reminder that we need no longer talk of the 'coaly Tyne' – perhaps the 'shoaly' Tyne would be more appropriate!

After a couple of hundred metres or so, at a road junction, turn sharp left. Walk ahead, past *Spiller's Forest* (Nick James, 2005), an artwork created from redundant quayside timbers. After fifty metres, on the right-hand side you will see The Mushroom Works, an art gallery and studios housing a wide range of creative businesses **(Qu 6)**.

Take the narrow path immediately to the right of The Mushroom Works. Walk ahead alongside the stone wall on your right to reach a main road (Walker Road). Cross the road with care. (If necessary use the pedestrian refuge one hundred metres or so further along on the left.) Turn left and walk to the wide entrance of **Hoult's Yard**. Turn right and go into the yard. A site map provides details of the present occupants. Hoult's Yard is a redevelopment of the Ford B site of the former **Maling Pottery** and incorporates many original buildings including the Clock Tower, which has a café **(Qu 7)**.

Hoult's Yard

This is the headquarters of Hoults Estates Ltd, a family-owned company set up in the 1940s. Originally, the site was the Ford B factory of Maling pottery. In 1947 Hoults took over Maling and, as well as carrying out its own removals and storage business, operated the pottery until 1963. In recent years the Yard has been transformed from an industrial estate into a complex of small businesses, mainly media, digital, marketing, legal and manufacturing, which are located in tastefully-reconditioned original factory buildings. Available space was increased in 2009 with the completion of The Kiln, a £3 million brand new office development which received financial support from the local regional development agency.

The Yard includes a café, open until mid-afternoon. It is located in the original Clock Tower and is open to the public. A visit to the café gives the opportunity to see the remaining buildings of the original Maling Ford B factory.

Maling Pottery

A plentiful supply of coal contributed to the growing importance of potteries, of which Maling was the most famous, in Newcastle's industrial development during the 18th and 19th centuries. In 1762 the family's first pottery was opened in Sunderland. In 1815 the business moved to Ouseburn Bridge in Newcastle; here, coal and clay were mined locally and other materials could be imported cheaply in the form of ballast from coal ships returning from the south of England.

From the 1850s there was a rapid expansion in output and range of products. Vastly superior production and profit levels were achieved from 1859 from the new Ford A pottery, financed by Mary nee Ford, wife of Christopher Thompson Maling. Expansion continued and in 1878 Ford B was built in Walker. Until the 1920s the Ford A and Ford B sites employed over 1,000 workers, mainly female.

Original Maling

Although the profits derived mostly from basic commercial ware, the firm is perhaps best remembered, especially by collectors, for its decorated domestic pottery. Some decorated pottery was manufactured as early as the end of the 18th century. Bell (1986) reports that the account books of Thomas Bewick and Ralph Beilby, between 1788 and 1798, include orders from Maling for engraved copper plates, from which designs were transferred onto the pottery. Designers in the 20th century included Lucien Emille Boullemeir and his son, also Lucien.

Examples of Maling ware can be seen in the Laing Art Gallery. There is a Maling Potteries Collectors' Society which can be contacted by email at info@maling-pottery.org.uk.

The beginning of a long, slow decline started in the 1920s. The firm was sold to Hoults Estates Limited, a furniture removal firm, in 1947. Under the leadership of Frederick Hoult, the company's chairman there was an initial recovery and production increased. However, international competition, especially from the Far East, proved too great an obstacle and C. T. Maling and Sons closed in 1963.

Retrace your steps to the entrance, turn right and proceed along Walker Road. Turn right and go up Rodney Street. After fifty metres, take the path on the left into St Lawrence Park, which merges with another path almost immediately. At the crossing of paths, walk ahead with the metal railings on your left until you reach a T-junction. Turn left and walk ahead to exit the park and carry straight on to the junction of St Lawrence Square and Walker Road.

Turn right and walk the short distance to Albion Row. Go straight across and turn right. Walk up Albion Row. On your left, you see a large ornate building, originally Ouseburn Schools (Frank West Rich, 1893). The two roof top cupolas were part of the building's ventilation system. The school closed in 1960. It is now occupied by the Newcastle Enterprise Centres.

Ahead in the distance you have a view of a section of the Byker Wall, an award-winning project by Ralph Erskine within the Byker redevelopment scheme (1969-1981). Walk ahead and turn left to the entrance to Ballast Hills Park where a plaque indicates the significance of the park's name and the gravestones path **(Qu 8)**.

(To avoid the difficult path through the park, walk ahead along Walker Road to the other side of the Enterprise Centres building. Turn right and walk along Ford Street where you will soon be walking parallel to Ballast Hills Park and arrive at the exit and the blue signpost.)

School by FW Rich

Walk ahead through the park taking either a clockwise or anticlockwise path over the gravestones until you reach the park exit into Ford Street where there is a blue signpost.

Proceed along Ford Street. The Ford A factory of Maling Pottery (see above) was situated on the right-hand side of Ford Street. You pass Raskl, a further example of the area's art and craft enclave, which specialises in custom-designed furniture and fittings.

At the junction with a main road (Byker Bank), turn left and walk to Ouse Street on the left. Proceed along this street where, on the right, you will see an entrance to the **Victoria Tunnel** together with display panels giving comprehensive information about the tunnel.

As you approach the junction with the busy City Road, you will see gates inscribed with the name of the Tyne Tees Shipping Company. The building was formerly the headquarters of this important business which was formed in1864 from the amalgamation of two local steam shipping companies. It is now occupied by the Hotel du Vin and Bisto. Notice the plaque on your right giving details of the exploits of the Craig family **(Qu 9)**.

At the junction, if you look over the road, you will see a monument to William Lisle Blenkinsopp Coulson (1841 - 1911), a noted supporter of child and animal welfare. To the right of this you can see the Sailor's Bethel opened in 1877; in the late nineteenth century it offered overnight accommodation to Danish sailors as their boat was being unloaded at the Ouseburn.

Turn right and walk past the Hotel du Vin and Bistro. Continue along City Road. You pass a metal pillar with references to rope making and 'the Byker sons who made the ships but never sailed the seas'. Take care in crossing the busy intersection. You pass the sculpture *Time to..* by Cate Watkinson (2006), which is designed to 'act as a link between the city, the Eastern Quayside and the east end'. St Nicholas' Cathedral can be seen ahead in the distance. Turn up the narrow road on your right. A plaque on the wall indicates that this was the former Ouseburn Mission Hall (1869) and commemorates local inventor and photographer Gladstone Adams **(Qu 10)**.

Victoria Tunnel

In 1835 the Spital Tongues Colliery opened. To get the coal from the pit to the staiths at Newcastle meant either using carts through Newcastle or building a waggonway. The former was opposed by the townsfolk and the Council, because of the disruption to traffic and the noise and dirt that would arise, and in any event would be expensive. Accordingly, a proposal for a waggonway across the Town Moor was made by William Gillespie, an engineer employed by the Colliery's owners. The Freemen of the Newcastle, who have oversight over the surface of the Moor, refused to allow this proposal to go ahead. Gillespie then came up with a plan for a tunnel to link the pit with the riverside. Permission was given by the Council. The tunnel was built in thirty months and was opened in January 1842. Its official opening by the Mayor being on 7th April 1842 when it was named after Queen Victoria.

Coal was transported by gravity in waggons which were hauled back to the pit by rope attached to a steam engine. Although the costs of transportation using the tunnel were much lower than the alternatives, the colliery itself was closed in 1860 and the tunnel became redundant. Subsequently, various short sections were lost with the development of new roads and housing. However, during World War II most of its length was converted into an air-raid shelter with seven entrances. For the Ouse Street entrance, it was necessary to install walls to act as blast deflectors in the event of a bomb landing nearby. Some years later part of it was used as a mushroom farm.

Today the tunnel, now a Grade II listed building, is fast becoming a tourist attraction with organised trips from the entrance in Ouse Street.

Further information is available from www.victoriatunnel.info

You might like to make use of the handrail as you climb up the steep path. At the top turn left and proceed past the elegant St Ann's Church (1768) on your left. Just inside the gate there is an information board about the church which was built on the site of a medieval chapel with stone from a demolished section of the Town Wall. The church was designed by William Newton (1730-1798) whose work includes The Assembly Rooms and Charlotte Square, where he lived for many years.

Cross the road when convenient and when you reach the crossroads, go straight across and immediately turn right and walk up the road (Crawhall Road).

Just before the busy intersection you will see, on your right, the Tanners pub, Also the Star and Shadow Cinema, which is entirely run by volunteers and as well as films has gigs, live art and exhibitions. Just before you turn left, look for the large yellow manhole cover, surrounded by bollards. This is the means of exit from the Victoria Tunnel, if for any reason an exit into Ouse Street is not possible – a comforting thought for the increasing number of visitors to the tunnel.

Now turn left and proceed past the Blackfriars Centre, containing Blackfriars Hall, a popular venue for social events, and also housing the St Vincent de Paul Society, a Roman Catholic charity, founded in Paris in the 1830s to relieve the poverty of those called by Victor Hugo, *Les Miserables* (the wretched ones). The Society has been active in the United Kingdom since 1844. The adjacent building (1897) is now occupied by the society. You pass the imposing bulk of St Dominic's Priory Church (1873). It is the largest Catholic church in the city and has been the home of the Dominican Order in Newcastle since its completion. Before you come to the next road on the left notice the men's and women's entrances to the former Gibson Street Public Baths.

Cross the road and continue in the same direction. Over to your right is the redeveloped site for further student residences for the University of Northumbria. You pass The New Bridge inn, with an information panel on the side which gives details of the construction of the Tyne Bridge. Next door is the Kings Manor pub which has an information board giving details of the area's ancient connection with royalty, particularly King Charles 1. A little further on you pass Manors Metro Station and Central Business and Technology Park, Kings Manor. Carry straight ahead, initially by a ramp, to cross over the motorway.

(There are steep steps ahead. To avoid these use the ramp to descend to a road. Cross the road with care, walk ahead for a few metres and then bear right to reach an open area.)

Go up a ramp, walk ahead and descend via steps to reach an open area. Walk ahead passing the Laing Art Gallery and the City Library. From there carry straight on towards Grey's Monument and the Monument Metro Station and the end of the walk.

Quiz questions

1. **Why is the Book Stack sculpture located where it is?**
2. **Which organisation funded the renovation of the clock on the spire of Christ Church?**
3. **What is the name of the restaurant which is next door to the Biscuit Factory?**
4. **Why was it necessary to build a culvert for the River Ouseburn to run through?**
5. **From here, how many bridges do you walk under before you reach the Ouseburn Village Green?**
6. **What do the Biscuit Factory and the Mushroom Works have in common?**
7. **When was the Clock Tower in Hoult's Yard built?**
8. **Why is Ballast Hills Park so named?**
9. **Why is there a plaque (at the end of Ouse Street) dedicated to the Craig family?**
10. **What did Gladstone Adams invent in 1911?**

12. Gateshead and Low Fell

Start: Gateshead Metro Station
Finish: Belle Vue Bank Bus Stop, Low Fell
Distance: 3.25 miles
Route: Gateshead Metro Station, Windmill Hills Park, Alexandra Road, Bewick Road, Prince Consort Road, Shipley Art Gallery, Saltwell Park, Low Fell
Accessibility: On pavements and paths throughout with ramped access to internal visits. However, there are several very steep sections
Refreshments: Gateshead Library, Saltwell Towers Visitor Centre, Tea Room and pub in Low Fell

To exit from Gateshead Metro Station follow the signs for Jackson Street, Bensham Road and Bus Station. In the Bus Station Concourse turn left to pass the Travel Shop to leave by the Jackson Street exit. A substantial artwork of glass and steel, *Opening line* (Danny Lane, 2004) serves as a safety barrier as well as a focal point for waiting passengers. Various images reflect aspects of the town's history and culture.

The wind blows on Windmill Hill

Cross over with care to Walker Terrace and turn right to proceed ahead. On your left is St Joseph's Catholic Church opened in 1859 at a time when Gateshead's population was rapidly expanding as industries attracted Irish Catholic immigrants in particular. The adjacent parish hall is known as the Emmaus Centre. The fine terrace of houses in Walker Terrace, with their stone gate posts, are now mainly occupied by offices that serve to maintain the professional tradition of this part of the town.

Cross the dual carriageway at the traffic lights to follow the sign 'Bensham Cycleway'. On your right you pass the now boarded up former Windmill Hills School of 1885. The building served as a school until 2000 before becoming a care home for some six years.

Walk a few metres and turn right to enter the Windmill Hills Park. In 1861 this became Gateshead's first public park occupying part of a much larger area on which once stood

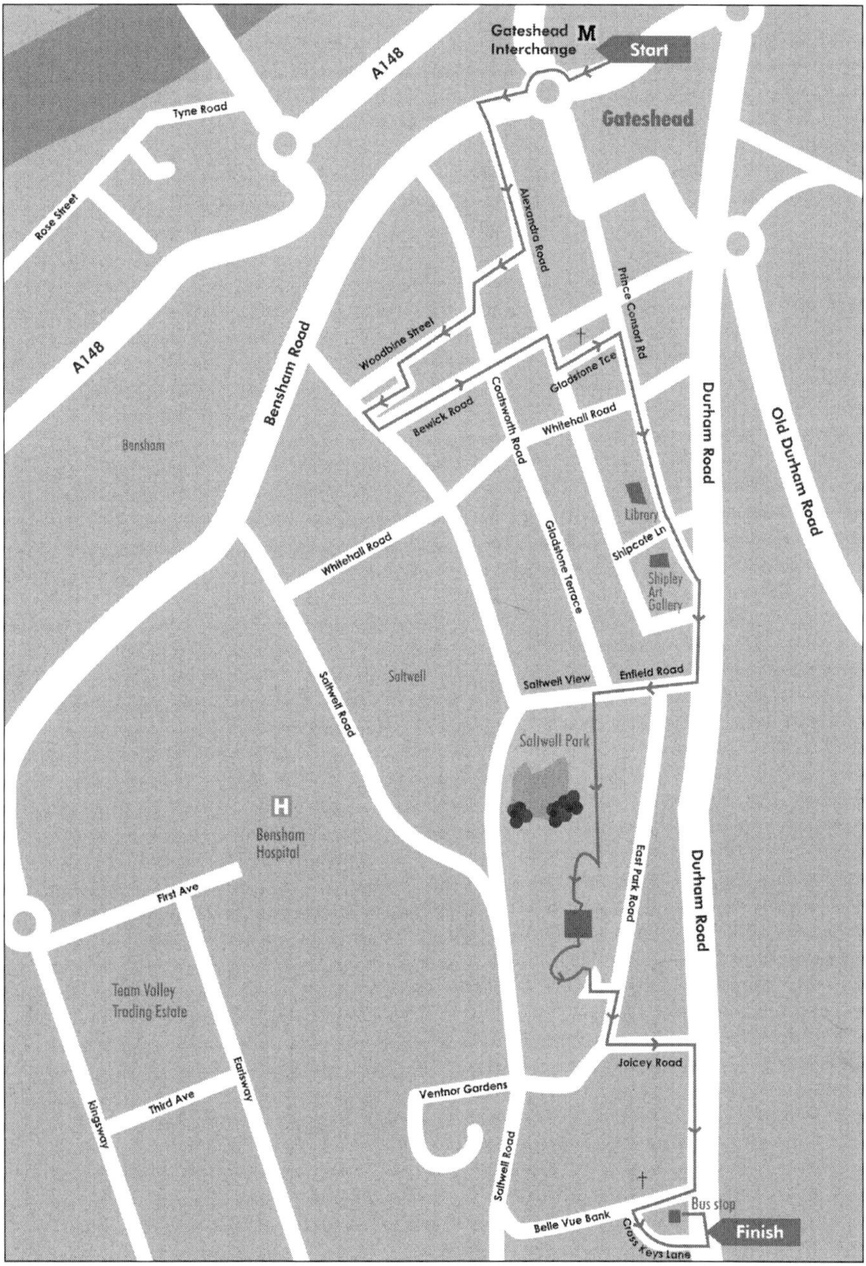
Gateshead Interchange
M
Start
A148
Tyne Road
Gateshead
Rose Street
Alexandra Road
Prince Consort Rd
A148
Bensham Road
Woodbine Street
Gladstone Tce
Bewick Road
Coatsworth Road
Whitehall Road
Durham Road
Old Durham Road
Bensham
Library
Whitehall Road
Gladstone Terrace
Shipcote Ln
Shipley Art Gallery
Saltwell
Saltwell Road
Saltwell View
Enfield Road
Saltwell Park
H
Bensham Hospital
East Park Road
Durham Road
First Ave
Team Valley Trading Estate
Earlsway
Joicey Road
Ventnor Gardens
Third Ave
Kingsway
Saltwell Road
Bus stop
Belle Vue Bank
Cross Keys Lane
Finish

some ten windmills. On your left is a statue dedicated to the first mayor of Gateshead. It is said that he was a popular mayor but one who admitted to not being assiduous in attention to his duties because of his work commitments in running the family ironworks. He is credited with granting the land to create the park. Although his name is missing from the monument itself, the answer to the first quiz question lies very close by **(Qu 1)**.

Follow the broad path past the tall metal weathervane to obtain excellent views across to Newcastle. It was from this vantage point in 1644 that the Battle of Windmill Hills took place when Scottish troops supporting the Parliamentarians in The Civil War bombarded the Royalists defending Newcastle.

Leave the park, following the path with the children's play area over to your right. Continue straight ahead up Mulgrave Villas to the main road. Use the pedestrian crossing on your right to get to the other side of the busy road. Turn left then immediately right and continue ahead (Alexandra Road). On your left you pass Gateshead Masonic Hall, base of the Gateshead group of lodges. Proceed ahead for a few hundred metres. passing on your left what is currently a playing field, formerly referred to as the **North Durham Cricket & Rugby Ground**..

Continue ahead until you reach Claremont North Avenue Turn right and walk down this pleasant pathway between the terraced houses. Turn left along the shop-lined road (Coatsworth Road) until you reach The Honeysuckle pub (currently boarded up). Cross over to Woodbine Street using the pedestrian crossing. (A few metres beyond the crossing is Woodbine Terrace where the founders of the Salvation Army, **William and Catherine Booth**, once lived.) Walk down Woodbine Street.

North Durham Cricket & Rugby Ground

This green space near the town centre has hosted sporting activities since the 19th century. A covenant in the title deeds decrees that the land should be used only for leisure purposes; hence, there has been no building development.

During the latter part of the 20th century the ground was the home of the North Durham Cricket and Rugby Club. In 1998 North Durham Rugby Club moved out following its earlier merger with Gateshead Fell Rugby Club to become Gateshead RFC. In 2000 the pavilion burnt down and the ground has since been used for youth football. Apart from cricket and rugby, the ground has been used for other sporting activities.

From the 1870s until the 1930s North Durham was well known for the athletics and cycling meetings held there. Runners used the grass track and there was a banked ash track for the cycling events. In the 1920s two Gateshead athletic clubs, Gateshead Congers (or Congregational) Harriers, whose relay team swept the board in 1929, and Saltwell Harriers achieved much success. Saltwell Harriers is still going strong but Gateshead Congers folded in the late 1960s possibly owing to the growth of Gateshead Harriers, founded in 1904 as St Mary's Church Running Club, which has achieved a great deal, particularly since it moved to the Gateshead International Stadium in 1956.

The latest plans for the North Durham ground involve professional football. Gateshead Football Club, currently using Gateshead International Stadium as its base, has announced that it has acquired the North Durham ground and proposes to build an 8000 capacity stadium on the site. In addition, having turned professional in 2010, the club aims to regain membership of the Football League which it lost in controversial circumstances in 1960.

William Booth (1829-1912) and Catherine Booth (1829-1890)

William and Catherine were married in 1858 and came to Gateshead to reside in Woodbine Terrace for three years from 1858 to 1861 while William was Minister of Bethseda New Connexion Methodist Chapel in Melbourne Road. He proved to be a powerful preacher and he attracted a large congregation. In that era it was not considered fashionable for women to take a prominent part in church services but Catherine, while in Gateshead, was inspired to preach for the first time. This had significant influence on William who thereafter became a great campaigner for women's rights. However William preferred to travel and preach rather than being settled in one place. This led to a break with the church authorities and to William becoming an independent evangelist. He and Catherine founded the Christian Revival Society (later renamed the Christian Mission) to work among the poor in the East End of London. This in turn in 1878 became the Salvation Army. It was organised on military lines with William as its first 'General' and women on an equal footing with men. The Booths returned to Gateshead in 1879 to conduct an impressive series of revivalist meetings in venues across the town and on Windmill Hills. This resulted in many conversions and the establishment of several Salvation Army Corps in Gateshead.

At the T-junction turn left towards Claremont Place and follow the road as it bears right. Turn left to take a path over a small park area passing a children's play area on your left and reach a road (Bewick Road). The building to your right, at the end of the road, is Gateshead Synagogue (1939), place of worship for Gateshead's large **Jewish community**.

Turn left and proceed up Bewick Road, named after the 19th-century engraver Thomas Bewick who lived the last sixteen years of his life in Gateshead. On your right you pass a terrace of the so-called 'Tyneside flats', that is, one flat upstairs one flat downstairs. Continue straight ahead over the busy road (Coatsworth Road). Bewick Road broadens out and you will notice see some fine refurbished family properties.

Go over the next crossroads, turn immediately right (Alexandra Road) and in a few metres turn left into Gladstone Terrace. Here as you walk up the street you will find an interesting mixture of religious establishments. In addition to a number of the Jewish educational establishments referred to above, on your right, you will see the tiny **Gateshead Consecration and Spiritualist National Union Church** and on the left **The Catholic Church of the Holy Name of Jesus (Qu 2)**.

Continue ahead and at the end of the street, turn right. Walk along this busier street (Prince Consort Road) with some shops and takeaways among some pleasant housing. Eventually, just beyond a sign for Gateshead Leisure Centre you pass a car park, shielded by a hedge and beyond which are some Gateshead Council Offices. You are now in the Shipcote area of Gateshead.

The Library's original entrance

You arrive at Gateshead Central Library which benefited from a multi-million pound refurbishment in 2009/2010 that included the development of a new café,

Jewish community

Gateshead's Jewish Community dates from the late 19th century when Zachariah Bernstone, a Lithuanian Jew believed to be of Polish stock who had settled in Newcastle, decided to move to Gateshead because he was dissatisfied with the standard of orthodoxy of the Newcastle congregation and concerned about attempts to convert immigants to Christianity. This was the beginning of the development of the present independent community of Orthodox Jews that started in humble surroundings near the Redheugh Bridge.

The community was led from its early days by dedicated, determined and scholarly men. It was boosted by the arrival of Orthodox Jews, displaced from many of the traditional centres of Jewish culture in mainland Europe, from the time of the First World War, the purges of the 1930s, World War II and its aftermath. This resulted in Gateshead becoming 'the great university town of Hebrew culture and study in Europe' (Olsover, 1981). Additionally, in the 1930s, German Jews with technical expertise, who had fled from persecution, took the opportunity to restart their manufacturing business in the newly created Team Valley Trading Estate.

Now several hundred Jewish families inhabit the Bensham-Saltwell area of Gateshead making this the third largest community in Britain. Here they are able to live according to their orthodox Jewish traditions. During the academic term the community may number some 4000 people due to the fact that Gateshead offers what is said to be the largest orthodox educational complex in the world outside of the USA and Israel. There is a comprehensive system of Jewish educational establishments from nursery and primary levels to high school and teacher training. The Talmudical College together with the Institute of Higher Rabbinical Studies enjoy a worldwide reputation and as such welcome students from many countries.

Gateshead Consecration and Spiritualist National Union Church

This Church was first established in Gateshead in the 1920s. Later needing to move to new premises, the Spiritualists were able to build the current church here on 'consecrated' land purchased from what was then Christ Church, located on the opposite side of the road, the entrance to which is on Bewick Road.

The Catholic Church of the Holy Name of Jesus

Christ Church on Bewick Road, built in the 1870s, was declared redundant by the Church of England in 2004. It was acquired in 2007 by the Society of St Pius X (SSPX) and reopened as The Catholic Church of the Holy Name of Jesus. The SSPX is a breakaway group of Roman Catholics, established in 1970 by the French Archbishop Lefebvre, who advocate the rediscovery of what they see as 'Catholic tradition'. The Society has refurbished the church and has included a stained glass panel of its founder.

adult learning spaces and a new children's library. It also houses Caedmon Hall, a concert and events venue, named after a 7th-century poet and monk at Whitby Abbey. After passing or visiting the café in the new extension, you pass the historic front entrance **(Qu 3)**.

Continue ahead, crossing the road via a pedestrian refuge. You pass the pillared doorway of the former Gateshead School board (GSB), later Gateshead Education Office which subsequently became the Sunderland Talmudical College, so-called because it was formerly located in Sunderland. Continuing ahead you soon arrive at the **Shipley Art Gallery**.

A few metres beyond the Art Gallery you will find a splendid statue of a local sporting hero, **James Renforth**, with information recorded on the plinth about his exploits and his tragic death recalled in the moving words: 'In the midst of life we are in death'.

A tragic event recalled

Retrace your steps and use the pedestrian refuge if necessary to cross the road to enter the small memorial garden. On the left is an all-inclusive memorial to 'all who made the supreme sacrifice' in 1939-1945. Now continue along the path with Shipley Gallery over to your right where above the end towers you will see two large sculptured male and female figures representing the arts and sciences **(Qu 4)**.

At the end of the path leave the garden, turn left and make your way to the very substantial Gateshead Cenotaph. Here you will discover further dedications on the wall. The memorial itself, designed by J.W.Spink, with the figure in bronze relief by R. Goulden, was inaugurated in front of a huge crowd in 1922. A roll of honour was placed within the monument, however, this was later transferred to the Gateshead Central library for safekeeping. It bears the inscription *Mors Janua Viae* (Death is the Gateway to (everlasting) Life) **(Qu 5)**.

Ahead is the junction with the main road (Durham Road). Turn right at the traffic lights, cross with care and proceed along Durham Road with St George's Church (1897) on your left.

Shipley Art Gallery

The Gallery was opened in 1917 thanks to a generous bequest from the solicitor Joseph Shipley, an avid collector of art. It seems the bequest was originally intended to benefit Newcastle but it appears that the executors could not reach agreement with the authorities and so Gateshead became the beneficiary. Admission to the gallery is free and it contains some fine paintings shown in both permanent and temporary exhibitions. In addition, it lays emphasis on the wide range of art and design that it has on show, stating that it is 'the North East's leading gallery of craft and design'. In 2010 it inaugurated the Henry Rothschild Study Centre which contains works by leading ceramicists since the 1950s, collected by Henry Rothschild (1913-2009) the founder of the shop Primavera. It has also forged strong links with London's Victoria and Albert Museum resulting in important visiting exhibitions and activities.

Even if time is pressing you might at least like to see W.C.Irving's painting *Blaydon Races - A study from life* (1903). An interactive video enables you to hear the famous song and to identify the characters involved. There are even some period dressing up clothes for young children.

James Renforth (1842-1871

Although evidence points to the fact that he was born in Newcastle, perhaps because his family was from Gateshead, it is generally claimed that he too was a Gateshead man. Of powerful build, having worked as a blacksmith and then as a ferryman, he took up rowing for money in his early twenties. He won races on the Tyne and the Thames and called himself the 'Champion of the world'! (Whitehead, 2002). Such was his fame that no one was prepared to challenge him and this led him to turn to competing as part of a four-man team. However, success came to an abrupt and tragic end when he died while racing in Canada against an American crew.

Such was his fame that 100,000 people were said to have turned out for his funeral. The sculptor George Burn who had made funeral monuments in the previous ten years for the noted Tyne oarsmen Robert Chambers and Harry Clasper succeeded in creating a striking and moving image of the tragic events of 23 Aug 1871. One hundred and twenty years later, after being vandalised, the monument was restored by Gateshead Council, and relocated outside the Shipley Art Gallery. An interesting memorial plaque to Renforth can also be found in St Mary's Visitor Centre.

Low Fell

Prior to the nineteenth century this was an area of farmland lying some distance from Gateshead itself. Streams ran down through a number of wooded denes to the River Team below. It was here in the mid-19th century that wealthy industrialists seeking the opportunity to reside in a splendid rural setting, a convenient distance from their collieries and their iron and chemical works, built substantial properties with large landscaped gardens. Nowadays there is little to see of these villas, several originally replaced by educational institutions, and these, in turn, by private housing.

Gateshead Cenotaph

You pass a parade of shops and takeaway outlets and in a short distance you reach Enfield Road. Cross to the other side. You are now in **Low Fell**.

Turn right down the steep Enfield Road and descend to the entrance to Saltwell Park. On the opposite side of the road is the Little Theatre. This is a popular venue for amateur dramatics and other activities A plaque indicates that it was built due to the 'enthusiasm and generosity' of the Dodds sisters. Hope, Ruth and Sylvia, of Low Fell'. It opened in 1943 and it is believed to be the only theatre built in Britain during World War II.

Beside the gates to **Saltwell Park** you will find a map that will help you to plan your visit. You may wish to spend some time exploring the splendour of this Victorian park while children may enjoy the wide grassy spaces, boating on the lake, the maze and the children's play areas. However, your ultimate destination today is **Saltwell Towers** at the far end of the park.

To begin your walk in the park, walk ahead for some 50 metres then turn left and proceed ahead past the Almond Pavilion and the statute of Alderman John Lucas, a former mayor who helped to develop the park. This is 'a park for all seasons' and you will discover a rich variety of plants, many of which are described in literature available in the Visitor Centre. As the path forks, bear right then left to the Rose Garden Information Board which will help you to locate the various varieties of roses **(Qu 6)**.

Proceed to the Rose Garden where you will find a stone monument that is much more recent than those generally found in the park. It commemorates Workers Memorial Day and recalls those lost through industrial accidents and illnesses. Perhaps it helps to recall those who died in harsh Victorian times as well as those since.

Saltwell Park and Saltwell Towers

William Wailes the noted glass manufacturer whose windows grace countless churches (see for example, St Nicholas' and St Mary's Cathedrals in Newcastle) bought the Saltwellside Estate in 1859. He is believed to have both designed and built Saltwell Towers in which he was to live from 1862 until his death in 1881. In 1875 he had sold the property to Gateshead Corporation on condition that he could remain in the house. The following year the Corporation opened the surrounding area as the 'People Park' as the second public park in Gateshead, the first being at Windmill Hills. The gardens of the mansion were enlarged to encompass a beautiful landscaped fifty-five acre site of open spaces, a lake, dense areas of vegetation, wooded denes, brick lodges and timber shelters.

Saltwell Towers was later acquired by Joseph Shipley (see above). During the First World War it was converted into a hospital and later it became a museum. However, it gradually deteriorated and no longer being considered to be a viable proposition it was eventually left to fall into disrepair at the beginning of the 1970s. Fortunately, some thirty-five years later, thanks largely to Heritage Lottery Funding, Gateshead Council were able to complete a major restoration project to bring both Saltwell Towers and Saltwell Park back to their former Victorian splendour. Such was the impressive reconstruction of the 19th century features that it was little wonder that in 2005 the complex won 'Britain's Best Park' award.

Now officially known as Saltwell Park Visitor Centre, the contemporary interior of the building houses a café and an exhibition gallery that includes a twenty minute video presentation outlining the history and restoration of the Towers and the Park. The exhibition room also contains a portrait of William Wailes by John Oliphant, on loan from the Shipley Art Gallery together with a glass painted portrait of Wailes son-in-law and successor to his business, Thomas Rantine Strang. The internal staircase is enclosed in a glass screen designed by local artist Bridget Jones and a lift facilitates access to the visitors' gallery. The former stables behind the house have been converted into an educational centre.

For further information see: www.gateshead.gov.uk/saltwellpark/welcome.htm

Carry on through the garden and then turn left. Proceed ahead and when the path forks, bear left and follow the path as it climbs to Saltwell Towers. You pass an ornate Victorian drinking fountain dedicated to George Charlton, Mayor of Gateshead 1874 and 1875. The pre-1975 Gateshead coat of arms, with its goat's head appears on two sides.

Leave the Saltwell Towers Visitor Centre via the café and make your way to the centre of the grassy area to the memorial to 'Gateshead Men' who died in the South African War (1899-1902). (Wheelchair users need to retrace their way back from the entrance to the Visitor Centre and continue to bear left until they arrive at a small wooden bridge that leads to the war memorial). Here, in addition to their names and the details of their numerous regiments you will be able to read a moving verse.

A modern memorial

Saltwell Towers

Continue ahead and then turn right to pass a seating area and monument, covering a wide span of years, in memory of several Durham contingents. It is interesting to note that it was built with stones from the Drill Hall in Gateshead **(Qu 7)**.

Continue ahead a short way and turn left to pass beneath an archway to arrive at the restored bandstand. Here on Sunday afternoons (May-September) you may be lucky enough to hear a band playing as people picnic nearby. You now need to make your way to the top right-hand corner of the field. Here you find a tree-lined path, uneven at first, that will take you in a short distance out of the park via Gate 4.

You are now in East Park Road also known as Low Road. Turn right and walk to the end of the narrow road to meet Joicey Road. Turn left and walk up the steep road. Opposite Chesters Park you will see the recently developed business premises of 3acrepark on the site of what was once the **Joicey Road Open Air School**.

At the top of the bank you return again to the busy Durham Road. Turn right and in a short distance you will see a driveway with a lodge on the left and on the right a board referring to Wing- Making Learning an Adventure . This is the entrance to what was the largest of Low Fell's grand villas and estates, **Whinney House**.

Continue along Durham Road and pass the gated entrance to a more modern dwelling thought possibly to be on the site of a former inn **(Qu 8)**.

At the traffic lights, turn right to descend Belle Vue Bank. On the left you will see a fine double-fronted building belonging to the Carlton Club, a social club **(Qu 9)**.

A few metres before reaching **St Helen's Church** you pass the Church Hall and a pleasant row of dwellings in St Helen's Terrace, set at right angles to the road.

At the church, cross to the other side of Belle Vue Bank to the Armstrong Building and the Belle Tea Room, to the right of which is Cross Keys Lane. Follow the lane as it

Joicey Road Open Air School

This school, opened in 1937 on land which had once formed part of the Whinney House estate (see below). It was also known as 'The Health School' and its purpose was to provide educational facilities 'for physically handicapped and delicate children', and was constructed according to a Swiss model with easy access to fresh air. It closed as such in 1969, after which it struggled on to fulfil various educational and Council uses until 2005 when it was no longer considered to be viable. Allowed to deteriorate, it was finally acquired from Gateshead Council in 2009 by the development company Adderstone which has created 'in-town' office accommodation.

Whinney House

This mansion house was built in the late 1860s for the colliery owning Joicey family. Edward Joicey lived here until his death in 1879 and his wife continued there until her death in 1906. The extensive grounds are said to have been landscaped by the renowned naturalist Albany Hancock. Edward Joicey was also responsible for financing the building of St Helen's Church (see below). Since the demise of its original occupants, it has served at times as a military convalescence hospital, during the First World War, and later as a residential home. The main house is now in private hands and as such may be restored. Diverse uses have been found for the stables and other outhouses within the grounds.

The family name is also recalled in Newcastle's Discovery Museum where the collection bequeathed by John George Joicey and formerly held at the Holy Jesus Hospital, is now housed.

St Helen's Church

St Helen's was built in the 1870s by the Newcastle architect John Wardle and totally funded by Edward Joicey (see above). It is in the Early English cruciform style with a nave, two transepts and a chancel with an apse. Its imposing tower and spire provide a local landmark. You may notice the trees behind the church which form part of the dene behind Whinney House. Edward Joicey built a bridge to provide a convenient way for his family and staff to go to church and there is an entrance, known as the 'Joicey Door', into the north transept of the church. The bridge to the church from the house was apparently accidentally destroyed in a training exercise during World War II! The church is justifiably proud of its fine array of stained glass windows by the famous manufacturers Wailes and Strang, Charles Kempe and William Morris. Information and photographs of the windows can be found on the church website: www.sthelenslowfell.com.

makes its way back to Durham Road and note the interesting properties on the right hand-side as the lane climbs more steeply. At the Belle Vue pub you will see shops and commercial outlets on both sides of the road making this the commercial heart of Low Fell. Turn left and in a short distance you pass the stone-built former premises of Lloyds Bank, once a reading room and school room established by **Thomas Wilson** in 1841.

Just beyond the former reading room you will see a statute of a solitary soldier on a war memorial 'erected by the inhabitants of Low Fell' in memory of local men who gave their lives in war **(Qu 10)**.

You are now at the end of the walk. From the adjacent bus stop you can take one of the many buses that will return you to Gateshead Interchange/Metro Station or to Newcastle.

Thomas Wilson (1774-1858)

Thomas Wilson, a native of Low Fell worked in local coal mines throughout his childhood. However, he saw the value of learning and became self-taught and appreciative of literature. He succeeded in obtaining work as a clerk in a Newcastle firm and rose to become a successful businessman. Elected as a councillor in Gateshead he was determined to provide better facilities for children than he had enjoyed. In 1841 he was responsible for the erection of a reading room and school room for children designed by the Newcastle architect, Thomas Oliver.

There is a bust of Thomas Wilson in the Shipley Art Gallery but this is not currently on show.

Quiz questions

1. Name the first Mayor of Gateshead
2. What is the date on the Gateshead Consecration and Spiritualist National Union Church?
3. What is the date above the historic front entrance of the Public Library?
4. As you look at the Shipley Art Gallery, on which side is the female sculptured figure and does she represent Arts or Science?
5. Whereabouts on the Gateshead Cenotaph can you find the name of the architect J.W.Spink?
6. What is the name of the rose at No 1 in the diagram of the rose garden?
7. What is the earliest date inscribed on the monument to the 5th Durham Rifle Volunteers?
8. What is the name of the house after the entrance to Whinney House?
9. What is the date inscribed on the Carlton Club?
10. In which war did these men die?

13. Gateshead to the Metrocentre

Start: Gateshead Metro Station
Finish: Gateshead Metrocentre/Bus Station
Distance: 3 miles
Route: Gateshead Metro Station, West Street, Pipewellgate, Riverside Park, Keelman's Way, Dunston Staithes, Dunston, Metrocentre and return by bus
Accessibility: On pavements and metalled paths throughout
Refreshments: Gateshead Centre, Dunston and Metrocentre

Leave Gateshead Metro Station by the West Street North exit and follow the ramp to the main road (West Street). Turn left and proceed to a large sculpture *Sport's Day* (Mike Winstone, 1986). This was the first work made specifically for Gateshead's Public Arts programme. It reflects the town's involvement in the promotion of athletics in its International Stadium, but also manages to convey the message that sport is for all. The tortoise and the hare possibly remind us that it's not always the naturally fastest who wins **(Qu 1)**.

Tortoise versus hare

Cross over to the other side of the road, turn left and walk ahead. At the time of writing, on your right you pass the construction site of the Trinity Square redevelopment.

You pass the former Post Office (1897); the site of the house where the famous engraver and naturalist Thomas Bewick lived and died. Adjacent is the Lloyds Bank building (George Reavell, 1914). You reach a clock tower and the former Town Hall **(Qu 2)**.

Opposite the Town Hall, the brown metal sculpture *Acceleration* (John Creed, 2005) is a pointer to the future as well as a reminder of the busy railway activities which took place nearby.

Continue ahead to arrive at a busy junction. Proceed ahead with care via the traffic lights and go under the railway bridge. Turn immediately right down Hill Street to pass a small pub with a rather grand title **(Qu 3)**.

Town Hall through 'Acceleration'

You go under another railway bridge after which, on your left, you will see one side of The Central, built in 1854 and carefully renovated in 2010 as part of the redevelopment of this area. The other side of the building is on Half Moon Lane, one of the ancient streets of Gateshead. The Tyne Bridge comes into view and you need to use the traffic island on your left to cross the road. Follow the sign for the Swing Bridge **(Qu 4)**.

You are now walking down the site of another ancient street, Bottle Bank (from 'botl' a Saxon word for settlement), once the main route from the old Tyne Bridge through Gateshead toward Durham. After some 75 metres, use the traffic island to cross to the other side where you can take a close look at the sculpture, *James Hill Monument* by Peter Coates (2006) **(Qu 5)**.

Now return to the other side and continue down the road to pass the 21st-century Hilton Hotel. It is worth pausing to appreciate the views across to Newcastle and to identify some of the places you may have encountered on other walks. You soon reach the Swing Bridge which we are not going to cross on this occasion. Turn left into **Pipewellgate** another of the town's ancient streets.

Proceed ahead, passing some currently closed leisure establishments, to go under the High Level Bridge (Robert Stephenson & T.E. Harrison, 1845-49) and come to the first of a series of riverside artworks on your route. On your left, *Rise and Fall* (Lulu Quinn, 2007), a glass and steel arch along which lights literally rise and fall at random, serves as an introduction or gateway to the Riverside Sculpture Park that lies ahead. You may be able to see some interesting reflections in the two lower panels.

Meanwhile on the right are the closed premises of Brett's Oil Ltd. This complex which was first established by the riverside in 1877 is, at the time of writing, the last remaining evidence of Pipewellgate's industrial past and it occupies an area that is likely to be the

Pipewellgate

This is the name given to an area around one of the 'seven ancient streets' of early Gateshead. Apparently the name is literally derived from the fact that a lane led to a well from which water was carried in wooden pipes. Pipewellgate occupied the riverside area from where the old Tyne Bridge once stood (more or less where the Swing Bridge now stands) to the west to the now tree-lined riverside sculpture park where it merged with another old area of Rabbit Banks. In the 19th century, like most of the Gateshead riverbanks, this was an industrial area with chemical works, coal mining, glass and brick works and locomotive engineering among other industries. These sources of employment attracted a large population and the area soon became known for its squalid and overcrowded living conditions. Fortunately as Gateshead spread southwards, those who could, began to move and this was completed in the 1930s following slum clearance programmes.

subject of redevelopment in the near future. Turn right just beyond the premises of the Gateshead sea cadets **(Qu 6)**.

Here you join the Keelman's Way, a 14-mile cycle and pedestrian route named after the keelmen who transported coal along the river (see below, Dunston Staithes). You will follow signs for this route as far as your destination. Stop here for a moment to get your bearings.

The bankside of the area was landscaped in the late 1960s. Above

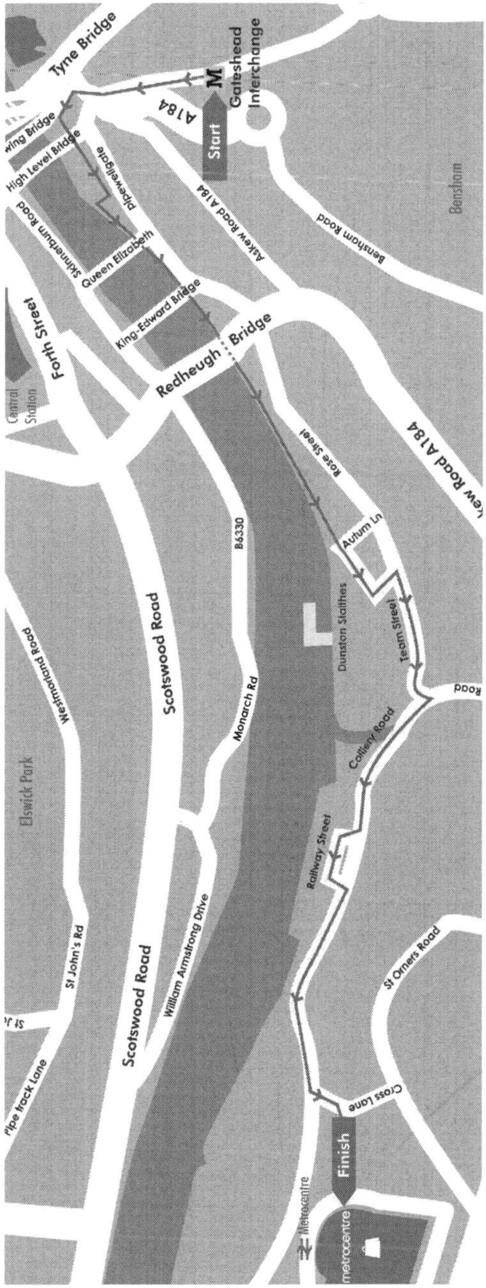

the current tree-line you may just be able to see the high stone walls of what was once **Greenesfields Locomotive Works** and Gateshead Station engine sheds.

Over the road on your left is one of the earlier artworks, a large steel arch and ball, *Rolling Moon* (Colin Rose, 1990). Beyond the river on your right you will get fine views across to Newcastle, the Copthorne Hotel (Arup Associates, 1991), the red bricked former Turnbull's warehouse (Frank Rich, 1881) , St Nicholas' Cathedral and the Castle. Ahead you will see three of the other bridges that cross the Tyne and in the distance are the wooden platforms of Dunston Staithes.

Now proceed ahead with the river on your right. Some 60 metres beyond the car park, turn left to walk up the stepped path to meet the road. To your left you will see some ornate railings, the *Thornbird Railings* (Marcela Livingston, 2005). The twenty-five panels are said to represent falling leaves or a winged bird. Look straight across the road and beyond the stone wall you should see some goats! Made from recycled materials they form the artwork *Goats* by Sally Matthews (1992) **(Qu 7)**.

Rising and falling

Greenesfield Locomotive Works

The North Eastern Railway Company developed its Greenesfield site adjacent to the station engine sheds in the mid-1850s and by 1900 with some 3000 employees it was the town's major employer. However, the site declined substantially when engine building was transferred to Darlington in 1910, although repair work continued until 1932. World War II resulted in Greenesfield being re-opened for repair work and this continued until 1959. Thereafter, parts of the site were put to a variety of engineering and warehouse uses until a major redevelopment project began about 2002 with the construction of the Ochre Yards apartments complex.

A fine assortment of bridges

Turn right and follow the path back to continue along the riverside path and walk beneath the Queen Elizabeth II Metro Bridge (W.A.Fairhurst & Partners, 1976-1980). You continue under the King Edward VII Rail Bridge (Charles Harrison, 1902) and then the slender more modern Redheugh Road Bridge (Mott, Hay& Anderson, 1980-83). If you look to the left you find a metal sculpture, *Once Upon a Time* (Richard Deacon, 1990) attached to an abutment of the demolished earlier Redheugh Bridge. This is said to represent links with the area's industrial past.

On the other side of the river you will see the long roof of the Telewest Arena, venue for major concerts and events. About a hundred and seventy-five metres beyond the bridge you will see a further sculpture, *Foliate Forms* (Gilbert Ward, 2010) carved in light coloured stone. Now is a good time to stop and look back and admire the bridges over the Tyne. The road parallel to your path is a designated route for the Express Bus from the Metrocentre so you may have another opportunity to appreciate some of the views on your return journey..

As the road curves away from the riverside path you arrive at an information board with details of the history of the area, its natural environment and the riverside park artwork. You pass an apartment block under construction at the time of writing. You then reach some pleasant housing at Riverside Row with views over the river to the Newcastle Business Park, the high rise flats of Cruddas Park and the spire of St Stephen's Church in Elswick. The river bears to the right and you may just be able to see Scotswood Bridge in the distance. Follow the riverside path as it arrives at an open area beside the remnants of the wooden structure, originally used for loading coal onto boats, known as **Dunston Staithes**.

From the open area beside the staithes, follow the sign for the Keelman's Way and Metro Centre and walk up the ramp to enter part of the Staiths South Bank, housing complex. The construction of housing began here in 2003 on what had been part of the site of the Gateshead National Garden Festival in 1990.

Dunston Staithes

There were several coal mines in this area from which coal was carried down river by the keelmen in their flat bottomed boats or keels to the larger vessels or colliers for transport in particular to London. Wooden platforms or staithes alongside the river had long been used to facilitate access to the keel boats and eventually these were erected further out into the river. This enabled coal to be dropped directly from wagons into larger vessels than had previously been the case and this in turn contributed to the demise of the keelmen. The Dunston Staithes were completed in 1893 and extended some ten years later. This huge wooden structure has been claimed by some to be the largest wooden structure in Europe! These staithes were in use until the late 1970s and while some dismantling followed shortly afterwards, some restoration was carried out for the Gateshead National Garden Festival of 1990. Unfortunately they have suffered from fire damage in recent years but their Grade II Listed Building status has at least ensured their survival.

Dunston Staithes

Continue ahead for about 100 metres and turn right just beyond a children's play area. After some 30 metres you will see a sign for November Courtyard. The dwellings in this modern housing development are arranged in what can seem a confusing set of streets named after months and seasons **(Qu 8)**.

Continue ahead along this roadway until eventually, after March courtyard, at February Courtyard you pass a small green area with a table and benches. At the end of the roadway take the path on the right that winds down to a service road. Turn left to the traffic lights, and then turn right to follow the road across a bridge over the River Team. Continue along the path with a fence on your right. The River Team (or the Gut as it is often referred to locally) becomes more obvious as you reach the older built-up area of **Dunston**. However, as the river bears away to the right to join the Tyne, keep on the pavement alongside the main road (at times: Clockmill Road/Collingwood Terrace/Colliery Rd/St Omers/ Handy Drive).

On the right, in Staithes Road, you will see the Dunston Excelsior Club. You pass a mock-Tudor building housing the Mamma Rosa Pizzeria and the Tudor Rose bar (open all day!). Here you will find a mixture of old and the new housing with a number of new streets on your right named after birds **(Qu 9)**.

Just after a small industrial estate (Dunston Workshops) turn right at the sign for Railway Street and go down Flour Mill Road (see reference above to the CWS). Walk towards to the entrance of Jewson, Building Materials. Just before the gates, turn left to follow the tree-lined cycleway. After a few hundred metres you rejoin the pavement alongside the main road and as you continue ahead the Tyne comes back into view. The Newcastle Business Park lies on the other side of the river. After a further 250 metres or so, turn right to follow the Cycleway 14 as it continues ahead behind the trees giving some relief from the busy road. You cross a road with international rather than local connections **(Qu 10)**.

Eventually you reach some traffic lights. Use the pedestrian lights to cross the road, turn right and then use further lights to cross the narrow road. Turn immediately left to follow the path beneath the railway bridge and then turn right to follow Cycleway 14 along a narrow path. The Metrocentre eventually appears ahead. Just beyond the roundabout turn left onto a short path and use the traffic island to cross the busy road with great care. Surprisingly

Dunston

This was originally a small farming community but like many areas of Tyneside the discovery and exploitation of coal made a major impact on this area. The staithes, described above, came to play an important part in the development of this industry. By the mid-1800s it was also the site of chemical works and iron and nail works. The Cooperative Wholesale Society later became the major employer following the opening of a flour milling complex in 1891 and a soap works in 1908. With its own wharfs, ships were able to use the Tyne to unload and load supplies and products. The CWS complex was finally demolished at the end of the twentieth century.

Dunston today is part of Gateshead Metropolitan Borough with Dunston Hill stretching to the south of the Western Bypass towards Whickham. It can claim at least two sporting heroes: Harry Clasper (1812-1870), who began his working life as a miner and later became a leading oarsman and then boat builder when rowing was a key sport not only on Tyneside but worldwide; and Paul Gascoigne, who was born in Gateshead in 1967 and moved to Dunston at the age of eleven to subsequently gain fame as a talented footballer, initially for Newcastle United and then further afield.

Gateshead Metrocentre

Said to be one of the largest, if not the largest shopping and leisure centres in Europe, the Gateshead Metrocentre was the brainchild of John Hall (later Sir John Hall), a miner's son from Ashington, owner of the property development company Cameron Hall and one time Chairman of Newcastle United. John Hall's dream of converting the waterlogged ash dump of a former power station into a state-of-the-art shopping and leisure centre was backed by Gateshead Metropolitan Borough Council which in 1984 hosted an exhibition that succeeded in gaining the enthusiastic support of some of the UK's major retailers. The Church Commissioners for England agreed to fund this innovative project and the first shopping mall was opened in 1986. Since then the Centre, now 90% owned by Capital Shopping Centres PLC, has gone from strength to strength with the opening of new malls, the remodelling of existing ones and the upgrading of the leisure facilities. It remains a target for other property developers

there is no better provision for pedestrian access here and even when you are over to the other side, you need to be aware of the bus traffic as you make your way into the bus station and the end of the walk.

Within the concourse there is escalator and lift access to **Gateshead Metrocentre** itself. The transport interchange information desk will provide you with details of return journeys to many locations including Gateshead Metro Station (to which the Centrelink X66 can return you in ten minutes). For rail enthusiasts there is also easy access to the adjacent station on the Newcastle to Carlisle railway line.

A modern mall

Quiz questions

1. **What sporting event does the sculpture represent?**
2. **What is the date on Gateshead's Old Town Hall?**
3. **What is the name of this pub?**
4. **What is the number of the road that leads to the Swing Bridge?**
5. **Which instrument did James Hill play?**
6. **What is the name of the sea cadets' headquarters?**
7. **How many goats can you see?**
8. **Which is the next month used for a Courtyard?**
9. **Which streets around here are named after birds?**
10. **What is the name of the road?**

14. Crossing the bridges

Start:	**St Nicholas' Cathedral**
Finish:	**Guildhall**
Distance:	**2 miles**
Route:	**St Nicholas' Cathedral, Mosley Street, Tyne Bridge, High Level Bridge, Swing Bridge, Gateshead Millennium Bridge, Newcastle Quayside, Guildhall**
Accessibility:	**On pavements throughout and mostly on the level. There is one descent via steep steps which can be avoided by following the alternative route presented in brackets below**
Refreshments:	**A café in the Cathedral (open Mon-Fri), pubs in Gateshead, a café in the Baltic and several facilities on Newcastle Quayside**

Before walking across four of the present bridges between Newcastle and Gateshead, you might wish to know a little about three earlier bridges, the **Roman bridge**, the **medieval bridge** and the **Georgian bridge**, which linked the north and south banks of the Tyne between these points.

Start from outside the Cathedral with the Queen Victoria statue on your left **(Qu 1)**.

Count the bridges

The landscaped area, incorporating the statue and a star on the ground, was opened in 2011 and designated 'St Nicholas' Square'. It is one of a series of 'pocket parks', a project by Newcastle NE1 to create more green spaces in Newcastle City Centre.

Walk ahead for a few metres. On the side wall of the first building, near the hairdressing salon, there is a plaque giving information about Thomas Cook **(Qu 2)**.

This building (No 42 Mosley Street) was built in the 1840s for the Newcastle Joint Stock Bank and was acquired in 2010 by the Cathedral for development as its administrative centre and shop. Now turn left and walk a few metres to Mosley Street.

Turn right and proceed along Mosley Street.

Mosley Street became Newcastle's financial centre in the late 19th century and most of the

Queen Victoria sets you on your way

Roman bridge

The earliest known bridge across the Tyne, between what we now know as Newcastle and Gateshead, was the Roman Pons Aelius. It probably consisted of a wooden deck mounted on stone piers and seems to have followed the line of the present Swing Bridge.

Medieval bridge

There is some uncertainty about how long the Roman bridge lasted as well as about the dates of subsequent replacements. It seems that the first stone Tyne Bridge was built in the late 12th century. This was a fairly typical medieval bridge, with towers, houses and commercial properties along its length. It underwent much rebuilding and restoration but survived until it was destroyed by a horrendous flood in 1771.

Georgian bridge

A temporary bridge was constructed in 1772. This was demolished in 1781 by which time a new Tyne Bridge, designed by Robert Mylne and erected on the same alignment as the medieval bridge, was completed and opened to traffic. This Georgian, stone bridge had nine low arches. At a time of growing industrialisation, the low arches prevented large vessels from sailing upstream. Hence, materials and merchandise needed for factories and other businesses located upstream had to be loaded onto smaller boats for transport up-river. At the same time, coal and other goods had to be carried in keel boats to be loaded onto waiting vessels downstream from the bridge. In addition, it had to be widened in 1801 by David Stephenson, because it was too narrow to cope with an increasing amount of cross-river traffic.

With the completion of the new High Level Bridge in 1849, the time had come to replace the Georgian bridge. It was demolished in 1868 and a temporary wooden bridge was used during the construction of a new (swing) bridge. The Swing Bridge was completed in 1876. This part of the river was now navigable for larger vessels.

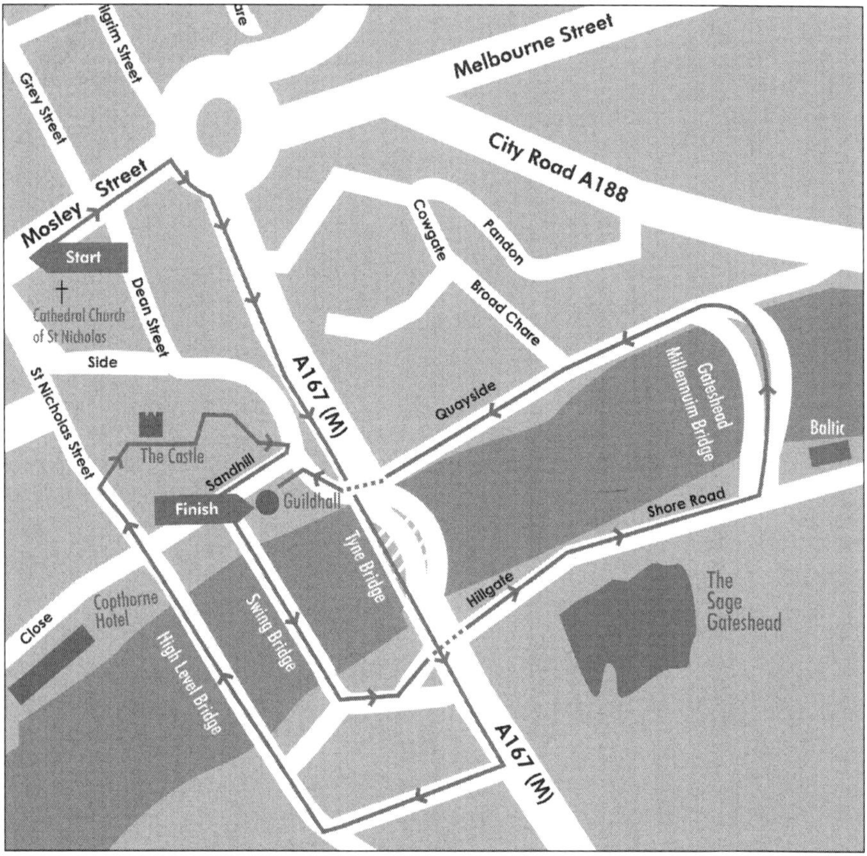

properties on both sides of the road were originally built for banks or insurance companies in the late 19th and early 20th centuries. Cross Dean Street and carry on to the junction ahead.

Bear right and walk towards the **Tyne Bridge**. Over to the left you have a good view of All Saints' Church. Go under the railway bridge. There is a tower block on your right **(Qu 3)**.

Proceed across the bridge. You need to stop at the first tall tower. It's usually very noisy along here with busy traffic but this is compensated for by the views across the roof tops and over the river, including the other bridges you will cross on this walk: Gateshead Millennium Bridge over to the left and the Swing and High Level bridges on the right.

This first tall tower has a matching tower on the other side. These are located on the bridge's supporting abutments. They were designed as warehouses and incorporate passenger and goods lifts to provide access to and from the quayside. A notice on the door informs you that the lifts have been withdrawn from service.

High up on the tower, a castle gate, from Gateshead's old Coat of Arms, is shown. (A new Coat of Arms was in adopted in 1974.) On the tower on the other side of the road the three castles from the Newcastle Coat of Arms are displayed.

Tyne Bridge

In the 1880s an increase in cross-river traffic together with high toll charges for road users of the High Level Bridge led to proposals for a new bridge. Discussions continued between Newcastle and Gateshead authorities but forty years elapsed before the Newcastle and Gateshead Corporations Bridge Act (1924) gave the go-ahead for a new bridge.

The design, by Mott, Hay and Anderson, was based on the Sydney Harbour Bridge. The contractor for the Sidney Bridge was Dorman Long of Middlesbrough who employed Sir Ralph Freeman as Consulting Engineer. The Sidney Harbour Bridge Act of 1922 was followed by initial land clearance in 1923 and construction between 1925 and 1932 when the Sidney Harbour Bridge was officially opened.

(There is some controversy as to whether the actual designer of the Sidney Bridge was Sir Ralph Freeman, who was responsible for the final detailed design, or Dr John Bradfield who, in 1916 as chief engineer of the project for a proposed bridge, had produced a formal design based on the New York Hell Gate Bridge. The roadway across the Sidney Bridge is called the Bradfield Highway.)

Dorman Long was appointed contractor for the Tyne Bridge project with Sir Ralph Freeman as the Consulting Engineer. Hence, contrary to some misplaced Geordie pride, although the smaller Tyne Bridge was completed in 1928, before the much larger Sidney Bridge in 1932, it was not the model for the Sydney Bridge.

Work on the Tyne Bridge started in 1925 from the Newcastle and Gateshead sides and the final joining sections were completed in February and March 1928.The overall length of the Tyne Bridge, including approaches, is 389 metres and the width of the bridge itself is just over 17 metres. The bridge was opened by King George V and Queen Mary on 10th October 1928, when it became part of the A1.

The bridge carries a great deal of local traffic. There was some reduction in through traffic when the Tyne Tunnel became the A1 in 1967. Subsequently, the Western Bypass became the A1 and much of the through traffic follows that route.

Carry on to the matching towers on the Gateshead side of the bridge **(Qu 4)**.

Over to your left you see The Sage and St Mary's Church with its clock which has an inscription **(Qu 5)**.

On the right you pass the Hilton Hotel (Red Box, 2004). A little further along on the left, next to the road, a small concrete building, a former public loo which has been converted into offices. When you reach the end of the railings, turn right and cross the road. Bear left and follow the pavement to walk along the street, Half Moon Lane, one of the ancient streets of Gateshead, with The Central pub on your left. Known by many as 'The Coffin' because of its shape, the Grade ll-listed building dates from the mid-19th century and it was very carefully refurbished in 2010 by the Head of Steam Company. Go under the railway bridge and at the junction turn right and proceed along Wellington Street.

The red brick building on the left at the end of the street, built in the 1880s as the Railway Workers' Club, reminds us of the importance of the railway in this part of Gateshead; locomotive workshops and a station were located nearby. You come to the entrance to the lower deck of the **High Level Bridge**. On the supports on either side of the pavement are two small square plaques commemorating the original engineers and contractors and the more recent refurbishment **(Qu 6)**.

Two information boards give details of the history and recent refurbishment of the bridge.

Walk across the bridge. It's usually a much quieter crossing for pedestrians than you probably found on the Tyne Bridge, because, since the completion of extensive repairs in 2008, road traffic on the High Level is one way and is restricted to local buses and taxis. You might, however, hear the rumbling of a train as it travels along the upper deck. You pass a plaque which has information about the refurbishment of the original lighting system. About half way across you will see three plaques. The middle one records the opening dates of the two decks and the other two relate to awards for the 2008 refurbishment **(Qu 7)**.

Over to the left are three other Tyne crossings: the **Queen Elizabeth II Metro Bridge**, the **King Edward VII Bridge** and the **Redheugh Bridge**. Viewed from here they almost seem to be touching.

On your right, just before the end of the bridge you will see a section of the Castle wall. After the end of the bridge, on

The Central restored

High Level Bridge

Before the opening of the rail deck of the High Level Bridge in 1849, rail passengers wishing to go to Newcastle had to leave the train at Gateshead and either make their way to the Georgian Tyne Bridge or, more likely, be taken across the river by rowing boat. There had been many proposals, dating back to the 1770s, for such a bridge but it was the need for a link to Newcastle, and ultimately to the north, that was the deciding factor leading to the construction of the High Level Bridge at that time.

The bridge, which has an upper rail deck and a lower road deck, was designed by Robert Stephenson with Thomas E Harrison being responsible for the technical drawings. Harrison was later described as the co-designer, but he acknowledged that the Stephenson was the sole designer (Manders and Potts, 2001). Harrison supervised the engineering work which was carried out by four local contractors. Overall, the bridge 425.6 metres long and its 'high level' gives it a 36.5 metre clearance above low water.

Queen Victoria carried out the official opening of the bridge, from a train, on 28th September 1849. The road deck was opened on 5th February 1850.

Remedial work was carried out on the piers in 1919. After that, apart from minor maintenance, no further work was done until a major restoration between 2001 and 2008.

Queen Elizabeth II Metro Bridge

This bridge, which is painted blue, was built between 1976 and 1980 to provide a Tyne crossing for the Metro rapid transit system. It was designed by W.A.Fairhurst and Partners who also supervised its construction. The contractors were Cementation Construction Ltd and Cleveland Bridge and Engineering Company.

At night the bridge is illuminated by the ever changing colours of Britain's biggest light artwork *Nocturne* (Nayan Kulkani, 2007).

King Edward VII Bridge

By the end of the 19th century the time had come to build a second high-level rail crossing between Newcastle and Gateshead. Apart from the steadily increasing amount of rail traffic using the 1849 High Level Bridge, there was also the problem that trains arriving from the High Level Bridge had to reverse out of Newcastle Central Station before continuing their onward journey. The construction of the new bridge enabled trains to enter and leave the station via a direct through-line.

The new bridge was built between 1902 and 1906. It was designed by Charles A. Harrison, Chief Civil Engineer of North East Railways and the contractor was the Cleveland Bridge and Engineering Company. It was opened on 10th July 1906 by King Edward VII.

Redheugh Bridge

There have been three road bridges on the site of the present Redheugh Bridge. The first, a toll bridge, was opened in 1871 to provide a crossing for the traffic expected from the development of the Redheugh area. It was designed by Thomas Bouch.

In 1901 this was replaced by a second toll bridge for which the consulting engineer was Sir Benjamin Baker. The contractor was Sir William Arrol & Co, bridge builders, whose previous work included the Forth Road Bridge and Tower Bridge, London. In 1937 the bridge was bought by Gateshead and Newcastle Corporations and tolls were abolished.

The third and present Redheugh Bridge was designed by Mott, Hay and Anderson and the architect was Holford Associates. Edmund Nuttall Ltd and its Dutch parent company HBM were the main contractors. It is an elegant, concrete structure, situated 25 metres downstream from its predecessor, and was opened on18th May 1983 by the Princess of Wales. Owing to its exposed position it is sometimes necessary to impose speed restrictions in times of high winds. A walk across can be most exhilarating!

your right you arrive at the area called Castle Garth, with the Castle Keep on the left and the Bridge Hotel on the right. The next section of the walk involves a descent down very steep steps. These can be avoided by following the directions set out in brackets below.

(From the High Level Bridge continue ahead until, just before you reach the Cathedral, turn right and walk down the steep street (Side). At the bottom, on the right-hand side, you arrive at the foot of the Dog Leap Stairs and can rejoin the main walk.)

Turn right and walk between the Bridge Hotel and the Keep. In front of you, on the right, is the Moot Hall (1812), formerly a county court and prison; on the left is the Vermont Hotel, formerly the Northumberland County Hall. Turn left and go through the right-hand side railway arch. The Black Gate is ahead but you need to go down the steps on your right.

At the bottom of the steps (Dog Leap Stairs) turn right and walk ahead down Side. At the junction, with the river ahead, use the pedestrian lights to cross the road to the Guildhall. Turn right to walk to the **Swing Bridge**.

There are two identical original tablets on the bridge and, next to each one, there is a small Port of Tyne panel giving historical information. One is on the right-hand side at the beginning. As you walk across this bridge you are and feel much closer to the river. You will see the other tablet and panel on your left at the end of the bridge. The tablets give details of the great and the good associated with the bridge's commissioning **(Qu 8)**.

At the end of the bridge, the small red brick house on the right-hand side was originally the police station for the river police. The force was established in 1845 with 21 policemen and six rowing boats. The building is now occupied by the O-de-V restaurant.

Proceed ahead and bear left and walk to a sign for HMS Calliope. Carry on, on the

An aptly-named pub

Swing Bridge

This bridge was built as a replacement for, and on the line of, the Georgian bridge (see above) whose low arches prevented larger vessels from sailing upstream. The Tyne Improvement Commission built the stone piers and abutments. W. G. Armstrong & Co. designed the bridge and also installed the iron superstructure and hydraulic machinery, both of which were manufactured at the firm's Elswick works. When the bridge opened in 1876 it was the world's largest swing bridge.

The bridge was extremely successful. Since 1876 over 300,000 ships have passed through; its most active year was 1924 with a daily average of 20 swings. Today it is used only rarely. However, although the original steam-powered pumps were replaced by electric pumps in 1959, when it does open, it is the original Armstrong hydraulic machinery which produces the swing.

Swing bridge

left-hand side of the road. You reach the base of a Tyne Bridge tower on the far side of which is a plaque with details of the disastrous fire which started in a factory near here **(Qu 9)**.

Continue ahead using the available pavements. The Sage is above on the right. On your left you reach HMS Calliope, the shore-based naval reserve headquarters. At the end of the building bear left to go down the ramp into the open area called Baltic Square with **Gateshead Millennium Bridge** ahead and, to your right, the Baltic Centre for Contemporary Art, usually referred

The sailing Sage

Gateshead Millennium Bridge

This exciting addition to the bridges linking Gateshead and Newcastle, designed by Wilkinson Eyre Architects and structural engineers Gifford, is the world's first tilting bridge. Spanning the Tyne between Newcastle Quayside and Gateshead Quays, it not only provides a crossing point for pedestrians and cyclists but also has become one of the area's iconic tourist attractions. Several prestigious awards have been made to the bridge and its designers.

On 20th November 2000 the bridge's steel deck was transported up the river from Wallsend, where it had been assembled, on one of the world's largest floating cranes. On arrival at its destination it was lowered onto its concrete foundations. The culmination of this spectacular feat of engineering was watched by thousands of onlookers. Members of the public were permitted to use the bridge from 17th September 2001 and it had its official opening by HM The Queen on 7th May 2002.

Tilting bridge

When the bridge tilts its two sections open up in a manner reminiscent of a blinking eye; hence, it is sometimes referred to as 'the blinking-eye bridge' or 'the winking-eye bridge'. The tilting of the bridge permits the passage of larger vessels and is carried out for special events such as the Northumbrian Water University Boat Race. You may be lucky enough to see the bridge tilt. At night, the changing colours of floodlighting produces a rainbow-like effect that enhances the attractiveness of this unique bridge.

For further information see: www.gateshead.gov.uk/bridge

to as the Baltic. Cross the Millennium Bridge. Ahead is the Malmaison Hotel **(Qu 10)**.

Turn left and walk along the Quayside. On your right you pass Wesley Square with its interesting artwork and then the modern Law Courts and several historic buildings including the Custom House (1776) which is next to Trinity Chare. Over the river on your left you have splendid views of the Baltic and The Sage. You arrive at the Guildhall and the end of the walk.

Quiz questions

1. **What is the address of the glass-walled building on the other side of the road?**
2. **When did Thomas Cook open his first travel business in Newcastle?**
3. **What is the name of the tower block on the right?**
4. **Which coats of arms is shown on the bridge tower you have come to?**
5. **What is the inscription on the clock face?**
6. **Who were the engineers of the High Level Bridge?**
7. **What award was presented to Network Rail, May Gurney and Mott McDonald?**
8. **Where is the Newcastle/Gateshead boundary?**
9. **How many people were killed in the 1854 fire?**
10. **Who previously used the building which is now occupied by the Malmaison Hotel?**

15. Gosforth

Start/Finish:	**South Gosforth Metro Station**
Distance:	**4.5 miles**
Route:	**South Gosforth Metro Station to Gosforth High Street, along the High Street, Rothwell Road, Gosforth Central Park, West Avenue to Kenton Road, then via Moor Crescent and Rectory Road, to South Gosforth Metro Station**
Accessibility:	**All on the level on pavements and metalled paths**
Refreshments:	**Lots of cafés and pubs on Gosforth High Street**

Before leaving South Gosforth Metro Station station, notice the 19th-century cast-iron footbridge, the sole reminder of the 1865 station, formerly on the Blyth and Tyne Railway, which was replaced when the Metro system was built.

Exit from South Gosforth Metro Station and turn left. The church on the other side of the road is **Gosforth Parish Church**.

Walk ahead along Station Road/Church Avenue. You cross Rectory Terrace, with its 19th-century terraces, and The Grove. Carry on to an Edward V11 pillar box on your left. It was from near here that Cullercoats women, who had travelled to Gosforth by train, used to sell their fish. Turn left into St Nicholas Avenue and proceed ahead. On your left you pass a

Arriving at South Gosforth

Gosforth

The most popular explanation of the name is that it derives from 'Gese Ford' meaning the ford over the Ouse (or Ouseburn), the narrow river which runs through Gosforth before continuing its journey through Jesmond to the Tyne. Since 1974, Gosforth has been part of Newcastle, but remains geographically distinct from the city centre by the existence of the Town Moor. The main A1 from Newcastle to Scotland once ran through Gosforth on what is now Gosforth High Street.

At the beginning of the 19th century Gosforth was largely a farming community. Most of the area belonged to the Brandling family who lived in the north of Gosforth in what is now Gosforth Park. (Their restored 18th-century property is incorporated into the grandstand of Newcastle Racecourse which is within the Park). Some Brandling land, to the west of the High Street was sold to Job Bulman, who built Coxlodge Hall in 1796.

In the early 19th century the development of quarries and particularly coal mines brought about an increase in the population. A number of collieries were developed on Brandling land. Coxlodge Colliery's Jubilee Pit, named for the 50th Jubilee of King George III, opened in 1810 and its Regent Pit, named after the newly-appointed Prince Regent, opened in 1812. The names survive in present-day Jubilee Road and Regent Road. Other Brandling coal mines included Fawdon Colliery and Gosforth Colliery, which was in South Gosforth. Owing to difficult underground conditions which were encountered, it was four years after the shaft was sunk at Gosforth Colliery before the first coal was extracted in 1829. In celebration a grand subterranean ball was held over 350 metres below the surface. The dancers were lowered in (clean!) baskets, this being before the introduction of cages. All the Gosforth coal mines were closed by the late 19th century.

The Bulmans built houses around what is now Gosforth High Street and for more than one hundred years the area was called Bulman Village. Later, like Fenham and Jesmond, Gosforth attracted professional and business families wishing to live away from the crowded centre of Newcastle.

From the latter half of the 19th century Gosforth has grown, initially by the infilling of spare land sold by large landowners, but subsequently by the development of new housing estates, the latest, to the north-west, being 'Newcastle Great Park'.

residential development of 2005, built on the site of the former headquarters of Proctor and Gamble (UK) which had operated from there from 1953 **(Qu 1)**.

At the mini-roundabout at the end St Nicholas Avenue, turn left and walk ahead. On your right is a recent example of infilling. The apartments and town houses were built in 2003 on part of the ground of South Northumberland Cricket Club. The winning entry in a competition to choose a name for the development was 'The Wickets'.

You come to a crossroads. Over the road to your left is one of the sites of the Newcastle School for Boys, which occupies one of the large, former residential properties around here. Turn right and proceed along the road (The Grove). On your right there is a mid-19th-century terrace of residential houses with their long gardens. No doubt the residents made use of the Victorian post box, embedded in the wall, which you soon reach. At the post box, cross the road and go into Roseworth Crescent.

You will see a variety of styles in the houses here as you proceed to the junction with

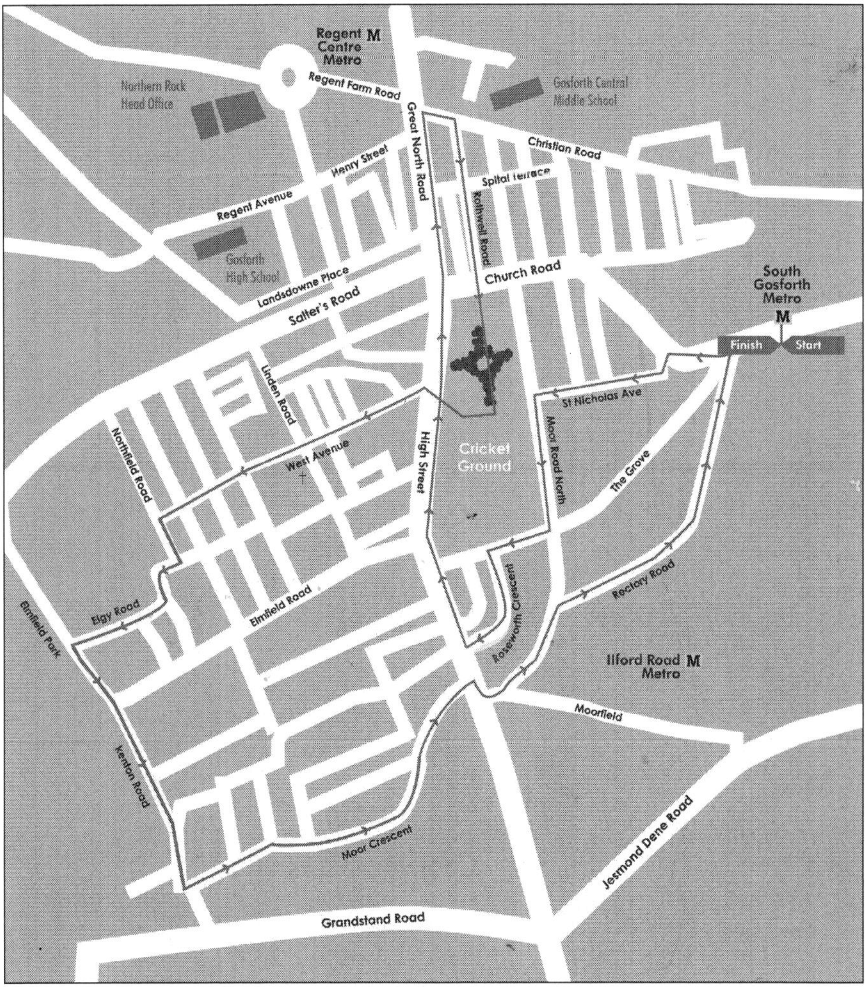

the main road (High Street). Gosforth's High Street remains the heart of Gosforth even though, like high streets in other towns, the butcher, the baker and the candlestick-maker have largely disappeared. Over the main road, at the bottom of The Drive, the small stone-built house was the lodge of the Bulman family's Coxlodge Hall property. The only other reminder of the estate is the former stable block, now used as offices, which is further up The Drive. Coxlodge Hall's later owners included Thomas Hedley the soap manufacturer and Andrew Leslie the shipowner. It was used as a school before it was demolished at the beginning of World War II.

Turn right and walk ahead. You come to a building now occupied by The Carphone Warehouse. Built in the mid-1920s for a motor engineering company, it has claims to be an

Gosforth Parish Church (dedicated to St Nicholas)

In 1799 a church was built (on the site of an Anglo-Saxon church) by John Dodds. The early parish registers record the marriage in 1805 of Edward Barrett Moulton Barrett and Mary Graham Clarke, the parents of the poet, Elizabeth Barrett Browning.

As the population of Gosforth grew, it became necessary to add to the building and extensions by John Dobson were completed in 1820. By 1880, the church was extremely crowded but, in addition, it had been allowed to fall into a dilapidated condition. Hence, the church 'was in urgent need of both restoration and expansion' (Hilton, 2001). Restoration in St Nicholas' was carried out by R.J. Johnson in 1884. He also designed the new daughter church of All Saints' (see below) which provided a place of worship for the growing population of Gosforth, most of whom lived outside the immediate vicinity of the Parish Church.

Further extensions to St Nicholas' were made in 1913 and 1959. Hence, the building we see today has changed a great deal since 1799. Nevertheless, the church presents a pleasing, dignified appearance.

Charles John Brandling (1769-1826) and Job Bulman (1746-1818) are buried in the graveyard.

The Church's patron saint is St Nicholas of Myra, a fourth century bishop after whom the Santa Claus legend developed. The ancient tradition in churches dedicated to St Nicholas, whereby a 'boy bishop' is appointed for a period to represent the real bishop, has been re-established by several churches including Gosforth Parish Church. Once a year a boy or girl is attired as a bishop and takes part in the Communion Service, including preaching a sermon!

St Nicholas' website indicates that its worship style is 'friendly/traditional Anglican with a vibrant choral tradition'. www.gosforthparishchurch.org.uk

early cinema because, in the pre-'talkie' era, the upstairs room was used to project silent films.

Before proceeding ahead look over the road. The block of flats on the left-hand side of Graham Park Road seems very plain when compared with the nearby Victorian and Edwardian properties. These local authority flats were built in 1951 at the time of the Festival of Britain. On the right-hand side of Graham Park Road, in Culzean Park, stands the United Hebrew Congregation Synagogue.

Now proceed ahead. A few metres further on is a small building occupied by Sanderson Young. Previously this was one of two branches of Midland Bank on the High Street. On each side of the doorframe, above the 'rare' sign, are reliefs of elephants, possibly copied from the crest of a family with local associations **(Qu 2)**.

A little further along on the left, you will see the Italian restaurant Basilico. This occupies the former Gosforth Assembly Rooms which moved here in the 1920s from its original location in West Avenue (which we see later). Carry on, passing another Victorian terrace, again with long gardens hidden behind high fences. At the end of the terrace you come to The County which has an information board giving details of its history **(Qu 3)**.

You are now on the main shopping area. In 2010 The Cooperative Society returned to the

High Street after an absence of many years, when it took over the premises previously occupied by Woolworths.

Proceed ahead, crossing St Nicholas Avenue and passing Gosforth Shopping Centre **(Qu 4)**.

Continue straight as far as the Brandling Arms **(Qu 5)**.

On the facade of the building on the other side of the road, the inscription 'Newcastle-upon-Tyne' is a reminder that this was originally purpose-built for the Gosforth premises of the Newcastle upon Tyne Cooperative Society.

Use the pedestrian lights to cross the road. Now look back over the road to the building occupied by the local branch of Halifax Bank **(Qu 6)**.

Turn right and walk ahead in the same direction as before (now on the left-hand side of the road). Over to your right there are three pubs: Barca, formerly The Earl Grey, which has a crest on the upper half of the building; the Blacksmith's Arms, on the site of an old smithy; The Queen Victoria, which has changed its name a number of times during the last few years, possibly to sound more trendy, but reverted to its original name in 2010. The present building dates from 1899 and replaced the original pub which had been converted from a house built in 1825, probably one of the earliest houses in Bulman village.

We are going to turn right here to cross at the pedestrian lights but before doing so notice, on your left, the small stone-built building, formerly Woodbine Road Methodist Church (built in 1882 by the Primitive Methodists as the Emma Robson Memorial Church), which has been tastefully refurbished as the registered office of the Northern Rock Foundation, the charitable arm of the former Northern Rock bank. The adjacent public car park is on the site of a former Church of England school before its relocation to Christon Road. Straight ahead you can see The Gosforth Hotel (an early venue for Sting), and, a little to the left of the pub, is Poon's Gosforth Palace Restaurant. The building was formerly a bingo hall but before that was the Globe Cinema which operated from 1910 to 1961. Although much altered internally, it is the oldest surviving cinema building in Newcastle.

Busy junction

Now, use the pedestrian lights to cross over to The Queen Victoria and the corner of Church Road. Cross Church Road and continue in the same direction. You pass a short parade of shops and come to stone-built council offices. These were occupied by the former Gosforth Urban District Council and are now used by departments of Newcastle Council. If the offices are open, go into the small entrance lobby where there is a War Memorial, dedicated to three employees of the Gosforth Urban District Council who lost their lives in the First World War.

You reach Homedown House, a block of retirement apartments which is on the site of Gosforth's second cinema, the Royalty, built in 1934. It was much grander than the Globe. However, although continuing in business for twenty years longer, it eventually succumbed to the decline in cinema-going and closed in 1981.

Carry on, crossing Spital Terrace, until you reach Christon Road. Pause on the corner here for a moment.

Christon Road follows part of the line of the old Coxlodge Waggonway which operated until the 1950s, latterly to transport coal from Hazelrigg Colliery to sidings at South Gosforth. On the other side of the road, a small stone gatepost is all that remains of the original crossing point, used by colliery locomotives to cross the main North Road. The playing fields behind the gatepost occupy the site of the former Gosforth Grammar School whose alumni includes the internationally-renowned guitarist Mark Knoffler.

Ahead on your left, the tall buildings are part of the Regent Centre office complex. Nearby there are three local authority buildings: Gosforth Civic Hall, Gosforth Customer Service Centre and Library, Gosforth Swimming Pool. Also nearby is the Regent Centre Metro Station and bus interchange. Straight ahead leads to Gosforth High School and on to Gosforth Park and Newcastle Racecourse.

Now, turn right and proceed along Christon Road. You soon reach Rothwell Road (which we are going to walk along). A little further along Christon Road is Gosforth Central Middle School and Archbishop Runcie Church of England First School. (State education in this part of Newcastle is provided by a three tier system of first, middle and high schools.) Further down is Gosforth Industrial Estate. Among the firms located on the Estate is Greggs plc. The company started as a small family bakery on Gosforth High Street and which, from the 1960s, has grown into the major business it is today.

Now, turn right and proceed along Rothwell Road with its terraces of family houses. At the junction with Church Road is St Charles Catholic Church (1911) and, adjacent, its modern parish centre built on the site of St Charles Primary School which was rebuilt near the Regent Centre. The notice board indicates that the church is a member of 'Christians Together in Gosforth'.

Use the traffic island on your right to cross to the other side of Church Road.

The building with the small clock tower is the Gosforth Memorial Medical Centre,

Turn left and walk a few metres then go into Gosforth Central Park, developed in 1932 on the site of a former nursery garden, and walk ahead. At a junction of paths bear left and after a few metres bear right past some steps then turn left and walk ahead. Beyond the tennis courts on your right the name on the park club house is Bulman Club Community Association - another reminder of the local Bulman family.

On your left is a children's play area. You reach the **Gosforth War Memorial**.

Walk past the Memorial to a junction of paths and a sculpture of five green oaks by Susheila Jamieson (2006). The rather stark building behind is the Newcastle Cricket Centre, one of only a small number of indoor cricket facilities in the UK. Turn

Gosforth remembers

Gosforth War Memorial

This memorial has two plaques, one for the 1914-1918 War and one for the 1939-1945 War.

In 1924 the Gosforth Memorial Medical Centre (originally a child welfare centre) was built with funds raised by public subscription. Inside the building a plaque records the names of the Gosforth men who lost their lives in the First World War. In addition, as a focal point, a small brick tower was built in the Memorial Centre's grounds but, after World War II, this was moved to its present prominent position in Gosforth Central Park.

In 1949 the Gosforth Central Hall, funded by public subscription, was built (on the site now occupied by the Gosforth Shopping Centre) as World War II Memorial. A plaque inside recorded the names of those who had lost their lives in that War. When the Hall was demolished to make way for the new shopping centre, the plaque was transferred to Gosforth Civic Hall near Regent Centre.

right and walk ahead to exit the Park into a street (St Nicholas Avenue). Walk ahead. On the left you come to **The Job Bulman**.

Walk to the junction with the High Street. For nearly one hundred years on New Years Day, the High Street was lined with spectators cheering on the runners in the annual Morpeth to Newcastle road race. Sadly this was stopped in 2004 because of financial and safety issues.

Cross at the traffic lights to the clock mounted on a tall post, on which there is a little plaque **(Qu 7)**.

Turn right and walk past the Loch Fyne restaurant then turn left in to West Avenue. The building occupied by Loch Fyne was built in 1907 as Gosforth Presbyterian Church which became Gosforth United Reformed Church in 1972. This church was one of three on the High Street along with West Avenue Methodist Church (originally built by the United Free Methodists in 1877) and Woodbine Road Methodist Church. In 2000 the congregations of the three churches made a decision to unite as Trinity Church and to develop a new **Trinity Centre**, which is on your right.

The Job Bulman

The Job Bulman, which occupies a splendid reconstruction of the former Gosforth Post Office, was opened in 2005. The owners, Wetherspoons, obviously thought more of the18th-century Gosforth land-owner than the pejorative comments seen on the information board outside The County.

Hero or villain?

It is well worth going inside where, apart from the available refreshments, there is a wonderful collection of material about people and places of old Gosforth as well as paintings by Emma Holliday and Peter Podmore. Verses by John Ward are displayed on the walls. John Ward (1919-1995) was born in Gosforth and became a high-ranking officer in the Civil Service. His poems 'are all a tender, wise and honest examination of the human seen condition' (Sean Body).

Trinity Centre

The three congregations decided that the former West Avenue Methodist Church would be redesignated as Trinity Church. The other two, now redundant, church buildings were disposed of, with the proceeds of sale going towards the £3.25 million cost of an ambitious redevelopment project culminating in a new Trinity Centre which is, as stated on the notice board outside the church: 'church, café, centre'.

Trinity Centre plans to offer a wide-ranging outreach programme to the wider community. As part of this plan a former Methodist Church in South Gosforth has been refurbished as The Trinity Christian Community Centre. Another part of the plan, working in partnership with the City Council, is to adapt the area in front of the church as a Town Square with a possible link to the Gosforth Shopping Centre and an overall aim to 'breathe much need vitality back into a tired high street'. In addition, Trinity is taking a leading role in the proposal to create a Business Improvement District (BID) for Gosforth. This will involve forming a company, established and run by local businesses, to address priorities set by the businesses.

Within the newly-adapted Trinity building, apart from the church, there is a café and several meeting rooms for community activities and functions. The church space itself can be used for music and theatrical performances. At the time of writing, two popular activities are a series of jazz concerts and a programme of lectures with emphasis on local issues. As the redevelopment continues it's a case of 'watch this space'.

Proceed up West Avenue. The first building on your left, after Loch Fyne, is the church hall of the former Gosforth United Reformed Church. The hall was built in 1877 and used as a place of worship by the Presbyterians until their church was built in 1907. This is currently in use as a children's soft-play centre. The next building (subject to redevelopment at the time of writing) served as Gosforth Magistrates Court until 2010. Previously, this was the location of the Gosforth Assembly Rooms until it moved to the High Street in the 1920s.

Next, you pass the Quaker Meeting House. The building was constructed in 1898 as a gentlemen's club. In 1922 it was bought by the Freemasons and used as a masonic meeting place until it was closed and taken over by the Quakers in 2011. It has been sensitively redeveloped to replace the Quakers' Archbold Terrace property. The 100 year-old front door of Archbold Terrace, which came from their earlier Meeting House at the foot of Pilgrim Street, is incorporated inside the Gosforth Meeting House.

Continue ahead passing, on the right, the Central Newcastle High School Nursery and Junior Departments. The purple front doors match the predominant colour of the School's uniform. At the crossroads is another site of Newcastle School for Boys. Over the road on your left you come to **All Saints' Church** with a notice board **(Qu 8)**.

Carry on in the same direction past the church on your left and Gosforth Bowling and Lawn Terrace Clubs on your right. At the junction proceed ahead along Furzefield Road. Turn left and then right to walk alongside the open space (Elgy Green). At the junction turn left and follow the road as it bears right. Walk along Elgy Road to a junction. Turn left and walk along the left-hand side of the road (Elmfield Park) until you come to a roundabout. Cross a road (Elmfield Road) and continue in the same direction to come to an entrance to Westfield School.

The School occupies the former Oakfield House, the home of the Cochrane family. In 1869 Mr and Mrs Cochrane planted two camellias to celebrate their 10th wedding

All Saints' Church

All Saints', designed by R. J. Johnson, was built in 1887 and the west tower, by W. S. Hicks, was added in 1896 as a memorial to Lyulf Cochrane, son of William Cochrane who was the driving force in the project to build All Saints'. Overall, the building presents a bold picture of strength in its suburban setting and has been described as 'Altogether a good, competent example of the large Late Victorian ecclesiastical building' (Pevsner and Richmond 1992).

Inside, the intricate wood carving by Ralph Hedley is particularly noteworthy and there are good examples of stained-glass windows. The splendid Harrison organ was installed in 1889, probably largely due to the influence of the music-loving William Cochrane.

All Saints'

Because of the inability of Gosforth Parish Church to cope with Gosforth's increasing population, a committee was set up in 1882 to look into raising funds for the construction of a new, daughter church. In 1883 William Cochrane took over the post of Honorary Secretary to the committee and 'There is absolutely no doubt that without him the Church would never have been completed in all its present glory' (Hilton, 2001). William Cochrane was a mining engineer whose family owned collieries. He had moved to Oakfield House in Gosforth in 1869. He was a generous benefactor to local institutions as well as to All Saints'.

All Saints' has been a training parish and many curates have gone on to high positions in the Church - not least Robert Runcie (1950-1952) who later became Archbishop of Canterbury.

anniversary. One of these survived, in a conservatory in the school building, until the 21st century, one of the oldest camellias in the country. The School emblem, which appears on the girls' uniform, is a pink camellia.

Continue ahead along the left-hand side of Kenton Road. After a couple of hundred metres of so you pass Montagu Avenue on your right. The wideness of the road is accounted for because this was originally part of the carriageway leading to the home of the Montagu family at Denton Burn. On your left you arrive at Westfield.

Before continuing the walk, which goes along Westfield, we can consider two nearby sites which have interesting historical associations. The building ahead, now occupied by Dukes Moor Garage, stands on the site of the former **Grandstand** and, over the road, **Kenton Lodge.**

Now proceed along Westfield, passing on your right a large apartment block of 1938, which has been described as being in 'the streamlined style' (McCombie, 2009) **(Qu 9)**.

Carry on for a couple of hundred metres or so then turn right into Moor Crescent. Continue until you come to the junction with the busy main road. Turn right and walk to the

Grandstand

The Grandstand was used until Newcastle Races were transferred from the Town Moor to Gosforth Park in 1882. A Roman Catholic industrial school for boys, the Bishop Chadwick Memorial School, took over the premises and remained there until 1905. The School had a highly-regarded band which often performed at the Temperance Festival on the Town Moor. The Grandstand stood empty for four years until its demolition in 1909 when it was replaced by a large hall to be used for leisure activities. In 1913 this was acquired by Armstrong Whitworths for the manufacture of aircraft and cars. From 1920 a riding school operated here until the building was sold to Lawsons, a sweet manufacturer. Latterly it has been used by garage businesses.

Kenton Lodge

The original Kenton Lodge was built in the 1790s for John Graham Clarke. His family remained here until 1809 when they moved to Fenham Hall. In 1805 their daughter Mary married Edward Moulton Barrett at Gosforth Parish Church. Elizabeth Barrett (late known as Elizabeth Barrett Browning) was their first child.

In 1908 Kenton Lodge was completely rebuilt by Max Holzapfel. He was born in Germany but moved to Tyneside and in1881, with his brother Albert and a local man Charles Petrie, started a paint manufacturing business which eventually grew into International Paints, including its landmark factory at Felling-on-Tyne. Holzapfel means crabapple and crabapples are incorporated into the design of the (now rather tired-looking) gates of Kenton Lodge near Grandstand Road.

From 1921 Kenton Lodge was a teacher training college. In the 1960s the college amalgamated with the new Newcastle Polytechnic, eventually becoming part of Northumbria University. Later, the building was used as one of the three centres of Trinity School, a special school. This centre closed in 2011. At the time of writing, the future of the building is under consideration by Newcastle Council.

pedestrian lights. The little area with seats on your right used to be known as 'Titty Bottle Corner' because this was where nursemaids from the nearby houses gave their charges bottles, possibly engaging in a little gossip at the same time!

Use the lights to cross the road. (If you wish to finish here, there is a bus stop a few metres along to your right where you can catch a bus back to the to the city centre).

To continue the walk, walk ahead for a few metres then bear left into Moor Road South. Proceed ahead. You pass the entrance to South Court, a residential home, then the entrance to The Bishop's House, the official residence and administrative offices of the Bishop of Newcastle. The next property, No 27, which has intricate cupolas is considered to be a good example of Edwardian domestic architecture. Walk ahead and turn right into Rectory Road. Proceed along the road **(Qu 10)**.

Continue ahead. At the junction with the main road, turn right and walk the short distance to South Gosforth Metro Station and the end of the walk.

Quiz questions

1. What is the name of the 2005 residential development in St Nicholas Avenue?
2. How many elephants are there?
3. How is the Bulman family described on the board outside The County?
4. Which national food retailer operates in Gosforth Shopping Centre?
5. Who do you think that the Brandling Arms was named after?
6. What is inscribed at the top of the Halifax building?
7. Why was the clock presented by the Rotary Club?
8. What does All Saints' have in common with St Charles Catholic Church?
9. What is the name of the large apartment block on Westfield?
10. What occupies the green space on the left-hand side of Rectory Road?

16. Jesmond

Start/Finish: **Jesmond Metro Station**
Distance: **3.75 miles**
Route: **Jesmond Metro Station, Fernwood Road, Jesmond Road, Jesmond Dene Road, Osborne Road, St George's Terrace, Forsyth Road, Great North Road, Brandling Park, Eskdale Terrace, Jesmond Metro Station**
Accessibility: **On pavements and tarmac paths throughout**
Refreshments: **Plenty of cafés and pubs on Jesmond Road and the Acorn Road area**

Before you leave Jesmond Metro Station take time to look through the glazed panelled concourse to view the sculpture *Garden Front* (Raf Fulcher, 1997). An information board provides details of this artwork, one of many commissioned by Nexus for the Metro network.

From the station, take the second path on the left that soon leads to a busy road (Jesmond Road). Follow the pavement as it bears left to the traffic lights. Use the lights to cross ahead to Osborne Road and turn left. Proceed along Osborne Road past some pleasant 1870s properties and then bear right into Fernwood Road. Now you will leave the sound of the traffic behind and be able to appreciate some of the fine properties in what estate agents describe as 'the most highly sought-after residential area of Newcastle'. In a short distance you will see a splendid building on the left with ceremonial street lamps outside the gates. This is the former home of Sir Arthur Munro Sutherland and now the **Mansion House**, the official residence of the Lord Mayor of Newcastle **(Qu 1)**.

Continue ahead, taking time to admire the variety of dwellings, now mainly divided into apartments, on both sides of Fernwood Road. At the T-junction, turn right and proceed down another interesting road (Akenside Terrace) to return to the busy hum of traffic on Jesmond Road. On the opposite side of the road you will see the impressive North Gate entrance to Old

Holy Trinity

Jesmond

Jesmond probably owes its name to the earlier version Gesemone meaning mouth of the Ouse (the river that runs through Jesmond Dene) and/or to Jesus Mount, the name given by the clergy of the medieval chapel of Our Lady of Jesmond. In the 18th century it was a separate settlement outside of Newcastle largely consisting of farms and pits. By the mid-19th century, wealthy land and colliery owners had decided that this was a desirable place in which to live and thus began the transition 'from mines to mansions' (Morgan, 2010). With a large influx of students since the 1960s it may well now be a case of 'from mansions to bed-sits'.

Mansion House

Originally built in 1876-1880 as two houses and then converted into one in 1900, this was to become the home of Sir Arthur Munro Sutherland (1867-1953), wealthy local shipowner, mining company director and benefactor. Among the beneficiaries of his generosity were his old school, Newcastle Royal Grammar School (see below), of which he was a governor, and Kings College (later Newcastle University) Medical and Dental Schools. On his death he bequeathed his home, Thurso House, to the City from whence it became the Mansion House, the official residence of the Lord Mayor. Sir Arthur's coat of arms and motto, *Sans Peur* (Without Fear) still adorn the building.

Official mayoral residence

The original residence of the mayor was the 17th - century Mansion House on the Quayside in the Close. Later it was to be in Ellison Place until the City had the good fortune to be given its present location in 1953. Unlike in earlier times, the Lord Mayor does not actually reside in the residence for his or her term of office. However, it is used to entertain important guests and is also available for private hire. There are several suites of rooms of differing shapes and sizes all tastefully decorated containing an excellent collection of paintings, furnishing and antiques, some of which belonged to Sir Arthur. Although the Mansion House is not open for general viewing, it does offer the opportunity for the public to attend a number of special events that have included musical concerts, murder mysteries and even match-day brunches.

For details of special events etc see, www.newcastle.gov.uk/mansionhouse

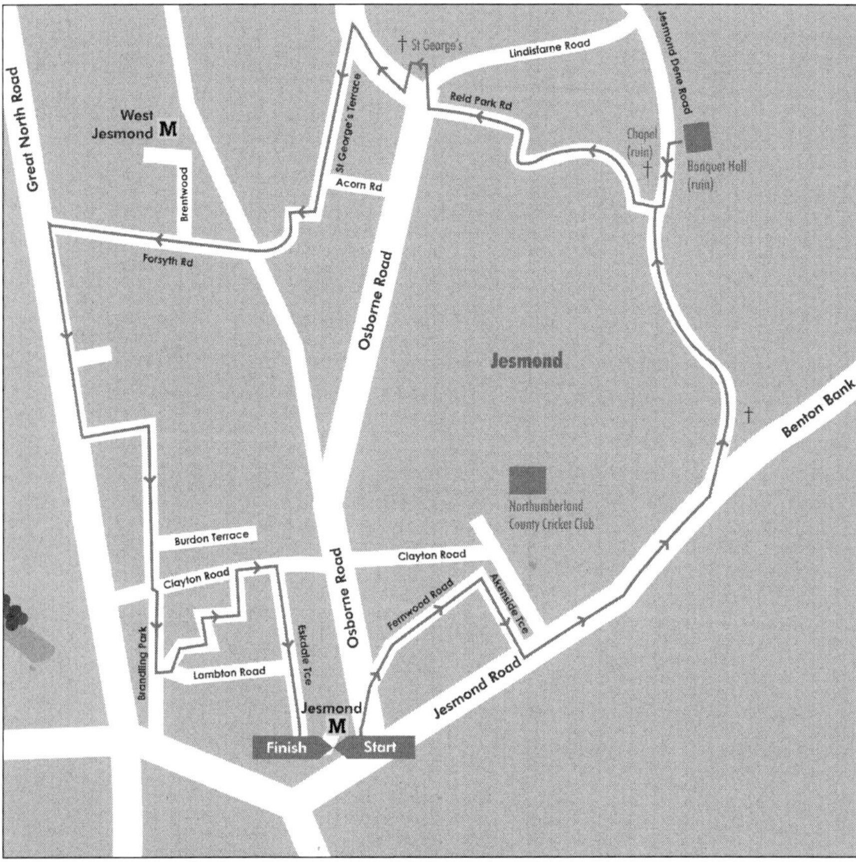

Jesmond Cemetery (1836) designed by John Dobson, where many of the famous citizens of Newcastle referred to in these walks, including Dobson himself, are buried,. This atmospheric cemetery, probably deserves a visit on a separate occasion when you may like to acquire Alan Morgan's excellent book *A Fine and Private Place: Jesmond Old Cemetery* (Morgan, 2000) or go on one of the organised tours.

To continue the walk turn left and in a short distance you reach the entrance to another old cemetery, All Saints Cemetery, with its fine arched entrance. This replaced the overcrowded cemetery of All Saints Church near the quayside. As Alan Morgan points out this was part of the trend towards 'out-of-town' burial places that had begun in Newcastle in 1829 with the opening of Westgate Hill Cemetery **(Qu 2)**.

Continue along Jesmond Road to pass the Punch Bowl and to head into the Cradewell area, so-named because apparently a stone drinking-well in the shape of a cradle once stood here. The Cradlewell pub (closed at the time of writing) stands on the corner of Deuchar Street, named after Robert Deuchar (1831-1904), formerly owner of the pub and a brewery nearby on Sandyford Road.

On the opposite side of the road amid the trees is an area known as The Minories the site of the Leonard Cheshire Care Home and some sheltered housing. You pass a number of business premises including Café Bar One. After crossing Osborne Avenue there are shops on both sides of the road. Then on your right is Holy Trinity Church (1922) as well as access to Armstrong Bridge and Jesmond Dene.

Follow the road as it bears left, and at a convenient moment, cross with care to the other side of the road. Now continue ahead keeping the wooded bankside of Jesmond Dene on your right. After some 450 metres, at Jesmond Dene Terrace, you need to cross back over the road in order to continue ahead on the pavement after the junction with The Grove. In a short distance, cross over to the right to look at the stone frontage to Lord Armstrong's Banqueting Hall. Armstrong, at one time, lived nearby and decided he needed somewhere suitable to entertain his numerous important guests. It was gifted to the City along with the Dene in 1883 and it was still used for functions at various times during the 20th century until it gradually fell into disrepair culminating with the collapse of the roof in the 1970s. The ruined hall itself nestles on the bankside below road level and may be glimpsed over the gate/wall to the left of the lodge or more fully viewed by taking the steep path to the left of the frontage. A commemorative plaque on the front provides some details of the building's construction by two architects **(Qu 3)**.

Banqueting Hall remains

Return to the main road and retrace your steps for some 50 metres to go through a wooden gate in the fence just beyond the gates of the property Ashbourne. Follow the path as it climbs to the ruins of the 12th-century Chapel of Our Lady of Jesmond or St Mary's Chapel, a medieval place of pilgrimage. It is lovingly maintained and still visited by pilgrims. A plaque gives historical details **(Qu 4)**.

St Mary's Chapel

(Alternatively for easy access in wet conditions or for wheelchairs proceed back to The Grove, turn right and follow the road as it bears right into Reid Park Road and climbs to arrive in front of the Chapel).

To continue on the walk, exit the Chapel grounds and turn right to follow Reid Park Road as it climbs quite steeply at first and then more gently, as it passes some very pleasant dwellings. As you approach a junction with the main road (Osborne Road), bear right to follow the pavement into Lindisfarne Road and then bear left to follow the access road into

St George's Church

St George's is a mainstream Anglican parish church which was consecrated in 1888. This splendid Grade 1*listed building is set in its attractive green space and is a focal point in this part of Jesmond. Its Italianate style bell tower is a landmark which, it is said, can be seen from as far afield as Rothbury, some thirty miles away.

Land and finance for the church and ancillary buildings were provided by Charles Mitchell (1820-1895) and he decided that no expense was to be spared in its construction. He was a shipbuilder, a business partner of W.G. Armstrong (later Lord Armstrong), and had, in common with other wealthier townsfolk, moved from near the centre of town to the pleasant and growing suburb of Jesmond. The designer was Thomas Ralph Spence, Mitchell's shipyard architect who had recently altered Mitchell's home, Jesmond Towers; he was assisted by Mitchell's son, C.W.Mitchell.

Outside, the gates at the main entrance, all that remains of the ironwork which surrounded the site, give some idea of the lavish, quality workmanship used in the church's construction. A later addition, to the left of the church, is the peaceful garden of remembrance, with a calvary by Leonard Evetts.

The interior is certainly eye-catching and impressive, with much Arts and Crafts influence. Noteworthy features include an ornate baptistry, a splendid ceiling and mosaics on the sanctuary wall. It is certainly well worth visiting if you happen to coincide with it being open.

For further details see: www.stgeorgesjesmond.org.uk

the grounds of **St George's Church**. Before you reach the church, you pass the Church Hall (Parish Office), Close House and then Tower House on which you will find a plaque **(Qu 5)**.

You may hear the sound of tennis balls being struck on the courts of the Northumberland Tennis Club that lies behind the church. Continue in an anti-clockwise direction to exit from the church grounds to come to Osborne Road. In recent years Osborne Road has seen the development of a considerable number of bars and bistros to the delight of the student population but to the dismay of the long-term residents.

Turn right and proceed a short distance to cross the road at a traffic island. Turn right and walk to the corner where the main road meets St Georges's Terrace. Turn left and proceed along St George's Terrace. At a convenient moment cross over to the other

Calvary by Leonard Evetts

side of the road and continue ahead to pass a number of shops and also **Jesmond Pool** and the branch library (1963).

Next to the library you will find Café 1901, part of the Jesmond Methodist Church building of that year which has been converted into public use and where you can 'enjoy café life as it should be'. This area around Acorn Road certainly provides good opportunities for refreshments.

Continue ahead, cross Coniston Avenue, take the next road on the right (Thornleigh Road) and then turn left (signposted Brentwood Avenue Shops) with St Hilda's Church (1905) on the opposite corner. Follow the road (Forsyth Road) as it climbs to cross the Metro line You pass West Jesmond School on the left and on the right you pass Brentwood Avenue. (Here you will find a further parade of shops and restaurants together with West Jesmond Metro Station should you not wish to go any further!).

Jesmond Pool

The swimming pool operated under the auspices of Newcastle Council from 1938 until the Local Authority decided to close it in 1991 due to financial constraints. However, with strong support from local residents it reopened in 1992 as a charitable organisation. With the aid of lottery funding it has been refurbished and it has gone from strength to strength, receiving a number of awards and frequently cited as an example of 'the inspiring story of a community's takeover of its swimming pool'. It offers a wide range of activities and facilities.

For further detail see: www.jesmondpool.co.uk

You cross Highbury, an elegant row of houses overlooking allotments and a sports field, before arriving at the T-junction with the busy Great North Road. Ahead is the wide expanse of the Town Moor with its metal gates bearing the symbols of the joint-keepers of the Moor, the Freemen of Newcastle **(Qu 6)**.

Turn left and walk parallel to the Moor for about 250 metres. Two stone posts mark the entrance to a narrow lane that leads to the third 'out of town' burial ground on this walk, St Andrew's Cemetery, consecrated in 1858 originally for the 12th-century church of St Andrew's in Newgate Street.

However, continue ahead for a further 250 metres or so and, immediately after a sign for the B1518 and Eldon Square, turn left down another narrow lane. At the end of the lane you reach the wrought iron gates of the Northern Counties School, originally Northern Counties Institution for the Deaf and Dumb (1861). At the gates turn right and continue along the narrow path. In a short distance, on the left, you will see the fine Princess Mary Court apartment complex that opened in 1997. 'Abbot Memorial' engraved in the stone work refers to one of the two benefactor families (the other being the Phillipson family) of the separate girls and boys Victorian orphanages which originally occupied the site. However, it will be best remembered as the Princess Mary Maternity Hospital (previously the Newcastle-Lying-in Hospital of 1760) which moved here in 1939 and was transferred to the Royal Victoria Infirmary (RVI) in 1993.

Former maternity hospital

Continue ahead, now on the pavement,

to pass another fine building. This was originally the Fleming Memorial Hospital for Sick Children, founded in the late 1880s by another local benefactor, the solicitor John Fleming, in memory of his wife. It closed in 1987 **(Qu 7)**.

Proceeding ahead, immediately on your left, you pass the end of Burdon Terrace, the street, where at No 20, once lived Thomas Burt (1837-1922), miners' leader and M.P. for Morpeth . It is interesting to note that he should have lived in a street named after a colliery owner and former mayor, Sir Thomas Burdon. Go straight over the crossroads (Clayton Road) and, on your right you will see Brandling Park with its bowling club and an underpass to Exhibition Park. This area is referred to as Brandling Village, named after another noted family of landowners and mine owners who provided mayors and MPs for Newcastle over several centuries.

Turn left into Lambton Road and keep left to go down the narrow lane, Brandling Pl. South. After some 175 metres, at lamp post 5B253, take the cut between the properties to go through the archway and then continue ahead a short distance to pass the music, drama and sports departments of Central Newcastle High School (locally known as Central High). This independent girls' school was founded in 1895 and its main premises are on Eskdale Terrace along which you will shortly walk. Among its many noted former pupils is Dr Miriam Stoppard, TV personality and health guru. Jesmond is also home to another independent girls' school, Newcastle Church High School (locally known as Church High) in nearby Tankerville Terrace and founded in 1885.

Turn right to follow the path beside The Collingwood Arms (1836) named by its first landlord, a naval enthusiast, after Lord Collingwood **(Qu 8)**.

At the end of the path, turn left and walk ahead to join Clayton Road with Willi's Coffee shop on the left. Clayton Road in this instance is named after the Reverend Richard Clayton, the younger brother of the town clerk, John Clayton who is recalled in a city centre street.

Turn right and then right again into Eskdale Terrace. On the left you pass the former Jesmond Synagogue (1915-1986), with its façade inscribed in Hebrew and the Star of David in the stained glass window, now Central Newcastle High School, Art School. As you continue along Eskdale Terrace you pass further educational properties including Newcastle University Easton Hall, and the Central Newcastle High School, Senior School. On the right you reach the long-established independent school **Newcastle Royal Grammar School**. The first school building you pass contains the indoor swimming pool (1930) with the school crest above the doorway **(Qu 9)**.

Continue ahead to pass the Reception Office with its semi-circular colonnaded entrance and the city crest and motto above. Some 30 metres further, behind the next set of metal gates, you will see two stones pillars (see next page).

The road bears left at Jesmond Parish Church, designed by John Dobson and built in memory of a notable preacher as indicated on a commemorative plaque **(Qu 10)**.

In a short distance you are back to Jesmond Metro Station and the end of the walk.

Newcastle Royal Grammar School

The school, generally known as RGS, is believed to have been founded in 1545 by Thomas Horsley, Mayor of Newcastle in a building next to St Nicholas Church (later Cathedral). It received its Royal Charter from Queen Elisabeth I and in 1607 it was sited in the former chapel of the Hospital of St Mary the Virgin in West Gate. The school remained there until a road-widening scheme resulted in the demolition of the hospital building in 1844 and the transfer of the school to Forth House. The architect John Dobson is said to have saved pillars from the chapel, one of which is located at the bottom of Westgate Road while appropriately another two have been placed at the current site of the RGS.

In 1848, the Forth House premises had to be demolished to make way for the construction of the Central Station and the school moved to Corporation property in Charlotte Square. The number of pupils began to increase and this resulted in a move to Rye Hill in 1870 and from there to its present premises in Jesmond in 1906. Since 2008 it has been fully co-educational and currently it has some 1260 pupils. In 2010 the school commemorated the bicentenary of the death of Admiral Lord Collingwood, one its many famous ex-pupils.

Royal Grammar School

Quiz questions

1. **How many ceremonial street lamps are there in front of the gates of the Mansion House?**
2. **What is the date of All Saints Cemetery?**
3. **Which was built first, the lodge or the banqueting hall?**
4. **Who sold the Chapel to Newcastle in 1540?**
5. **For how long was Canon Boot vicar of St George's?**
6. **What colour are the Town Moor gates?**
7. **What is now the name of the former Hospital for Sick Children?**
8. **What was the name of the first landlord of The Collingwood Arms?**
9. **Which creatures can you see on the crest above the doorway of the RGS swimming pool building?**
10. **What is the name of the 'notable preacher'?**

17. Ouseburn Parks: Jesmond Dene, Armstrong Park and Heaton Park

Start: Ilford Road Metro Station
Finish: Chillingham Road Metro Station
Distance: 3 miles
Route: Through Jesmond Dene, Armstrong Park and Heaton Park and parts of Heaton
Accessibility: Mainly on the level along riverside paths, with a few steep climbs out of the parks
Refreshments: A café in Jesmond Dene and one on Heaton Road

Leave Ilford Road Metro Station: from Platform 1, turn right and walk up Albury Road to the road junction (Moorfield); from Platform 2, with the houses on your right, walk to the road junction (Moorfield). Turn left, walk ahead and use the traffic lights to cross over the main road (Jesmond Dene Road). Turn left and walk ahead to where the main road bears to the left (Matthew Bank). On your right behind the gates is **Jesmond Towers**, the site of the former, **La Sagesse School**. Continue ahead to proceed down what is now the minor road (Jesmond Dene Road). After some 50 metres, over the stone wall

Ouseburn Parks: Jesmond Dene, Armstrong Park and Heaton Park

This walk is mainly through the green corridor formed by these three inter-connected parks which are now collectively referred to as the Ouseburn Parks (this designation also includes two other neighbouring parks, Paddy Freeman's Park and Jesmond Vale). The River Ouseburn rises at Callerton, near Newcastle Airport from where it runs for some eight miles before flowing through Jesmond Dene and skirting Armstrong and Heaton Parks. Numerous mills once harnessed the Ouseburn water long before the creation of the parks. It was largely William (later Lord) Armstrong in the second half of the nineteenth century, who having gradually acquired most of this land, created the parks we are visiting today. He also provided housing for his key business partners, Andrew Noble and Charles Mitchell within the same area. Armstrong, a generous benefactor to developments in Newcastle, donated the parks to the city for the benefit of its citizens. They are now managed by the City Council and were the subject of a £6m renovation project under the Ouseburn Parks Scheme of 2010-2011.

Heaton Windmill

Jesnond Towers and La Sagesse

The Sisters of La Sagesse, otherwise known as The Daughters of Wisdom founded a school for girls in Low Fell in 1906. In 1912 they acquired Jesmond Towers, the former home of the shipbuilder Charles Mitchell, a business partner of Lord Armstrong. The nuns established their convent here and created a very successful independent school for girls. However, falling numbers and the need to meet rent increases forced the school to close in 2008. The site including the Grade II listed Jesmond Towers was subsequently purchased by Freddy Shepherd (former Chairman of Newcastle United) of Shepherd Offshore. Its future is uncertain although its new owner has submitted plans to transform the site into a high-grade housing complex.

on your left, you will see the roof of Jesmond Real Tennis Club. Continuing a short distance further, on your left you pass **Jesmond Dene House**, formerly the home of Sir Andrew Noble, one of Lord Armstrong's collaborators, now a hotel and restaurant. **Jesmond Real Tennis Club**. continues to maintain the sport that the Noble family introduced here over a hundred years ago.

Continue ahead for about 150 metres, ignoring the first entrance on your left, until you come to North West Lodge. Now leave the road and follow the metalled path into Jesmond Dene. After a short distance, take a path on the left just before a covered area (with public conveniences) to go over a narrow bridge. This is a favourite spot for photographs!

At the end of the bridge, turn right to the ruins of the Old Mill. On your left, an entrance gives you access to a plaque and two information boards which provide plenty of details of the mill's history **(Qu 1)**.

Go down the steps beside the mill and continue ahead on the path close to the river (alternatively to avoid the steps, retrace your way back over the bridge, turn left, proceed ahead and cross the second bridge to rejoin the route). You pass a small bridge down on your right and then a larger bridge where the alternative way rejoins the route. Don't cross this bridge but look over to see another small bridge below. The walk continues alongside the river on your right.

Jesmond Dene House

A popular view

Jesmond Dene House and Jesmond Real Tennis Club

Originally called Black Dene House, it was designed by John Dobson in 1822 for Thomas Hedlam, a surgeon, who was twice Mayor of Newcastle. In 1871 the house was acquired by Sir (later Lord) Andrew Noble (1831-1915) another business partner of Lord Armstrong. Captain Noble, educated at the Royal Military Academy at Woolwich, was a physicist and expert in ballistics and therefore of great significance to Armstrong's armament factory in Elswick where he rose to become the Company Chairman.

Jesmond Dene House was extended and altered by the renowned architect, Norman Shaw, at the same time as he was building Armstrong's Cragside residence (1870-1885). Subsequently, as a result of further work, in the mid- 1890s, by the local architect Frank Rich, the house looked as though it had been 'completely rebuilt' (Faulkner & Gregg, 2001).

At the same time, Rich built a Real Tennis court for Andrew Noble in the grounds of the house. Lord Noble's widow, who died in 1931, bequeathed the house and the grounds to the City Council. The Noble family kept up the tradition of the sport but during World War II the court building was used as a Council workshop and storeroom. Subsequently, until 1981, it was used for badminton. Since then it has reverted to its original use and club members and their guests continue to enjoy the original form of tennis in one of the twenty-three or so clubs in the UK. The name 'real' is said to be derived from 'royal' as the game was popular among royalty, and a favourite of King Henry VIII at Hampton Court Palace where it is still played (for further details of the game see: www.irtpa.com).

Meanwhile the house itself has been used for several purposes, including, as a college, a Civil Defence establishment and a residential school. It opened as an hotel and restaurant in 2005 after sensitive restoration and extension work (Darbyshire & Kendall). The alterations included the addition of a conservatory that provides a very pleasant dining experience overlooking the gardens that run down to the dene. The hotel also contains a number of art works from the university gallery of Northumbria University. It is open daily to non-residents for coffee and afternoon tea as well as meals. (For further information see:www.jesmonddenehouse.co.uk).

Eventually you pass the Fisherman's Lodge restaurant at what was once the site of Heaton Cottage corn mill and then a flint mill. After you pass beneath a bridge look beyond the trees on your right and you should be able to see part of the remains of the Banqueting Hall (1860-62), designed by John Dobson for Lord Armstrong for entertaining.

Continue ahead until you come to Pets' Corner, a popular venue for families with its aviary, animal pens and adjacent play area. Opposite this you will find the Millfield House Café, Jesmond Dene Conference Centre and the Ouseburn Parks Visitor Centre. Millfield House was once the site of the Busy Cottage Ironworks, later replaced by another corn mill. The Visitor Centre contains maps and information about both the industrial heritage and the natural environment of the parks. A plaque on the outside wall of Millfield House commemorates Lord Armstrong's gift of Jesmond Dene, 'an area of outstanding beauty', to the citizens of Newcastle while another plaque pays tribute to the founder of the Friends of Jesmond Dene.

Continue ahead for about 100 metres to take the path on your left leading from a turning circle. Turn almost immediately right to follow the path that then climbs steeply to the right and leave the park through a brick gateway. On the right is Armstrong Bridge, built by Lord Armstrong's company in 1876-8 to carry traffic across the dene and is now pedestrianized. Turn left and after a few metres turn right, to cross a bridge over the busy road and enter Armstrong Park.

Adam or John's house?

Follow the broad path between the mature woodland. After some 450 metres you cross a small bridge with metal railings, shortly after which look out on the left, beyond the trees, for the remains of what is known as Heaton Windmill.

You arrive at a lane (Jesmond Vale Lane) at the exit of Armstrong Park. Turn left and walk uphill for some 150 metres to find the ruined House of Adam on your right. This is sometimes referred to locally as King John's Palace because of an unsubstantiated tradition that King John stayed in Heaton. A plaque provides some information about its history **(Qu 2)**.

Bear right and descend on the surfaced path. At the car park take the path on the left to reach a path near an entrance to Heaton Park. We are going to turn left to walk along the broad path, but first look at the information board to your right which provides some historical details and a map of the park`**(Qu 3)**.

Now begin your way through the park on the broad path for a couple of hundred metres. On the right is the ornate Heaton Pavilion, now a restaurant, and the bowling green. When you reach a crescent with seats on your left and a children's play area over to the right, leave the broad path and turn left to climb steeply out of the park to Heaton Park View.

Heaton Pavilion

Cross over the road, with care, and continue along Stannington Grove to the second road on your left (Cardigan Terrace). Turn left and walk to the crossroads with a busy road (Heaton Road). On your right is St Cuthbert's Church, a United Reformed and Methodist Partnership. On your left, motoring enthusiasts will enjoy looking at the noticeboards and window of Northumbrian Leather, housed in part of what was once the substantial Heaton Branch of the Newcastle Co-operative Society **(Qu 4)**.

Cross over the busy road (Heaton Road)

at the traffic lights to Café One 20 Coffee Lounge, turn right and then immediately left to continue up the same road as before (Cardigan Terrace). At the T-junction (Second Avenue) turn right and walk a short distance before turning left to walk along Third Avenue. There are in fact ten so-called 'Avenues' in this area.

On your right, at No. 44 you pass a blue plaque, indicating that the author, **Jack Common** was born here **(Qu 5)**.

Jack Common (1903-68)

He spent his early life on Tyneside before moving to London at the age of twenty-five where he thought he might better pursue his political ideals and obtain employment. In the 1930s he worked for The Adelphi and other left-wing journals and became friendly with George Orwell. He published two popular autobiographical novels about his upbringing on Tyneside, *Kiddar's Luck* and *Ampersand.* The rest of his writing consisted of film scripts and articles for journals. Newcastle University Library holds a collection of his papers. A sheltered housing complex in nearby Mundella Terrace bears his name

At the T-junction, with The Chillingham pub on your right, cross with care over the busy road (Chillingham Road) and turn right. Go over the pedestrian bridge, turn left and walk the short distance to Chillingham Road Metro Station and the end of the walk. To the right, beyond the station, you will see Siemens. This was formerly the site of the world famous engineering works created by Charles Parsons in 1889.

Quiz questions

1. **What was the name of the mill in 1739?**
2. **When was the House of Adam given to Newcastle?**
3. **Who gave the land at Heaton Park to William Armstrong?**
4. **What is the date of the Heaton Branch of the Newcastle Co-operative Society?**
5. **In which flat was Jack Common born?**

18. Heworth to Gateshead International Stadium

Start: **Heworth Metro Station**
Finish: **Gateshead Stadium Metro Station**
Distance: **4.5 miles**
Route: **Heworth Metro Station, Sunderland Road Villas, Dilly Line, Pelaw, Bill Quay Community Farm, Keelman's Way, Friars Goose Marina, Gateshead International Stadium & Metro Station**
Accessibility: **On pavements and surface paths. Some steep inclines and a descent on a track from Bill Quay Farm which can be slippery**
Refreshments: **Bill Quay Farm café, the Elephant on the Tyne Hotel, Gateshead International Stadium**

At the exit of Heworth Metro Station walk straight ahead to the car park, turn left to cross the access road and then turn right to the traffic lights opposite The Swan pub. Cross the road and turn left to find a small gated entrance to **St Mary's Church**. Once through the gateway, immediately on your left you will see an obelisk memorial 'in memory of 91 persons' killed in the **Felling Colliery disaster** of 1812. Due to their unstable condition great care needs to be taken in approaching any of the memorials.

Walk to the left of the church until you reach the path from the lych gate to the main door of the church. The lych gate was built in 1937 by the Pelaw CWS Cabinet Works (see below) as a memorial to King George V. On your left, you will see three small gravestones dating from the beginning of the seventeenth century. Next to these is the Haddon Memorial Tomb of 1717. It attracts a lot of attention as it depicts small children tucked up in a four-poster bed and so it is often referred to as 'The babes in the bed'. It was designed by the children's father, a master mason who died some 4 years later. This together with the adjacent tomb recalls the Haddon and Makepeace family **(Qu 1)**.

Babes in the bed

Continue around the church then turn left at the side entrance. Now walk ahead through the graveyard to arrive at a road. Do not cross the road, but note the small stone house opposite, The Old Mill House. This was the site of one of a number of watermills driven by the Heworth Burn which is now culveted.

Turn left to walk along Sunderland Road Villas with the long stone wall of the cemetery on your left. You cross Field Lane and after some 40 metres turn left to walk through an underpass beneath the Felling by-pass.

St Mary's Church

The present church dating from 1822 is on the site of a former chapel belonging to St Paul's at Jarrow. The narrow gateway through which you passed is believed to be the original entrance. The church was built by J Stokoe for the Rev. Joseph Hodgson who was Rector of Jarrow-with-Heworth. It was not until 1843 that it became a separate parish under his successor the Rev. Matthew Plummer. The clock was added in 1883 and in the 1890s some modifications to the building were made by the W.S Hicks, the Diocesan Surveyor for Newcastle whose firm specialised in the building and restoration of churches. However, the church largely remains as it was originally. The graveyard is an important source of local family and social history.

St Mary's Heworth

For further information see:www.stmaryschurchheworth.com

Felling Colliery disaster

Unfortunately, explosions and accidents and loss of life have been all too commonplace in the coal mining industry. The explosion at the Felling Colliery in the Parish of St Mary's on the 25th May 1812 was particularly devastating with such a huge loss of life of both men and boys. Boys as young as eight years old were engaged underground as 'trappers' to open and close the trap doors which provided ventilation and three boys under 10 years of age are listed on the Felling Colliery memorial. The Vicar of St Mary's, the Rev. John Hodgson published an account of the disaster which had an important impact on the industry. Mine owners preferred to keep quiet about accidents in their mines and previously little had been known about such events. Several important outcomes stemmed from the publicity that John Hodgson gave to the Felling disaster. The press began to report mining accidents more widely and coroners were obliged to hold inquests into such deaths; The Society for the Prevention of Accidents in Coalmines was established and safety lamps were developed by George Stephenson and Humphrey Davy.

Here there is some artwork, created by local school children, which sadly appears to have been vandalised but hopefully you should still be able to identify the name of the original waggonway. This was one of the numerous waggonways for the transport of coal from the mines to loading staithes on the Tyne. This line, built in 1805, originally relied on rope and wire haulage mechanisms but this was replaced by a railway serving several local collieries until it was closed in 1959 **(Qu 2)**.

Continue ahead on the tree-lined tarmac path between the houses and at the end of the path turn left to cross the bridge over the Metro line at Pelaw Station. Continue ahead to the main road (Shields Road) at Croxdale Terrace. To your left some of commercial premises formerly belonged to the Cooperative Society. Due to its location as an important railway junction, Pelaw became a major manufacturing centre for the Cooperative Wholesale Society. Factories stretched along Shields Road producing clothes, textiles, cabinets, furniture and household cleaning materials, together with print works and laundry facilities. However, foreign competition largely led to the decline of the Pelaw complex from the 1970s until its demise in the 1990s.

Cross the main road and proceed straight ahead down Fisherwell Road. As the road bears left, turn right and follow the track that leads ahead between paddocks to **Bill Quay Community Farm**. Notice the artwork between and on the sides of the barns as you make for the entrance at the far end of the buildings **(Qu 3)**.

The café with an outdoor seating area overlooking the Tyne is to your right. To the right of the café there is a section of dry stone wall together with a plaque which gives information about the art of dry stone walling.

After your visit, retrace your steps along the track for some 100 metres and take the right-hand fork. Follow the track as it bears right and descends steeply towards the river. The narrow path can be slippery in wet weather and due care needs to be taken. You soon reach a metalled path on the Keelman's Way. This fourteen mile route from Bill Quay to Dunston serves as a reminder of the keelmen who used to play a vital role in the coal trade as they ferried coal in their flat-bottomed boats (called keels) to the colliers lower down the Tyne.

Turn left and proceed along the path. After a short tree-lined section you are soon walking alongside the River Tyne which is about to sweep to the right past an industrial

Bill Quay Community Farm

The Farm was established in 1986 on 40 acres of reclaimed land. It is a member of the Federation of City Farms and Community Gardens that promotes farms in urban areas to encourage strong community relations and an awareness of farming and gardening. The Farm is particularly interested in providing opportunities for young people to gain experience of agriculture, conservation and environmental issues, for example, through a trained volunteers programme.

Bill Quay proudly specialises in the conservation of rare and traditional breeds of livestock and is a Rare Breed Survival Trust Approved Conservation Centre. Here you will find Longhorn cattle, Tamworth pigs, Hebridean sheep and Bagot goats.

In addition to the covered barns and pens, the site includes a variety of environments, including woodlands, grasslands, and wetlands through which the visitor can enjoy a leisurely stroll. The site now attracts a diversity of bird life as well as wildflowers and butterflies. Today it is hard to imagine that this was once the site of brickworks, a clay pit, a quarry and a possible spoil heap from the adjacent chemical works, bottle works and paint factory.

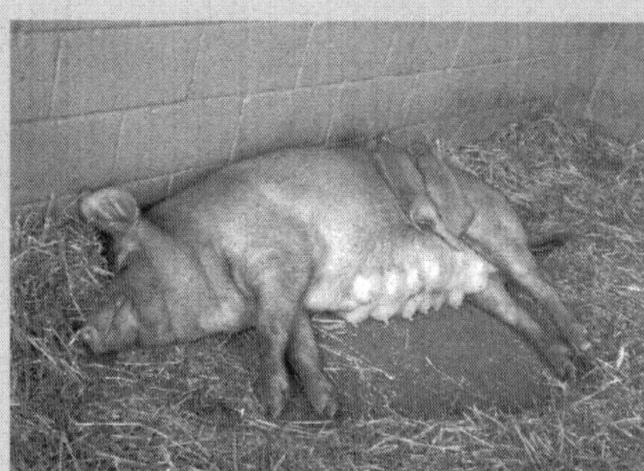

Content with life at Bill Quay Farm

For details of special events and to check the opening times of the café see:www.gateshead.gov.uk/leisure/billquayfarm or Tel 0191 4335780.

complex belonging to the multinational company Akzo Nobel, world-leader in the manufacture of paints and protective coatings. This plant is said to be the largest private sector employer in Gateshead.

The skyline of Newcastle soon comes into view. When you reach the industrial complex follow the 'Cycleway 14 Newcastle Gateshead C2C' signs in order to take a loop inland and then return back to the riverside. You bear left and climb steeply to a road where you turn left to continue the steep ascent past a corrugated-iron fenced area. After some 200 metres leave the road and turn right between the bollards to climb further to join a road (Abbotsford Road). Proceed ahead as the road levels out as you pass Corrofell Gardens on your right and some industrial units on your left. At the junction turn right and walk downhill to pass the main entrance to Akzo Nobel. Turn left along Nest Road and then just beyond a workshop, turn almost immediately right to continue on the 'Cycleway 14 Newcastle Gateshead C2C'.

Friars Goose Marina

You are now on a pleasant path known as Friars Goose Riverside Footpath and you soon have the river below on your right. However, you need to remember, particularly at the bends, that this is also a popular route for cyclists. Eventually the path meets a road and you continue a few metres to a T-junction. Turn right and walk for about 100 metres to find an anchor resting on a stone with a plaque that explains that this area, known as Friars Goose, was reclaimed from former industrial use. It was in this area that **Thomas Hepburn** gained famed as an early miners' leader. Beyond the anchor you will see some modern apartments named after a local landing stage **(Qu 4)**.

On the right is a small marina and the Elephant on the Tyne hotel, bar and bistro, (open all day for refreshments).

Thomas Hepburn

This was a heavily industrialised area in the nineteenth century and of course this included coal mining where working conditions and safety were particularly bad. Thomas Hepburn, a miner himself and Methodist lay preacher, took a major role in creating the Northern Union of Pitmen in the early 1830s. Although he advocated peaceful means he was unable to prevent violence breaking out in May 1832 when the colliery owners tried to evict striking miners from their pit cottages. Such was the extent of the conflict that the army had to be called in to quell the miners and end the so called 'Battle of Friars Goose'. Hepburn continued to work for improved conditions until his death in 1864 and is remembered as an early founder of trade unionism. Such is his significance that he has a school named after him, The Thomas Hepburn Community School, Felling and Gateshead Council hosts an annual Thomas Hepburn Memorial Lecture. His memorial is in St Mary's churchyard at Heworth.

Continue ahead past The Elephant on the Tyne on your right to rejoin the riverside path. On the other side of the river you will see the St Peter's Basin housing and marina complex. After several hundred metres follow the metalled path as it bears left and rises sharply for a short distance. Then follow the C2C to the right. Walk along the broad path parallel to the river until eventually you come to a junction of paths just before a car park.

St Peter's Basin

Turn sharp left to climb steeply again. You pass The Schooner pub before arriving at a road (Tyne Main Road). Turn right, walk a few metres and then turn left to cross the road and walk up Neilson Road. On you right is the Saltmeadows Trade Park and on your left is Gateshead International Stadium. At an appropriate point, cross the road and continue ahead on the left-hand side pavement. At the end of the stadium building turn left and follow the path to the main entrance of **Gateshead International Stadium.**

Gateshead International Stadium

The original stadium with a cinder track and an asphalt cycle track was officially opened in 1955 by the famous marathon runner, Jim Peters. The stadium gradually underwent several improvements but it was the 1970s which first witnessed the development of the stadium as we know it today. In 1974, a synthetic 'tartan' track was laid and the inaugural meeting was crowned by the fact that Brendan Foster broke the world 3000 metre record. Since then the stadium has gone from strength to strength, with improved indoor and outdoor facilities for both athletes and spectators, and Gateshead is now recognised as a major national and international athletics venue. It is home to Gateshead Harriers, one of the leading local and national athletics clubs, formed in 1904 as Gateshead St Mary's Church Running Club, now with Brendan Foster as its President. It is currently also home to both football (Gateshead FC) and rugby league (Gateshead Thunder) teams. However, there are plans to develop a new football stadium at the former North Durham Cricket and Rugby Ground, opposite Gateshead Civic Centre, on Prince Consort Road.

Sport for all

The stadium's fine facilities are open to the public and it plays host to many events for school children. The café, which looks out on the track, is open in line with stadium activities.

Continue ahead for some 50 metres then turn right and walk to the main road (A184 Felling by-pass). Turn right and use the pedestrian lights to cross over the busy road. After a few metres, at the crossing of paths, continue diagonally ahead to follow the sign for Gateshead Stadium (Metro Station) and bear left through a circular fold.

Now walk ahead along the broad path. On your left you will see what is probably Gateshead's most recent church building, which was officially opened in 2008 and is associated through the Jesmond Trust with Jesmond Parish Church in Newcastle **(Qu 5)**.

You cross Holmes Drive (Kelly won gold medals in the 800m and 1500m in the Athens Olympics, 2004). You are now on a walkway that takes you through the St James Village housing estate. There a several circular folds and you may notice motifs on the railings that relate to sports activities. Although the names are not visible on you route, adjoining streets bear the names of sporting heroes such as, Radcliffe Close (Paula, outstanding marathon runner), Foster Drive (Brendan, Commonwealth and Olympic medals winner), Redgrave Close (Steve, gold medals for rowing in five consecutive Olympics, 1984-2000) and Renforth Close (James, world champion rower in nineteenth century).

After some 200 metres you cross Ovett Gardens (Steve Ovett won a gold medal in the 800m in the Moscow Olympics, 1980). At the end of the pedestrian walkway turn left, walk across the bridge to Gateshead Stadium Metro Station and the end of the walk.

Quiz questions

1. **How many babes are there in the bed?**
2. **Can you tell the local name given in the artwork to this waggonway line**
3. **Which unusual 'flying' animals can you see in the artwork?**
4. **What is the name of these apartments?**
5. **What is the name of the church?**

19. Derwent Walk Country Park

Start/finish:	**By bus: from bus stops at Winlaton Mill. By car: from the Country Park car park at Winlaton Mill on the A694**
Distance:	**2.25 miles**
Route:	**A circular walk through Derwenthaugh and Derwent Walk Country Park including a red kite area**
Accessibility:	**On a mixture of surfaced paths and tracks. There is one long fairly steep ascent**
Refreshments:	**A pub in Winlaton Mill**
Outward bus:	**From Newcastle Eldon Square 45, 46, 47. To Spa Well Road bus stop (No 13031) which, approaching from Newcastle, is the stop just before the traffic lights at Winlaton Mill**
Return bus:	**To Newcastle Eldon Square 45, 46, 47 from Spa Well Road bus stop (No 13032)**

The Derwenthaugh Park has been reclaimed from the site of the former Derwenthaugh Cokeworks. The Derwent Walk Country Park provides a main walk which follows the line of the former Derwent Valley Railway, which ran from 1867 to 1962. Alternative walks are available. You will find routes for these in the maps in the information panels.

On the multi-user route

From the car park, which is just beyond the traffic lights, proceed to the information panel about the Red Kite Trail **(Qu 1)**.

Go through the metal barrier where there is another information panel **(Qu 2)**.

Follow the path to a junction of paths. Turn right. On your right there is a low-level notice **(Qu 3)**.

Walk ahead. At a crossing of paths proceed ahead, in the direction indicated for Consett and Rowlands Gill, along the broad path. Keep to the main path as it bears left and runs alongside Clockburn Lake on your right. Look out for a small notice on your right near the lake side **(Qu 4)**.

You come to a bridge on your left. Turn left and cross the bridge. Now turn left and walk ahead. Carry on along the path, which eventually climbs quite steeply, until you reach a collection of directional signs and a metal Royal Bank of Scotland milepost **(Qu 5)**.

Turn right and join the multi-user route. After 150 metres or so, just before a seat on the right, over to your left you can see in the distance the 140 feet tall *Column of British Liberty*, completed in 1757 as a major feature of the Gibside Estate (National Trust). Nearer to you, through the trees, you might be able to see the Nine Arch Viaduct, a feature of the former railway.

Continue ahead. At the junction of paths turn left, go over the bridge and turn left to follow the path past Clockburn Lake on your right. Carry on to a junction of paths. Turn left and proceed to a crossing of paths (which you came through earlier).

(If a refreshment stop is needed you can turn left and go through the gateway. Walk ahead for about 300 metres to arrive at the Golden Lion pub. From here you can turn right and walk along the main road to the Winlaton Mill car park).

To continue the walk, bear right and retrace your steps along the Derwent Walk path. Turn left as indicated to return to the car park and the end of the walk.

Down by the riverside

Quiz questions

1. **How long is the Red Kite Trail?**
2. **When did the Derwenthaugh Cokeworks operate?**
3. **Who should remain on the multi-user route?**
4. **What should you not do at the lake?**
5. **How far is it to Consett from here?**

20. Watergate Forest Park

Start/finish:	**By bus: from bus stops on Lobley Hill Road. By car: from the car park at Watergate Forest Park on Whickham Highway (B6317)**
Distance:	**2 miles**
Route:	**Through Watergate Forest Park going around the lake**
Accessibility:	**Almost all on the level on tracks and surfaced paths**
Refreshments:	**There are no refreshment places on this walk**
Outward bus:	**From Gateshead Interchange Nos X30, X31, X70, 70, 97** **From Newcastle Eldon Square Nos X30, X31, X70, 70** **From Newcastle Monument Market Street No 97** **To bus stop no.14021 on Lobley Hill Road. It is the second stop after the roundabout over the A1 dual carriageway and before the brow of Lobley Hill Road**
Return bus:	**To Gateshead Interchange/Newcastle Eldon Square X30, X31, X70, 70 from bus stop No 14043**

Walk uphill from the bus stop to the pedestrian lights. Cross the road at the lights and turn left. Walk ahead and cross Whickham Highway at the traffic lights. Turn right and walk for 200 metres to a sign for 'Watergate Forest Park'. Turn left into the large car.

The park is on the site of the former Watergate Colliery which operated from 1924 to 1964. From 1993 to 2000 Gateshead Council undertook a comprehensive reclamation of the area, which culminated in the attractive park to which you are introduced on the present walk. You will find suggestions for alternative, waymarked, walks in the leaflet available at the start of the walk, as well as in the information panels which you will encounter en route. In addition, there are lots of small 'nature watch' panels and some interesting sculptures to add to your enjoyment.

Walk to the end of the car park. Before you go through the metal barrier it's worth looking at the information panel **(Qu 1)**.

Go through the barrier. From here there are three paths. Take the middle path, which has red and blue waymark arrows, in

Symbolic sculpture

the direction indicated 'To the lake' and walk straight ahead. Keep to the main path. You pass a metal sculpture on your right **(Qu 2)**.

At a crossing of paths bear right and walk uphill and then descend. Carry on to a crossing of paths and an information board. Continue ahead with the lake on your left. You reach a metal seat on your right **(Qu 3)**.

Turn left and follow the narrow path which leads to an observation point at the side of the lake **(Qu 4)**.

Turn right and walk to the main path. Turn left and walk ahead, passing a bridge on your left. Continue to a second bridge. Turn left and go across the bridge. Turn left and walk to a T-junction. Bear left and proceed ahead until eventually you come to a bridge on your left **(Qu 5)**.

Continue in the same direction. You soon reach some sturdy metal railings on the right. Walk a couple of metres then turn right and follow the railings on your right to a point where you can look over to the waterfall and the artwork *Floating Rocks* (Colin Rose, 1996).

Swans' haven

A novel rock pool

Retrace your steps to the main path. Turn right and continue ahead with the lake on your left. Keep on the main path, ignoring two paths going off to the left near an information board. The path soon runs parallel to another broad track on the right. After about 100 metres turn right then left and carry on along the broad track.

The track is part of the Tanfield Railway Path, a recreational walk which follows the line of the original Tanfield Railway. The railway opened in 1840 to transport coal from pits in north-west Durham to Dunston on the River Tyne.

Carry straight on. After a few hundred metres, a narrow path on the left goes up to the car park. However, to reach the bus stop, carry on along the broad track to exit from Watergate Forest Park. Turn right and walk ahead. At the traffic lights turn left to cross Whickham Highway. Proceed ahead to bus stop no. 14043 and the end of the walk.

Quiz questions

1. What is the name of the wood which joins Watergate Forest Park?
2. What type of worker is commemorated in the sculpture?
3. How many people are seats provided for?
4. Which two birds might you see here?
5. Which creature is represented in the small metal sculpture?

21. The Angel of the North

Start/finish:	**By bus: from bus stops near the Angel of the North. By car: from the Angel of the North car park on the A167**
Distance:	**1 mile**
Route:	**Around the Angel of the North**
Accessibility:	**On pavements and tracks**
Refreshments:	**There are no refreshment places on this short walk**
Outward bus:	**From Newcastle Eldon Square and Gateshead Interchange Nos 21, 22**
Return bus:	**To Gateshead Interchange and Newcastle Eldon Square Nos 21,22**

Alight from the bus at the Angel of the North bus stop, which is immediately after a pedestrian bridge and before the statue. Walk back to the bridge and, using steps or the ramp, cross over the dual carriageway. Follow the ramp to the pavement. Walk ahead towards the Angel. You reach the car park. Walk along the pavement on the right to arrive at an information panel **(Qu 1)**, **Qu 2)**.

Turn right and walk towards the statue. After 30 metres take the narrow path on the right to walk round the statue. You came to a plaque **(Qu 3)**.

Guardian Angel

Carry on and complete your circuit. You may wish to wander around to see this iconic sculpture from various angles.

Walk to the information panel which you saw as you entered the grounds. Turn right and walk along the footpath (which runs parallel to the main road) with the hedgerow on your left, (If the path is muddy you can turn right to walk on the pavement alongside the main road).

At the end of the path turn left to join the main road and walk the few metres to the Angel of the North bus stop **(Qu 5)**.

You can catch the return bus from here. If travelling by car, proceed ahead for 350 metres or so to the car park.

Quiz questions

1. **How tall is the Angel of the North?**
2. **What is the third function of the Angel?**
3. **Which organisations funded the Angel project?**
4. **When did the Team Colliery operate here?**
5. **Which wood can be visited from here?**

22. Whitley Bay to St Mary's Island

Start/finish:	**Monkseaton Metro Station**
Distance:	**4.5 miles (or 3 miles with bus along The Links)**
Route:	**Marine Avenue to sea front, promenade/beach, causeway to St Mary's Island, return along The Links and Marine Avenue**
Accessibility:	**On paved paths/promenades with a section along the beach depending on tides (alternative on pavement along The Links)**
Refreshments:	**Rendezvous Café and Links Gallery on promenade, Briar Dene pub on return route**

Leave Monkseaton Metro Station: from Platform 1, through the covered ramp onto a busy road (Marine Avenue); from Platform 2, turn left to the busy road (Marine Avenue). Turn right and proceed ahead. On your right is Souter Park and on your left, Churchill Playing fields with facilities for bowls, football and cricket. Here there is one of the very few synthetic running tracks in the NewcastleGateshead area and it is home to North Shields Polytechnic Athletics Club (founded 1903).

Follow Marine Avenue for about half a mile to the sea front. You pass the Whitley Bay Playhouse, a parade of food outlets and amusements. As the pavement bears right you see the white landmark-dome of the Spanish City.

Dominant dome

Whitley Bay had developed as a major seaside resort following the opening of its railway station in 1882. The Spanish City then opened in 1910 to become a major tourist attraction with its theatre (later to become a ballroom), restaurant and permanent fairground. However, as fashions changed so did its appeal and it finally closed in the early 2000s. However, it is hoped that the major regeneration scheme currently underway to develop a leisure and entertainment complex, will help to bring life back to this area. The white-domed building itself has been refurbished and the two copper dancing- girl figures were restored and replaced in 2010, a hundred years after they were originally installed.

Use the pedestrian lights to proceed straight ahead and make your way to the War Memorial commemorating the fallen in two World Wars **(Qu 1)**.

With the War Memorial behind you, follow the path on the right, between the benches, to head towards St Mary's Island and Lighthouse which you can see in the distance. At a junction of paths turn right to pass the Panama Skatepark to arrive at the promenade. Turn left and proceed along the promenade passing the Panama Swimming Club hut. The Club organises an annual New Year's Day swim that attracts over a hundred swimmers to venture into the invigorating North Sea. As you continue ahead look out on your left for a small fountain with a connection to a certain King's Speech **(Qu 2)**.

Whitley Bay war memorial

A little further along the promenade is the Rendezvous Café with the Links Gallery/café on the other side of the same building. When you reach the end of the promenade follow the path to the left for some 75 metres then turn right onto the narrow path and cross the bridge to arrive at a junction. Here you have a choice of routes. Depending on the tide you may like to walk on the beach for a short section. In this case turn right and follow the path to the beach. Turn left and continue ahead until you reach some steps that will take you up to a further section of promenade.

To the lighthouse

(If you decide not to go along the beach, then turn left then left again at a further junction and then right to join a road (The Links). Turn right and proceed ahead on the pavement until the road turns left. At this point turn right and follow the access road to St Mary's Island. As the access road bends to the left take the steep path on the right to join the promenade and the route from the beach.

On the promenade on the left you will find an information board *Tide Wrack* with interesting details of the importance of some forms of flotsam and jetsam. Proceed head and just before the causeway to St Mary's Island you will find two other boards, one with information about the Waterside Trail, and the other about the moon and tides, crabs, periwinkles and limpets **(Qu 3)**.

Before crossing the causeway you need to make sure that it is safe to cross and you are not in danger of being cut off by the fast incoming tide. If there are no tide tables at this point then you should find them in the car park a short distance behind you. If the tide is right you can cross the causeway, where there is access to many rock pools, to visit the tiny island and view the lighthouse and visitor centre (admission charge and seasonal openings) and shop. (For details of the history of St Mary's Island see: www.friendsofstmarys island.co.uk)

To return, follow the access road. Almost immediately on your right is a stone plinth marking the spot where a murderer was executed in 1739! You then pass an information board about the island and arrive at the car park with its 'Welcome to St Mary's Island' board and timetables **(Qu 4)**.

Continue along the access road, past the car park and the public conveniences, to another car park with an information board and a hide. Here you can observe the wildlife that is attracted to a fresh water pond **(Qu 5)**.

Continue ahead to the main road (The Links) and turn left to arrive at a bus stop opposite Whitley Bay Cemetery. If you prefer to confine your walk to 3 miles then you can take a bus from here to near the War Memorial (Bandstand stop) and then walk back up Marine Avenue to the Metro Station.

Otherwise walk along the pavement past the mini-golf course until eventually you pass the Briar Dene pub and a roundabout. Continuing ahead, on your right, you pass Waves, with its child-friendly pool facilities, before reaching the junction with Marine Avenue. Turn right and return to Monkseaton Metro Station and the end of the walk.

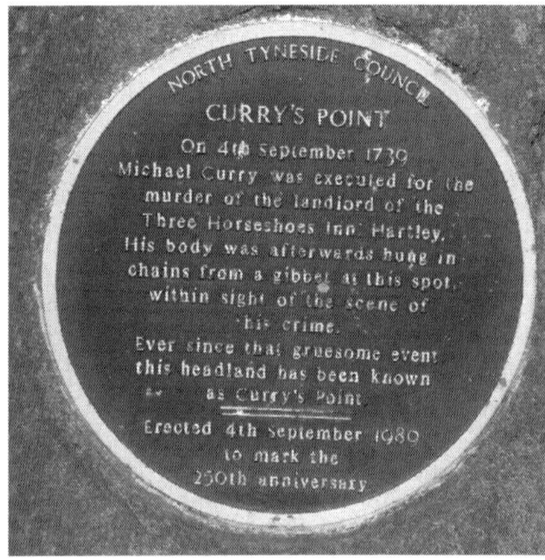

Execution site

Quiz questions

1. **What are the dates given for those who died?**
2. **Which King's coronation does the fountain commemorate?**
3. **How long is the Waterside Trail?**
4. **How many steps are there to the top of the lighthouse?**
5. **How many different kind of birds may visit here?**

23. Whitley Bay to Tynemouth

Start: Monkseaton Metro Station
Finish: Tynemouth Metro Station
Distance: 3.5 miles
Route: Marine Avenue to sea front at Whitley Bay, promenade/beach along the coast via Cullercoats to Tynemouth
Accessibility: On paved paths/promenades throughout
Refreshments: Cafés and pubs throughout the walk

Leave Monkseaton Metro Station: from Platform 1, through the covered ramp onto a busy road (Marine Avenue); from Platform 2, turn left to the busy road (Marine Avenue). Turn right and walk ahead. On your right is Souter Park and on your left, Churchill Playing fields. You pass the Whitley Bay Playhouse, a parade of food outlets and amusements. As the pavement bears right you see the white landmark-dome of the Spanish City (see Walk 22).

Use the pedestrian lights to proceed straight ahead and then turn immediately right. On your left is a small landscaped area and on your right is the Spanish City **(Qu 1)**.

Cross the access road, Watts Road. (Alternatively, if you turn left down the access road, you come to the Boardwalk Café and Restaurant and soon find yourself on the beach from where you can turn right and continue ahead towards Tynemouth. It is not possible to walk

Contemporary castles

the whole way along the seashore and you will need to use ramps at various points to take you up and down the adjacent promenades. If you enjoy beach walking, and the tide is out, then here is an opportunity).

You arrive at the paved upper-promenade. Almost immediately ahead you pass a metal sculpture *Sand Castles* (Richard Broderick, 1999).

Carry along the upper promenade parallel to the road. You pass a large hotel with a royal connection **(Qu 2)**.

Make sure you enjoy the views of the bays and the rock formations as you make your way along the promenade for the next mile or so. Look out for a sign on your right that advises you to be discreet if you decide to take a dip in the sea at any time you fancy!

A discrete sign

At a fork, as the path goes left at South Cliff, bear right to follow the main road and in about 100 metres you pass a sign for Cullercoats. This one-time fishing village was a favourite place for painters and photographers. (A few of the fishermen's cottages can still be seen by crossing over to the road that leads up from the Cullercoats Methodist Fishermen's Mission and then turning almost immediately left. Turn left beyond the cottages to return to the sea front). Information panels provide details of its artistic significance and the contribution of one 19th-century American artist in particular **(Qu 3)**.

You pass the former fisherman's look-out and below, on the edge of the beach, the Cullercoats Lifeboat Station. In close proximity is Newcastle University's Dove Marine Laboratory.

A short distance ahead you pass a small fountain and after a further 50 metres on your left you will see a tall mast with a basket-like structure on it. Across the road peering over a house is a similar navigation mast. You will notice that the house had to be built deliberately lower than its neighbours so that the beacon could be seen! As you continue ahead you pass St George's Church (1884) with its landmark tower and spire and a First World War memorial outside its east end. From this point on you will see a fine stretch of sand, the Longsands, where the sea waves provide a noted attraction for surfers. On your right you pass the Blue Reef Aquarium and the Park Hotel.

Longsands and St George's

On your left are a small number of outlets that include the Childhood Memories Toy Museum (seasonal opening: Tel 01912591776 or www.tynemouth toymuseum). These stand next to the site of what was once billed as 'the Showplace of the North', Tynemouth Plaza. This impressively grand building opened in

1878 and after serving many functions including as a theatre, a roller skating rink and nightclub, it was engulfed in flames in 1996 and almost immediately demolished.

Cross the road at the pedestrian lights and enter Tynemouth Park with its lake, Clocktower Café, crazy golf, synthetic ice rink, bowling greens and children's play area. Walk around in an anti-clockwise direction, exit the park near the end of the lake and return to the other side of the road. Turn right and continue ahead towards another splendid local landmark, The Grand Hotel (1877) which boasts an interesting history describing itself as 'a grand old lady who has gone through good times and bad times' (see: www.grandhotel-uk.com). Opposite the hotel, a ramp leads down to the beach and the popular Crusoe's Café.

Continuing ahead you may see the former outdoor swimming pool now rather sadly a rock pool and then on your right the elegant lines of Percy Gardens. You then soon reach the Gibraltar Rock pub beyond which is the imposing headland on which stands Tynemouth Priory and Castle. You can visit the remains of the 13th-century priory with its 15th-century chapel that after the Reformation became a royal castle. Its strategic position resulted in it being a coastal gun battery in World Wars I and II. A noticeboard gives details of opening hours **(Qu 4)**.

Ahead lies a delightful bay, the Collingwood Monument and the mouth of the River Tyne (see Walk 24) but our route now turns right to continue along the left-hand side of Front Street. Behind the railings of the first property you will discover the remains of an important doorway. You then pass Our Lady and St Oswin's RC Church (1890, Hansom & Dunn), St Oswin being King of Deria (Southern Northumbria) who was buried at the Priory (AD 651).

At the other end of Front Street is the Green Ginger Shopping Arcade occupying a former church, evidence of which can still be seen in the words 'God is love' above the internal gallery. Varied outlets including a café can be found among its nooks and crannies.

Cross the busy road with care and proceed ahead along Huntingdon Place. You pass a park on your right with two war memorials and a statue of Queen Victoria (1902) by Alfred Gilbert whose work includes the famous statue of Eros in London. On your left, at No 8, a plaque indicates that Giuseppe Garibldi once stayed here. Next door is a well-regarded independent school for pupils between 4 and 18 years of age **(Qu 5)**.

Follow the road on your left to Tynemouth Metro Station and the end of the walk.

Quiz questions

1. **How many dancing-girl figures adorn the Spanish City?**
2. **What is the name of this hotel?**
3. **Who was the American artist?**
4. **Which organisation is responsible for managing the Castle and Priory?**
5. **What is the name of the school?**

24. Tynemouth to North Shields

Start: **Tynemouth Metro Station**
Finish: **North Shields Metro Station**
Distance: **3 miles**
Route: **Through Tynemouth village and along the River Tyne to North Shields**
Accessibility: **Mainly on the level on pavements and metalled paths. Towards the end there is a steep ascent via steps. The steps, but not the steep ascent, can be avoided by taking the alternative route presented**
Refreshments: **A wide variety of places in Tynemouth and North Shields**

Leave Tynemouth Station from Platform 2. (Platform 2 can be accessed from Platform 1 either by steps and a bridge, or, exit the station and follow the sign 'Access via road bridge'). Near the exit there are some notice boards with interesting information, including details of markets which are held on the station concourse on Saturdays and Sundays. Emerge opposite Kings School. Turn left and follow the road as it bears right past a pleasant terrace. There is a plaque on Number 8 explaining that Garibaldi stayed there **(Qu 1)**.

The small park on your left has two war memorials and a statue of Queen Victoria (1902) by Alfred Gilbert whose work includes the famous statue of Eros in London. Cross at the traffic lights and walk ahead. On your right is the Green Ginger Shopping Arcade occupying a former church, evidence of which can still be seen in the words 'God is love' over the internal gallery. Various outlets including a café can be found among its nooks and crannies.

Gatehouse

Carry on along Front Street. You pass Our Lady and St Oswin's RC Church (1890) by Hanson & Dunn. St Oswin being King of Deria (Southern Northumbria) who was buried at Tynemouth Priory in AD651. Behind the railings of the last property you will discover the remains of an important doorway.

On the headland you will see the gatehouse of Tynemouth Castle beyond which lies the Priory. A plaque provides some details of this burial ground of Kings **(Qu 2)**.

Turn right and proceed down the road to Tynemouth Haven. On your left you will get good views of the ruins of both Tynemouth Priory and the Castle. Over to your right is the Collingwood Monument (1845) designed by John Dobson (1787-1865) the famous architect who was born in North Shields. The tall statue is by John Lough (1798-1876), the highly-regarded Northumbrian sculptor. The monument was paid for by a grateful public, proud of one of the heroes of Trafalgar.

Now, follow the path by the side of the road as it ascends to the Spanish Battery car park. You might like to go left, through the car park, onto the headland to enjoy the views. However to continue the walk you need to leave the path and follow the access road to the right to walk past (and/or visit) the Watch House and Museum. Carry on in the same direction and follow the path which soon descends towards the river. On reaching the riverside you will see a plaque and a milepost referring to the National Cycle Network **(Qu 3)**.

Proceed along the riverside path with the river on your left. Above on the right is the Collingwood Monument. (Should you wish to visit the monument, see the cannons from Collingwood's ship, the Royal Sovereign, and read about him, you may like to take the path on your right. Then return to the promenade).
Further along the promenade, towering above you on the bankside, you pass a clock on the wall of the James Knott Memorial Flats (1938). You can read, later in the walk, about Sir James. Carry on, eventually you will see two large white towers ahead. These are the Low Light and the High Light, former navigational aids for vessels sailing into the Tyne. You come to a small sandy beach and a car park. Here you will see one of a number of interesting North Shields Heritage Trail information panels on this walk **(Qu 4)**.

Collingwood's cannon

Just beyond the car park you will see three colourfully-restored navigational buoys. Turn right onto the road and just after the bus stop you will find the heritage trail panel *River Life* where you can read about Lowlights among interesting things. Carry on to the junction, turn left and follow the road to walk past the New Dolphin pub with a modern sculpture and a whale jawbone outside.

Walk ahead, passing the fish quay on your left. On the right is a miscellany of fishmongers, pubs and cafés. Wm Wight Ltd's shop usually displays some amusing messages and a board gives some information about the history of the shop.

Just before the tall blue corrugated metal building (the ice house), on the right you arrive at the narrow entrance to Ropery Stairs. Although this provides a steep climb, it will enable you to see more of North Shields.

(However, If you don't wish to climb the 115 or so steps (!) and you prefer to go direct to the Metro Station, continue straight ahead to a junction near The Porthole pub, turn right and walk up the steep hill. At the T-junction, turn right and proceed to North Shields Metro Station and the end the walk. If you want to link up with Walk 25 (North Shields to South Shields), continue straight ahead and follow the signs to the Pedestrian Ferry. Ferries depart at 30 minutes past the hour. Mondays to Saturdays from 7.30 a.m; Sundays from 10.30 a.m.).

Take your time and carefully ascend Ropery Stairs. At the top, turn left and walk along Tyne Street. Looking back you get a good view of the High Light. Looking ahead in the distance on the right you may be able to see a ship docked at the International Ferry terminal at Royal Quays terminal. At the end of the street you come to an anchor, serving as a memorial 'For all those lost at sea'. There is also a heritage trail panel *The Gorge* where you can read about the generosity of Sir James Knot and his wife. A plaque on the nearby Registry Office outlines the history of the building and the significance of the Stag emblem.

A poignant reminder

Turn right and walk along Howard Street. At the junction with Saville Street an information panel provides details of this area in the 18th and 19th centuries. Continue along Howard Street for a few hundred metres until you come to Northumberland Square. A heritage trail panel *Wooden Dollies* provides some information which will help you to appreciate the significance of the sculpture a short distance ahead within the park. Go into the little park and bear left at the sculpture **(Qu 5)**.

Follow the path diagonally through the park to the crossroads. Beyond the crossroads to the right you may catch a glimpse of Christ Church (1668), built as the parish church of Tynemouth. However you need to bear left to follow the road (Northumberland Place). Cross Church Walk and then turn left at Bedford Street. Walk to the clock tower outside the Beacon shopping centre and turn right to arrive at North Shields Metro Station and the end of the walk.

Quiz questions

1. **In what year did Garibaldi stay here?**
2. **How many Kings are buried here?**
3. **How far is it to the Irish Sea?**
4. **What is the name of the fort near here that once guarded the Tyne?**
5. **Who does the statue represent?**

25. North Shields to South Shields (via Tyne Ferry)

Start:	**North Shields Metro Station**
Finish:	**South Shields Metro Station**
Distance:	**3.25 miles**
Route:	**From North Shields to the River Tyne and across by the pedestrian ferry. (The ferry departs on the hour and at 30 minutes past the hour). Then, via Arbeia Roman fort, North Marine Park and Ocean Road, to South Shields Metro Station**
Accessibility:	**There is a steep descent near the start and a short steep ascent from the river at South Shields. Otherwise, mainly on the level on pavements and surfaced paths**
Refreshments:	**Several pubs and cafés in North Shields and South Shields town centres**

Leave North Shields Metro Station. In front of you there is an information panel (No 17 on the North Shields Heritage Trail) with details of local events and personalities, including Thomas Burt, one of Tyneside's greatest working class heroes, and Dr Hastings Banda, Malawi's first Prime Minister **(Qu 1)**.

Turn right and after a few metres turn right again to follow the sign 'Pedestrian Ferry'. Proceed ahead and turn left into Borough Road. Follow the road, using the left-hand side pavement, as it descends towards the river. At the bottom of the hill, on your left, is another Heritage Tail panel which has fascinating comments about 'A nest of vice'.

Turn right and cross to the other side of Borough Road. Proceed ahead. A plaque on the first building indicates that this was originally the Sailors' Home (Benjamin Green, 1856) financed by the 4th Duke of Northumberland. Like the other properties here it has been converted into residential apartments.

You reach an information panel which includes details of the former Smith's Dock located nearby. It is said that workers who were returning to South Shields used to stop at the Crane House Vaults pub before crossing by ferry. However, not wanting to waste precious drinking time, they always left it to the last second before leaving the pub so that unwary fellow passengers were almost mown down in the rush to get onto the boat.

Ready to sail

Cross the road, go along Ferry Mews and follow the walkway to the terminal, where there is a waiting room. A further Heritage Trail panel gives local information including the history of '700 years of crossing the Tyne'. Board the ferry. Enjoy the crossing! After disembarking, walk up the ramp to a paved promenade. On your right an information panel 'Ferries and Tugs' provides some historical background.

Turn left. Walk for 25 metres and then turn right and walk to the Alum Ale House pub on your left. Turn left at the T-junction and proceed ahead. At the roundabout bear right and follow the road, climbing quite steeply, as it bears left and crosses a bridge.
You can also enjoy some extensive views of the river where despite the disappearance of its traditional trade there are still signs of activity. Just beyond the bridge, turn left onto the metalled path.

Follow the path past the statute of Dolly Peel (1782-1857) whose fascinating story is told on the accompanying information panels **(Qu 2)**.

Continue on the path. Below on the left there are several little boatyards on the riverside. The path rejoins the main pavement. From here, looking over the river to North Shields, the two tall white buildings in the foreground are the High Light and Low Light, which for many years served as navigational aids.

Cross the road and proceed along Mile End Road for a few metres and then turn left and follow the path past the beautifully maintained war memorial and graveyard. Unusually, the memorial itself honours the men from just one South Shields street, who fought and died in the First World War **(Qu 3)**.

The church over to the right is St Stephen and St Aidan (1846). At a junction of paths turn left, walk about 50 metres and at the railings turn right. Walk ahead and go up three steps. Turn left and follow the road round to the right with the railings on your left. At the end of the railings, turn left and follow the railings on your left towards the church. Continue ahead to the junction at the People's Mission. Turn left and walk to Arbeia Roman Fort and Museum on the right (see www.twmuseums.org.uk/arbeia for details of opening dates and times).

Today's Arbeia

After visiting Arbeia leave the grounds, turn right and walk towards the river. You pass an information panel 'Gateway to a frontier' which has details of the early history of the area. At the T-junction turn right and proceed along Greens Place. You pass Wellesley Court, formerly the River Tyne Pilot Offices, and The Beacon pub. Walk ahead to an information panel about The Lawe Top **(Qu 4)**.

A few metres further on you reach the Lawe Beacons (1832) with a plaque which outlines its significance. Ignore the gateposts on your left as you bear right for 30 metres before turning left into parkland.

Follow the pink line which takes you left at a crossing of paths. You come to a small plaque at The Lawe Top. From the top of the nearby steps there are splendid sea views. On the beach below you can see the bronze figures of the sculpture *Conversation Piece* (Juan Munoz, 1999).

Keep following the pink line (which needs repainting in places). Where a path comes in from a road on your right, follow the path you are on as it bears left and gently descends between bushes. Carry on to a crossing of paths with a lamp post in the centre. Carry on for a hundred metres or so to another crossing of paths with a lamp post in the centre. Turn right and follow the path to exit the park.

View from Lawe Top

Turn left and walk the short distance to the lifeboat memorial where several panels tell the story of the development of early lifeboats. The adjacent clock tower dates from 1887. A few metres along, on the right, is another information panel which outlines stories about 'The sands of Tyne' **(Qu 5)**.

With the clock tower behind you, walk ahead to the crossroads. Cross over and continue in the same direction along the road (Ocean Road) with its fascinating collection of ethnic restaurants and takeaways on the left and neat boarding houses on the right.

The road becomes pedestrianized as you come to the town centre. On your right there is statue in memory of John Simpson Kirkpatrick (Robert Olley, 1988). John Simpson Fitzpatrick (1892-1915) served with the Australian and New Zealand Army Corps (ANZAC) as a stretcher-bearer during the Gallipoli campaign in the First World War. He used a donkey to carry soldiers to safety, ignoring danger to himself, until he was killed. His grave is in a small cemetery in Gallipoli. In 2011 a play based on his life was premiered in South Shields' Customs House theatre.

On your left you reach the Museum and Art Gallery. Its major collections cover the natural and social history of the area and include an exhibition celebrating the life and achievements of celebrated local author Dame Catherine Cookson (1906-1998). There is also a café. Entry to the Museum is free and further information can be obtained from: www.twmuseums.org.uk/southshields.

Carry straight on to the South Shields Metro Station and the end of the walk.

Quiz questions

1. **What was Dr Hasting Banda's connection with North Shields?**
2. **What was Dolly Peel always determined to fight against?**
3. **Which South Shields street is named on the War Memorial?**
4. **What did Mr Green establish near the Lawe Top in 1792?**
5. **How any lives are said to have been saved by the Tyne lifeboat?**

26. Howdon to Jarrow (via Tyne Pedestrian Tunnel)

Start: Howdon Metro Station
Finish: Jarrow Metro Station
Distance: 3.5 miles
Route: Through Howdon and the Tyne Pedestrian Tunnel then via St Paul's Church and Bede's World to Jarrow
Accessibility: Not for the faint-hearted. The walk goes through the tunnel and, because it is much less used than in its heyday, you might feel rather lonely if you are the only pedestrian going through. After a gentle descent the walk is mainly on the level on metalled paths and pavements
Refreshments: A café in Bede's World and several cafés and pubs in Jarrow

Leave Howdon Metro Station: from Platform 1, turn right to cross the Metro line; from Platform 2, turn left. Walk ahead, passing Howdon Park on your left. When the road completes its descent, about 75 metres after the 'Welcome to Willington Quay' sign, turn left to walk along Norman Terrace. On your left, you come to a sign for 'Tyne Cycle & Ped Tunnel'. Turn right to follow the direction indicated and pass the east end of St Paul's Church (1876). The absence of a notice board might give the impression that the church is closed. However, at the time of writing, it still is in use for Sunday and other services.

Carry on along the road (Cumberland Street). At the junction, turn left and walk a few metres, then use the traffic island to cross the road with care. Walk ahead to follow the metalled path, with railings on your right. You reach an information panel which gives details about North Tyneside Waggonways. Just beyond this you arrive at a road. Turn right and walk towards the entrance to the Tyne pedestrian and cycle tunnels. On the right, in the aptly-named Stephenson Street, there is an information panel with details of local connections with George Stephenson the railway engineer. Just before the entrance there are two sculptures by Fiona Gray (2004): *The ones that got away* and *Echo*. Details of the Tyne crossings are incorporated in the latter.

At the Tunnel entrance there is an information plaque with details of its fascinating history **(Qu 1)**.

A fishy introduction

Use the escalator (one of the longest in the world at the

time of its construction) or, if this is not operating, the lift to enter the tunnel. Go through the tunnel. Its length clearly confirms that you are passing underneath the River Tyne. You know when you are half-way across when you see the Northumberland and Durham coats of arms, which are displayed on the wall.

Near the exit there is an exhibition of photographs about the construction and opening of the tunnel and a panel with technical details. Walk ahead and go up the fairly steep steps or use the ramp to come to a red-brick road. You can see a tunnel ventilation funnel ahead. Walk straight ahead to arrive at a main road (Chaytor Street). At the time of writing there is a great deal of building activity in this area.

Turn left and proceed along the left-hand side of the road. Where the road bears to the right, turn left at a Keelman's Way sign, Walk ahead, passing storage tanks on your right and carry on. Continue ahead to come to a road and the River Don.

Turn right and proceed ahead along the riverside path, or the road if the path is slippery. The path rejoins the road. Carry on in the same direction and follow the road as it turns to the right. After a hundred metres or so you come to an entrance gate to the grounds of St Paul's Church and a notice board welcoming you to the church and the site of St Paul's Monastery.

Go into the grounds and follow the path to arrive at the main entrance. The church has 7th-century foundations and a Saxon chancel. During daylight hours, church members are normally on hand to answer questions you may have. Beyond the main entrance you come to the remains of the monastery and one of several information panels. Here you enter the area where the Venerable Bede (c673-735), monk and historian, lived and worked **(Qu 2)**.

St Bede's place

Leave the church grounds by the gate through which you entered. Cross the road and walk ahead, along the path which runs through the parkland. You arrive at steps. Go up the steps to arrive at Jarrow Hall.

(To avoid the steps, bear left and walk past the children's play area to a road (Church Bank). Turn right and proceed ahead for about a hundred metres to arrive at the entrance drive to Bede's World. Turn right and walk ahead to Jarrow Hall.)

Jarrow Hall (1785) was built by Simon Temple, a local businessman. It is now part of the Bede's World complex and has a café.

A few metres to the left of the Hall is the entrance to Bede's World. Its attractions include an Anglo-Saxon-style farm with animals and crops appropriate to those times. There is an admission fee. (For further details see www.bedesworld.co.uk). You can go into the entrance lobby, without charge, where you will find some interesting details displayed on panels **(Qu 3)**.

Walk along the driveway to the exit of the grounds of Bede's World at a road (Church Bank). Cross the road via the pedestrian lights. Bear right and walk along the pavement.

Carry on to a junction with a busy road (Priory Road). You need to take extreme care as you cross this road. Walk ahead along Cloister Walk.

You pass The Alexandra Hotel on your right. A little further on, turn right into Staple Road. Walk ahead for about 50 metres and then turn left to walk along the footpath through the supermarket car park. At the end of the path you will see the bold sculpture *Spirit of Jarrow* (Graham C. Ibbeson) 2002, with its Jarrow Crusade banner which seems to evoke both times past and a looking ahead to the future.

Campaigning crusade

Bear slightly right and go through The Viking Shopping Centre gateway. Turn right and proceed through the shopping complex. Go through another gateway and after about 30 metres turn left. The apartment block on your right, Wilkinson Court, is named after Ellen Wilkinson, the local M. P. who strongly supported the unemployed men who marched to London in 1936 in what has become known as the Jarrow Crusade. Walk ahead to the red-brick building surmounted with a clock **(Qu 4)**.

This building, now used by South Tyneside Council, is the former Jarrow Town Hall (1902). A plaque on the wall commemorates the start of the Jarrow March from here.

Go across the road to a statue of Sir Charles Mark Palmer, shipbuilder, whose yards provided local employment **(Qu 5)**.

Walk ahead to an information panel 'Jarrar lads'. A little further on you come to a sculpture *The Vikings* (Colin Davidson, 1962). Turn left at the crossroads. The church over the road is Christ Church (1868). Now proceed along the road (Grange Road) for 175 metres then turn right and go through the underpass. Turn immediately left and follow the ramp to Jarrow Metro Station and the end of the walk. In the station there is an information panel with details of local walks embracing places of historical interest. On Platform 2 there is a sculpture *Jarrow Crusade* (Vince Rae, 1984).

Quiz questions

1. **When was the Tyne pedestrian tunnel opened?**
2. **What was St Paul's twin monastery?**
3. **Who was the first Patron of Bede's World?**
4. **When was the clock added to the building?**
5. **Who provided the monument of Sir Charles Mark Palmer?**

Answers to quiz questions

The answers to the quiz questions are based on the information that was available at the time of writing and users may find in the meantime that signs and even buildings have disappeared. Likewise, as with the questions, the answers may need to be adapted to suit the ages of the participants.

Walk 1
1. 1881, 1899 (interwoven numbers) and 1898
2. Think and Look
3. 1893
4. Six on Grey Street (but there is another around the corner on Hood Street!)
5. King Charles I
6. King George V
7. Dirty Burn
8. Hero of the naval battle of Trafalgar
9. Because he translated the Holy Scriptures into Chinese
10. Anne Huxtable

Walk 2
1. To assist in preserving public health, following the 1831 cholera epidemic
2. Rotary Watches
3. Tyne Bridge
4. Great North Run
5. Around 1706-1710
6. Greene family
7. Outside the east entrance (Performance Square)
8. Level 5
9. Lindisfarne Community Primary School (1966-2007)
10. 1925

Walk 3
1. A sword and a garland.
2. King's Gate
3. Armaments and hydraulics: on the left a crane and a gun; on the right the Swing Bridge
4. The giraffe
5. The Military Vehicle Museum
6. Two
7. Inside the church porch
8. 1975
9. Framlington House
10. Robin (Telford)

Walk 4
1. 43rd and 49th Battalions of the Royal Tank Regiment
2. Hate evil love good
3. For excellence in the provision of library services
4. Victoria Square
5. 4 St Mary's Terrace
6. The Stone Firms, i.e. firms which supply Portland stone
7. Nine
8. William Straker (1855-1941)
9. The Centenary of the Northern Architectural Association
10. Six: St Thomas's Church, Jesmond Parish Church, Carlton Terrace, Drill Hall (Northumberland Road), Dobson's House, Lying-in Hospital

Walk 5
1. The Newcastle Breweries
2. To transport the beer (in barrels) on carts, called drays, pulled by horses driven by draymen
3. A young looking Queen Victoria
4. 1885
5. The TA (Territorial Army)
6. Chinese Restaurant (Dragoni)
7. 60th Jubilee of Queen Victoria in 1897. She came to the throne in 1837 and died in 1901
8. Lions
9. Basketball
10. No 14

Walk 6
1. Music for everyone: printed music, musical instruments, CD/DVDs,etc.
2. The bookshop that was once on this site
3. Six
4. 30p (September 2011)
5. The Duke of Northumberland (an early one!)
6. The Mile Castle
7. He became organist at the Churches of St John's and St Nicholas'.
8. 1894
9. Carliol Croft and Cutler Tower
10. Sunderland

Walk 7
1. Because strawberries were grown around here in the grounds of St Bartholomew's Nunnery
2. Because it was built outside the Town Wall

3. 5th October 1892
4. Because they were used by the Gallowgate Lead Works which was located here
5. The Irish. The Irish Club is near the Chinese Arch
6. A football
7. 55 years (1861-1916)
8. Because he held his first public subscription concert here
9. 1985
10. Three: one parallel to Stowell Street, one in Bath Lane, one in the grounds of St Andrew's Church

Walk 8

1. H.M.The Queen to commemorate the 150th anniversary of the Station.
2. It is free for the under fours.
3. The daughter of Richard and Rachel Grainger
4. Turbinia, the fastest vessel in the world in 1897
5. 1907
6. The Newcastle Amateur Vocal Society
7. 1979-1983.
8. Adam Wakenshaw died bravely in battle at Mersa Matruh in North Africa on 21st June 1942
9. St Aidan and St Cuthbert
10. The Chillingham Wild Bull

Walk 9

1. Thirty
2. Butcher Bank
3. An anchor, on the crest, and a ship, on the noticeboard
4. Nearly five past three (unless the clock has been restored since the time of writing!)
5. Four or five: Gateshead Millennium Bridge, Tyne Bridge Swing Bridge, High Level Bridge and possibly the supports of the Queen Elizabeth II Metro Bridge
6. People and animals
7. Nine: Hamburg, Genoa, Aberdeen, Rotterdam, Copenhagen, Malmo, London, Antwerp, Hull
8. 6000 kilometres
9. May
10. A schoolroom

Walk 10

1. A medieval house and warehouse complex with a private quay
2. The Close
3. A Stone Tramway
4. There was a walled orchard here
5. Circus
6. Clavering House
7. The Robert Stephenson Bi-centenary
8. A sphere (representing the Orb, one of the signs of her authority)
9. Crests of the County of Northumberland; the area was once part of that County
10. Castle Stairs

Walk 11

1. Its location in Northumbria University is appropriate because it denotes learning
2. Northumbria University
3. NE2 Food Social
4. To enable a filling- in of the valley here
5. Three: Rail bridge, Metro viaduct, Byker Bridge (road bridge)
6. Spaces for artists to work
7. 1879
8. It was created on piles of ballast, dumped here from incoming boats
9. They were brave men who took part in life-saving
10. Windscreen wipers

Walk12

1. George Hawks -see memorial stone on the ground beside his statue.
2. 1935
3. 1925
4. On the left and with a book in her hand to represent the Arts
5. On the base to the left of the door of the monument
6. Wendy Cousins
7. 1886-the date of the foundation of the regiment
8. The Great House
9. 1901
10. The South African Campaign (1899-1902) also known as the Boer War

Walk 13

1. A tortoise racing a hare in a sack race
2. 1868
3. The Station Hotel
4. B1600
5. The fiddle
6. TS Flamingo
7. Depending on the vegetation, five are usually fairly obvious and then there are a further two higher up
8. September (Courtyard)
9. Cormorant, Kingfisher, Grebe, and Bittern
10. Mandela Road: presumably named after famous South African political leader Nelson Mandela

Walk 14
1. No 1 Cathedral Square
2. 1875
3. Cale Cross
4. Newcastle's three castles
5. Gateshead Visitor Centre
6. Robert Stephenson and Thomas E. Harrison
7. National Railway Heritage Awards: The First Group Craft Skills Award
8. Half-way across the Swing Bridge
9. 53
10. The Co-operative Society

Walk 15
1. Grove Park
2. Two
3. Notorious, reputed to be the local mobsters
4. Sainsburys
5. The Brandling Family of Gosforth House
6. Bulman Village
7. In appreciation to the community for supporting Rotary Club projects 1941-1991
8. Member of Christians Together in Gosforth
9. Moor Court
10. Allotments

Walk 16
1. Four
2. 1856
3. The Banqueting Hall in 1860-62
4. King Edward VI
5. Twenty-seven years
6. Blue
7. Fleming Business Centre
8. Robert Howlett
9. Two seahorses and a lion
10. Richard Clayton

Walk 17
1. Mabel's Mill
2. 1879
3. Armourer Donkin (1779-1851), a Newcastle solicitor to whom Armstrong had been articled as a young man
4. 1892 (the date is on the corner of the building)
5. Upstairs

Walk 18
1. Three: two boys and a girl
2. Dilly Line
3. Pigs
4. Friars Wharf
5. Holy Trinity

Walk 19
1. 18 kilometres (11 miles)
2. 1928-1986
3. Cyclists and horseriders
4. Swimming and diving
5. 10 miles

Walk 20
1. Washingwell Wood
2. A coalminer
3. Three
4. Tufted Duck, Common Tern
5. A frog

Walk 21
1. 20 metres (65 feet)
2. As a focus for our hopes and fears
3. National Lottery, European Community Regional Development Fund and Northern Arts
4. 1720s -1960s
5. Longacre Wood

Walk 22
1. 1914-1919 and 1939-1945
2. The coronation of King George VI (1937)
3. 13 kilometres
4. 137 steps
5. 15 kinds of birds are listed

Walk 23
1. Two
2. The Rex Hotel
3. Winslow Homer
4. English Heritage
5. The King's School

Walk 24
1. 1854
2. Three: Oswin, Osred, Malcolm
3. C2C- Sea to Sea (Irish Sea to North Sea) also called Coast to Coast
4. Clifford's Fort
5. A North Shields fisherwoman

Walk 25
1. Practised as a doctor in North Shields 1942-1945
2. The pressgang
3. Wellington Street
4. An industrial ropery
5. 1,028 lives

Walk 26
1. 1951
2. St Peter's, Wearmouth in Sunderland
3. Dame Catherine Cookson
4. 1951
5. The workmen of Palmer's yard & a few friends

Bibliography

Adams, Max (2005) *Collingwood: Northumberland's Heart of Oak*, Tyne Bridge Publishing

Allen, Joan and Buswell, Richard (2005) *Rutherford's Ladder: The Making of Northumbria University,1871 - 1996*, Northumbria University Press

Bell, R. C. (1986) *Maling and other Tyneside Pottery*, Shire Publications Ltd

Chapman, Robert H. (1997) *A View from the Chair: A History of Chapman's Siesta Furniture,* 2nd edn. Chapmans

Charleton, R. J. (1882) *A History of Newcastle-on-Tyne*, William H. Robinson

Cole, Grenville S. (1996) *Arms and the Man: W.G. Armstrong First Baron of Cragside*, Lady Armstrong

Donaghy, Peter and Laidler, John (2006) *Metro Walks*, Nexus

Faulkner, Thomas and Greg, Andrew (2001) *John Dobson: Architect of the North East*, Tyne Bridge Publishing

Friar, Stephen (2000) *The Companion to the English Parish Church*, Chancellor Press

Grundy, John et al (2006) *Tyneside's Finest*, Tyne Bridge Publishing

Hall, Marshall (2005) *The Artists of Northumbria*, Art Dictionaries

Heslop, D. H., Jobling, B. and McCombie, G. (2001) *Alderman Fenwick's House*, The Society of Antiquaries of Newcastle upon Tyne

Hilton, Patricia (2001) *Pennies from Heaven*, All Saints' Church, Gosforth

Histon, Vanessa (2006) *Unlocking the Quayside: NewcastleGateshead's historic waterfront explored*, Tyne Bridge Publishing

Histon, Vanessa (2007) *Keys to the City: Walks exploring Newcastle's hidden history*, Tyne Bridge Publishing

Howard, Anthony (2005) *Basil Hume: the Monk Cardinal*, Headline

Laidler, John (2008) *Bus Walks Booklet 1: North and West Newcastle upon Tyne*, Nexus

Laidler, John (2009) *Bus Walks Booklet 2: Gateshead*, Nexus

Lovie, David (2001) *The buildings of Grainger Town: Four townscape walks around Newcastle*, 2nd edn. Grainger Town Partnership

Manders, F. W. D. (1973) *A History of Gateshead*, Gateshead Corporation

Manders, Frank and Potts, Richard (2001) *Crossing the Tyne*, Tyne Bridge Publishing

Maw, W. (1964) *The Story of Rutherford Grammar School*, Northumberland Press

McCombie, Grace (2009) *Newcastle and Gateshead*, Yale University Press

Middlebrook, S. (1950) *Newcastle upon Tyne: Its Growth and Achievement*, Newcastle Journal

Moffat, Alistair and Rosie, George (2005) *Tyneside: A History of Newcastle and Gateshead from Earliest Times*, Mainstream Publishing

Morgan, Alan (2000) *A fine and private place: Jesmond Old Cemetery*, Tyne Bridge Publishing

Morgan, Alan (2004) *Beyond the Grave: Exploring Newcastle's Burial Grounds*, Tyne Bridge Publishing

Olsover, Lewis (1981) *The Jewish Communities of North East England 1755-1980*, Ashley Mark

Pevsner, Nikolaus (1983) *The Buildings of England: County of Durham*, 2nd edn. (revised by Williamson, Elizabeth), Penguin Books

Pevsner, Nikolaus and Richmond, Ian (2002) *The Buildings of England: Northumberland*, 2nd edn. (revised by John Grundy, Grace McCombie, Peter Ryder, Humphrey Welfare), Yale University Press

Pickering, W.S.F. (ed.) (1981) *A Social History of the Diocese of Newcastle upon Tyne 1882-1992*, Oriel Press

Taylor, Simon and Lovie, David B. (2004) *Gateshead: Architecture in a Changing English Urban Landscape*, English Heritage

Walton, John and Irving, Miles (2006) *100 years of the RVI 1906-2006*, The Newcastle upon Tyne Hospitals NHS Trust

Whitehead, Ian (2002) *The Sporting Tyne: A history of professional rowing*, Portcullis Press

Index

Page numbers in **bold** refer to boxed vignettes